Conversing in Paradise

Awake Awake Jerusalem! O lovely Emanation of Albion
Awake and overspread all Nations as in Ancient Time
For lo! the Night of Death is past and the Eternal Day
Appears upon our Hills: Awake Jerusalem, and come away

So spake the Vision of Albion & in him so spake in my hearing
The Universal Father. Then Albion stretchd his hand into Infinitude.
And took his Bow. Fourfold the Vision for bright beaming Urizen
Layd his hand on the South & took a breathing Bow of carved Gold
Luvah his hand stretchd to the East & bore a Silver Bow bright shining
Thammas Westward a Bow of Brass pure flaming richly wrought
Urthona Northward in thick storms a Bow of Iron terrible thundering

And the Bow is a Male & Female & the Quiver of the Arrows of Love
Are the Children of this Bow: a Bow of Mercy & Loving-kindness: laying
Open the hidden Heart in Wars of mutual Benevolence Wars of Love
And the Hand of Man grasps firm between the Male & Female Loves
And he Clothed himself in Bow & Arrows in awful state Fourfold
In the midst of his Twenty-eight Cities each with his Bow breathing

Conversing in Paradise

Poetic Genius and
Identity-as-Community
in Blake's Los

Leonard W. Deen

University of Missouri Press
Columbia & London
1983

Copyright © 1983 by
The Curators of the University of Missouri
University of Missouri Press, Columbia, Missouri 65211
Library of Congress Catalog Card Number 82–20307
Printed and bound in the United States of America

Library of Congress Cataloging in Publication Data

Deen, Leonard W., 1926–
    Conversing in paradise.

    Bibliography: p.
    Includes index.
    1. Blake, William, 1757–1827—Allegory and symbolism.
2. Blake, William, 1757–1827—Characters—Los.
3. Identity (Psychology) in literature.   4. Community in
literature.   I. Title.
PR4148.S95D43   1983   821′.7   82–20307
ISBN 0–8262–0396–5

Frontispiece: detail of *Los with the sun,* plate 97
of *Jerusalem* (copy E), reproduced courtesy of
Mr. and Mrs. Paul Mellon, Upperville, Virginia.

For Rosemary

Acknowledgments

Everyone who reads Blake and writes about him is deeply indebted to his editors, especially Geoffrey Keynes and David V. Erdman.

Mark Schorer's *William Blake: The Politics of Vision* and Maurice Friedman's "image of man" in *To Deny Our Nothingness* have influenced my treatment of community, and J. Middleton Murry's *William Blake* my treatment of identity. My view of Romantic poetry has been shaped by Harold Bloom's *The Visionary Company* and by M. H. Abrams's *Natural Supernaturalism* and *The Mirror and the Lamp*. My most pervasive debt is to Northrop Frye, in *Fearful Symmetry*, *The Anatomy of Criticism*, *Fables of Identity*, *The Stubborn Structure*, and *The Educated Imagination*.

Louis Crompton and David Erdman read most of the manuscript and offered very helpful advice and criticism. My colleagues Martha England, Bette Weidman, Marie Ponsot, Fred Kaplan, and Thomas R. Frosch also listened to or read parts of the manuscript, and made valuable and immensely encouraging suggestions; and Susan Fox's *Poetic Form in Blake's "Milton"* was very enlightening indeed. I owe most of all to Rosemary Deen. The better part of it is hers.

L. W. D.
Bayside, New York
January 1983

Contents

. . . Chaucer makes every one of his characters perfect in his kind, every one is an Antique Statue; the image of a class, and not of an imperfect individual. . . . The Franklin is one who keeps open table, who is the genius of eating and drinking, the Bacchus; as the Doctor of Physic is the Esculapius, the Host is the Silenus, the Squire is the Apollo, the Miller is the Hercules, &c. Chaucer's characters are a description of the eternal Principles that exist in all ages. . . . Visions of these eternal principles or characters of human life appear to poets, in all ages; the Grecian gods were the ancient Cherubim of Phoenicia; but the Greeks, and since them the Moderns, have neglected to subdue the gods of Priam. These Gods are visions of the eternal attributes . . . which, when erected into gods, become destructive to humanity . . . when separated from man or humanity, who is Jesus the Saviour, the vine of eternity, they are thieves and rebels, they are destroyers.

—Blake's "Descriptive Catalogue"

The common end of all *narrative,* nay of *all* poems is to convert a series into a *Whole*; to make those events, which in real or imagined History move on in a *strait* line, assume to our Understandings a circular motion—the snake with its Tail in its mouth. Hence indeed the almost flattering and yet appropriate term, Poesy—i.e. *Poiesis—making.* Doubtless to *his* eye, which alone comprehends all Past and Future in one eternal Present, what to our short sight appears strait is but part of the great Cycle—just as the calm Sea to us *appears* level, tho' it be indeed only a part of a *globe.* Now what the Globe is in Geography, *miniaturing* in order to manifest the Truth, such is a Poem to that Image of God, which we were created with, and which still seeks that Unity, or revelation of the *One* in and by the *Many,* which reminds it, that tho' in order to be an individual Being it must go forth *from* God, yet as the *re*ceding from him is to *pro*ceed toward Nothingness and Privation, it must still at every step turn back toward him in order to be at all—Now, a strait Line, continuously retracted forms of necessity a circular orbit.

—Coleridge to Joseph Cottle, 7 March 1815

1

Introduction

Identity and Community in English Romantic Poetry

Persons identify themselves with and through groups or communities, and it is often asserted that as solitary beings they have no identity. Blake's prophecies show a community of "Eternals" falling asunder, but surviving and recreating itself through the love and labors of the figure he calls "Los." Paralleling and imaging this fall, the four Zoas who constitute the active powers of Albion the Eternal Man fall asunder, but reorganize themselves as a single body through Los's love and labors for Albion. For Blake the community may not only act or recreate itself in the individual person: it may *be* that person, as Jesus is for Blake the community of mankind. Identity is community. For Blake, community achieved as a conversing in paradise is Jesus; struggling to create itself, it is Los.

Blake's Los, like Shelley's Prometheus, reveals active Poetic Genius in the single person as the source of human culture and humanity itself. But Blake's Los, unlike Shelley's Prometheus, brings his creator's ideal of art, of prophecy, and of humanity to life in a figure as far from abstract allegory as one can imagine—in a character as "real" as any in Shakespeare and Dickens. Los not only signifies but also embodies and enacts "divine humanity" and the ideals and salient characteristics of Blake's own poetry; and identity-as-community describes the form of a body of poetry as well as an ideal of brotherhood. The unfolding of the abstract Poetic Genius of 1788 into the character Los and into the brotherhood of the risen poem-man at the end of *Jerusalem* is the work of most of Blake's life and has to be treated chronologically. But I agree with Northrop Frye that Blake's myth forms one body. My account thus aims to be genetic, both chronological and holistic.

1

We can begin with the idea of personal identity that Romantic poets inherited from the seventeenth and eighteenth centuries, and define Blake's idea of identity and community by putting it beside that of other Romantic poets.

Philosophers of the Enlightenment were much concerned with the problem of personal identity. Taking *personal identity* to mean consciousness of being the same person throughout one's life, Locke and Hume subject the belief to a skeptical logical and psychological analysis.[1] Bishop Butler and Leibniz, most notably, defend it, largely through logical and psychological analysis. Both respond to Locke: Butler insists that personal identity is not constituted by *consciousness* of personal identity, Leibniz that personal identity is not always fully conscious—that it is larger than conscious awareness. To Butler and Leibniz, personal identity means a reasoned belief in the single and indestructible life of the individual person.[2] They are defending traditional belief in the immortality of the soul.

---

1. As Robert Langbaum has observed, *identity* "did not begin to be applied to the self until the unity of the self became problematic. As long as men believed in a soul created and sustained (continuously *known* and *seen*) by God, there could be no question about the unity of the self. It is significant that *identity* is first used to mean personal identity by the empiricist philosophers Locke and Hume, who use the word ... to cast doubt on the unity of the self" (*The Mysteries of Identity,* p. 25).

2. "Locke thought there could be nothing in the mind of which the mind was not conscious. Leibniz pointed out the absolute necessity of unconscious mental states. He distinguished between perception, which consists merely in being conscious of something, and apperception, which consists in self-consciousness, *i.e.* in being aware of perception. An unconscious perception *is* a state of consciousness, but is unconscious in the sense that we are not aware *of* it, though in it we are aware of something else. How important these unconscious perceptions are, appears from the Introduction to the New Essays. It is in consequence of these that 'the present is big with the future and laden with the past, that all things conspire, and that, in the least of substances, eyes as penetrating as those of God could read the whole course of things in the universe' (*New Essays* 48). They also preserve the identity of the individual, and explain the pre-established harmony ... and it is in virtue of them that no two things are perfectly alike" (Bertrand Russell, *A Critical Exposition of the Philosophy of Leibniz,* p. 156).

Bishop Joseph Butler's views on identity are to be found in "Of Personal Identity," Dissertation I appended to *The Analogy of Religion Natural and Revealed,* of which there are several one-volume editions. The handiest is the Everyman.

For English Romantic poets, as for Locke and Hume, Butler and Leibniz, the problem of identity still occurs in time, as the paradox of sameness or continuity through time and change. And for them, as for Butler and Leibniz, identity is a matter of belief—but it is a belief given by imagination or prophetic vision. Romantic poets, that is, see identity not simply as knowledge or consciousness but as power; they treat it mythically. Unlike the philosophers, who are interested in logical problems of whether it is the same or "identical" person who remembers or survives or who is resurrected after death, they look at the active powers of memory, vitality, awakening. They are less interested in the personal identity that exists as an ideal datum of conscious and inward-turning memory than in the identity that is implied in the source and emerges as working or interaction.

If the personal identity of Locke and Hume is both a vanishing awareness and a logical-epistemological problem, Romantic poets respond by finding identity not in thought or in passive and isolated consciousness but in productive act or imagination: I act or make, and see that it is good; therefore I am. Their preferred model of identity is not the philosophic thinker but the Creator God of Genesis, the I am who begins time by an initiating act. If the philosophers' personal identity is a problematic end in consciousness, Romantic poets seek a balancing source in creative act. And the active powers of man are to be found in—or can best be signified by—youth, of the individual or the race: "The ancient Poets animated all sensible objects with Gods or Geniuses."

Though my subject is not personal identity, in what follows I use the word *identity* often—largely because it is Blake's word, chosen deliberately to allude to and react against the image of man implied in Locke's and Hume's concept of personal identity: that man knows himself as consciousness, and that consciousness is isolated, passive (except in its inspection and choice and combining of given ideas), and memorial.[3] For Blake, personal identity is a kind

3. Owen Barfield distinguishes usefully between Locke and Hume in the matter of the mind's "passivity":

> Hume's philosophy differs from Locke's in the much smaller role

of nadir or "limit of contraction" in the fall, as in Tharmas's lament in *The Four Zoas*:

> I am like an atom
> A Nothing left in darkness yet I am an identity
> I wish & feel & weep & groan Ah terrible terrible.
> (Night I, p. 4/E298/302)[4]

Against this atom-minimum, Blake increasingly uses *identity* to signify his own active and communitarian image of man. For Blake, full humanity emerges only in a community in which each of us is free to identify himself by unique act. In the following chapters I trace the gradual perfecting of this myth of identity-as-community in Blake's poetry from the "Tractates" of 1788 to *Jerusalem*.

* * *

If we can agree that the image of man in Romantic poetry emphasizes source or genesis, two different forms may be distinguished in the Romantic protagonist's relation to the source of his own being. His turn or growth away from the origin gives us a history of identity that traces the gradual

---

which it assigns to the activity of the human mind. Locke begins, certainly, by denying the doctrine of "innate ideas" and affirming the principle *nihil in intellectu quod non prius fuerit in sensu*. But although he says that there can be no idea without a previous perception, he does not quite take the further step of identifying the two. He writes of ideas as though they were something which appeared in the mind as a kind of response to sense-perceptions and—what is perhaps more important— his interest is concentrated on the activity of the mind in dealing with these ideas. The Wit, which combines, and the Judgement, which distinguishes them, are for him realities.

For Hume, on the other hand, the ideas *are* the percepts or, as he calls them, *impressions*. When a sense-impression loses its first vivacity, it becomes an idea, and there is no content of thought which was not originally a sense datum. The activity of the mind in memory or imagination is limited to "retaining" the original impression; the memory with more, and the imagination with less "force and vivacity." For Hume therefore man, as knower, is above all a passive recipient of impressions.

(*Poetic Diction*, "Preface to the Second Edition," p. 17)

4. All references to Blake's works refer to David V. Erdman's edition, with commentary by Harold Bloom, of *The Poetry and Prose of William Blake* (1965) as *E*. I cite this edition first, after a slash (/). After a second slash, I give the page number in the Newly Revised Edition of Erdman's text, titled *The Complete Poetry and Prose of William Blake* (1982).

development of a separated awareness, known by memory, as continuity and growth of consciousness in time—what Keats calls "identical soul." (Here Keats is closer than most Romantic poets to the Enlightenment view of personal identity.) The protagonist's turn back to the source, seeking a renewed energy or oneness, gives us a myth revealing his original identity with God and stressing the eternal origin and end. The history identifies man as mortal creature and conscious, individuated person; the myth identifies him as impersonal—though often unique—participant in creative power or the divine source. Romantic poetry as a whole mediates between the myth and the history, the eternal and the time images of man, and many Romantic poems are constituted by the interweaving or the stress and counterstress of both forms. Here the "Immortality Ode" is typical. In it, time as divine rebirth is matched by time as earthly maturation, the two times interwoven in the implied myth of Eos and Tithonus: one reborn daily, the other infinitely aging, the one inhabiting a perfectly correspondent and perpetually renewed world of vision, the other adjusting more and more to an alien world of sense and common sense.

Because it violates the normal or commonsense view of the direction of time and the Enlightenment view of the development of a conscious sense of identity, the myth of identity is likely to be the more striking form; and for most readers, the turning back of the protagonist to source or origin is one of the signs marking a poem or plot as Romantic (as in *Wuthering Heights, Great Expectations, St. Mawr*, "Fern Hill"). In most of the great Romantic odes, to take a familiar example, the speaker turns from the fallen self in an effort to touch again original or innate powers—the powers by which each person helps to create his own world. Insofar as the effort to link the late or fallen self with original power succeeds, the origin reasserts its place in the present self, and the form experience takes in the poem becomes spiral or "revolutionary," the end being a transformed origin.[5] When it does not

5. Northrop Frye remarks, "The limit of imagination is a totally human world" which "recapture[s], in full consciousness [thus, recaptures with a difference], that original sense of identity with our surroundings" which we call paradise (*The Educated Imagination*, p. 29). M. H. Abrams says something

succeed, the speaker measures his distance from the origin as loss (Coleridge in "Dejection," Shelley in at least one moment in "Ode to the West Wind") or as a severing into a new and more personal identity (Keats in the "Ode to a Nightingale" and "Ode on a Grecian Urn"). But even in Keats the origin is always in view and becomes a defining pole for the new awareness created or revealed in the poem. The turn back remains essential.

This turn back leads toward a more primary psychic level and toward a world that can be represented in images—in what Wordsworth calls "the language of the sense," or in what Blake calls the "enlarged and numerous senses" of the "ancient Poets": visionary sense. Both views, but especially Wordsworth's, are akin to what Freud calls "transforming thought into images."[6] Wordsworth's contemplative turning back to origins arouses an emotion kindred to the original one, together with the images bonded to it, as if the development of sense-feeling into thought could be reversed, and sense-feeling resurrected. In Blake's analogous formula from "A Vision of the Last Judgment," "the Imaginative Image returns by the seed of Contemplative Thought."

---

similar: "...In the most representative Romantic version of emanation and return, when the process reverts to its beginning the recovered unity is not, as in ... Plotinus, the simple, undifferentiated unity of the origin, but a unity which ... incorporates the intervening differentiation." Fusing "circular return" with "linear progress" yields "a distinctive figure of Romantic thought and imagination—the ascending circle, or spiral" (*Natural Supernaturalism*, pp. 183–84).

6. *The Interpretation of Dreams*, trans. James Strachey, p. 597. The Romantic turning back to source or past is like the turning back in dreams to man's "archaic heritage," to "what is psychically innate" in man, and to "motive force," in Freud's terms. And, like dreams, it often leads us into the future:

> Dreams are derived from the past in every sense. Nevertheless the ancient belief that dreams foretell the future is not wholly devoid of truth. By picturing our wishes as fulfilled, dreams are after all leading us into the future. But this future, which the dreamer pictures as the present, has been moulded by his indestructible wish into a perfect likeness of the past. (*The Interpretation of Dreams*, p. 621)

The reality envisioned by Romantic poets is not a "perfect" likeness of the past, but it is a likeness, and often a progressive one. Thus qualified, the passage is a useful account of the time-structure of "Tintern Abbey," *The Prelude*, "Frost at Midnight," "The Rime of the Ancient Mariner," and "Kubla Khan"; and it tells us much about the spiral shape of the Romantic ode, *Endymion*, *The Fall of Hyperion*, *Prometheus Unbound*, and even *Jerusalem*.

As in these examples, conscious turning back to the source implies that the source has become other—a person not-one's-self. Parent, lover, friend, or God, the other is a figure with whom the agent or speaker in the poem identifies himself—but only through a kind of dialogue, so that turning back to the source is turning back to the seed of community. Conscious identity is never simply one; it is always at least twofold, so that the movement toward community is marked by evolving styles of address, by a growing communicativeness and civility of speech: *soliloquy*; *soliloquy address*; *dialogue* or *"mental fight"*; and *conversation*. The last two are more developed in Blake, as the expression of his greater emphasis on identity-as-community.

Romantic soliloquy is a communion of self with self, often former self with present self or projected self with observer, as in "Kubla Khan" or "A Night-Piece." Soliloquy is the mode in which continuity or deepening of consciousness expresses itself— "the language of the sense," which (in Coleridge's phrase) composes "the tunes that each calls I." It is often imaged as a reflective lake or a murmuring river, with the river often the source of the tune. Soliloquy moves very gradually into soliloquy-address, a communion of self with self and also with an other. "Frost at Midnight," "Tintern Abbey," "There Was a Boy," "Mont Blanc," and Keats's odes begin or end as soliloquy-address: speech addressed to an other (often a personified other) as well as to the self. Thoreau's address to Walden Pond—"Walden, is it you?"— shows it beautifully.

In Blake, soliloquy and soliloquy-address tend to be replaced by solitary struggle, as in *The Book of Los*, or solitary dramatic lament, as in *The Four Zoas* (where the laments are often set like arias in a recitative context). Identity is reasserted in the confrontation of visions Blake calls "Mental Fight"—the moving force in most of his prophecies—and achieves full identity-as-community in *conversation*: speaking to another as to the image of God.

If the other has been projected or diffused into the world of the poem, as in Coleridge's conversation poems or "Ancient Mariner" or in Wordsworth's *Prelude*, community appears as a community of being where "in all things I was one life, and felt that it was joy" (as Wordsworth says), or where "each Thing has a Life of its own, & yet they are all one Life" (as Coleridge says).[7] Such a community is implied also in Blake's "For every thing that lives is Holy." But for Blake, as for Shelley in *Prometheus Unbound,* the other is not diffused into the world; it is part of the individual identity, and yet is a separate agent—as Asia is a state or power of Prometheus, and turns to and moves Demogorgon; and as Enitharmon and the Spectre of Urthona are separated but linked parts of Los.

Blake's prophecies imply a disintegrated community reflected in the parts of a single figure. In Los, then, the inner order of identity is itself an implicit community of psychological powers and preserves community in its external disintegration, as the acorn preserves the oak. If identity is the offspring and embodies the remnant of community, it also recreates community in a new form.[8] Community both fosters and needs the unique powers of the individual person; and having begun anew in the individual imagination, it appears finally as one man.

In Blake's Los and Shelley's Prometheus, the whole of mankind learns to act as one person, is "identified." Both poets enlarge the integrity and the completed development of the single person—"I am I"—to the world and to mankind: "I am I and the world"; "I am I and mankind." Though the protagonist remains single and uniquely individuated— identified as himself—he is also identified with the whole through a turning back to the origin in which no unique

7. *Collected Letters of Samuel Taylor Coleridge,* ed. Earl Leslie Griggs, 2:866. Abrams points out that Wordsworth in *The Prelude* speaks to Coleridge and "often supplements this form with an interior monologue, or else carries on an extended colloquy with the landscape in which the interlocutors are 'my mind' and 'The speaking face of earth and heaven' (V, 11–12)" (*Natural Supernaturalism,* p. 139).

8. Romantic poets enlarge our conception of the mind to include all its forces—reason, the passions, will and desire, and what we now call the unconscious. This enlargement reveals an organic creative process that is proof against domination by one power, so that Romantic psychology is neither a tyranny nor an anarchy but a kind of democracy of the mind, in which the most varied elements interact in orderly freedom. Mark Schorer envisions men achieving "a democracy of their faculties" in *William Blake: The Politics of Vision,* p. 277.

quality is lost, and yet all is one. This ideal many-in-one identifies the person with humanity and reveals the world as human.

Community in this sense is of course not only a social-political ideal but also an imaginative and aesthetic construct, and has its ideal home in a poem. The identification of person with world and human community is the identification of unlikes or incommensurables that we find in metaphor, and it parallels the identification of part with whole in the organic structure of a poem. Thus the poem as a unique identity made of interacting parts reveals the ideal of community in every part, and Los and Prometheus are not only figures of identity but also figures of "Poetic Genius"—poets as prophets or legislators who create human community in their poems. As both creators and preservers of community, Los and Prometheus show us that poet-prophets and poet-legislators form a kind of apostolic succession from the first poet, they themselves being both the first and the latest members of this succession. In them, the turning back of history to its source in myth becomes a leap forward that transforms divided mankind into community.

*　　*　　*

Whether or not they appeal to Nature, Romantic poets, like Rousseau, turn back to a state they image as before established society in order to re-envision and renew the nature of man and, in this way, recreate community. The turning back seeks the future.[9]

> From crowded streets remote,
> Far from the living and dead wilderness

9. Rousseau needs to be understood as Kant understood him. For Kant, Rousseau's "state of nature" was "not ... a theory of what exists but of what should be ... not ... a retrospective elegy but ... a prospective prophecy." "Kant never takes the idea of the *homme naturel* in a purely scientific or historical sense, but rather ethically and teleologically. What is truly permanent in human nature is not any condition *in which* it once existed and *from which* it has fallen; rather it is the goal for which and toward which it moves ... And Kant credits Rousseau the ethical philosopher with having discerned the 'real man' beneath all the distortions and concealments ... that man has created for himself and won in the course of his history" (Ernst Cassirer, "Kant and Rousseau," pp. 10, 20).

> Of the thronged World, Society is here
> A true Community, a genuine frame
> Of many into one incorporate. (*Recluse,* I, "Home at
>   Grasmere," lines 612–16)

Romantic poets turn back not simply to a pastoral community, but to a community discerned through its destruction, like Milton's England-Isis picking up the scattered limbs of Truth-Osiris: "We have not yet found them all, Lords and Commons." Blake's myth in *The Book of Urizen* is about the fall of the energetic community of the Eternals into faction, and it derives isolated and divided humanity from this fall. *The Four Zoas, Milton,* and *Jerusalem* also present the destruction of community and expect or enact its renewal: "Perfect Unity / Cannot Exist but from the Universal / Brotherhood of Eden, / The Universal Man" (*The Four Zoas,* I:4–6/E297/300). "The Ruined Cottage," *The Borderers,* many of the *Lyrical Ballads,* Coleridge's conversation poems, and such poems as *Prometheus Unbound* and *Hyperion* also concern the destruction of a community that once embraced man and man, man and nature, or Titan and Titan. The problem in all these poems is to convert into community a world fallen into loss and division.

Often resembling the model of religious conversion, community begins with the single person when he turns away from isolation or self-division toward the innate powers by which he helps create his own world, and then toward others.[10] In *The Marriage of Heaven and Hell,* community is formed by recognizing the divine in all men and "loving the greatest men best." It will be a democratic community rather than an elitist society, for the poem establishes the authority both of the individual point of view (in the "Proverbs of

---

10. My idea of Romantic community derives partly from comedy and from the comic "society" in Northrop Frye's account of comedy in *Anatomy of Criticism,* pp. 163–71. *As You Like It* shows it in pure form, and furthermore gives us the definitive comic formulation of identity-surviving-conversion. In act 4, scene 3 the once villainous Oliver explains his change. To Celia's question, "Was't you that did so oft contrive to kill him?" (Oliver's brother Orlando), Oliver answers,

> 'Twas I. But 'tis not I. I do not shame
> To tell you what I was, since my conversion
> So sweetly tastes, being the thing I am.

Hell") and the out-of-power point of view (in the devil's "opposition" account of identity and the fall from it in *Paradise Lost*). Community is an awakening to truth *and* to brotherhood, as in the conversion of an angel first to a flaming Elijah and then to a devil who is Blake's particular friend; in the Ancient Mariner's conversion, followed by his awakening a wedding guest to spiritual wisdom; in Wordsworth's turning in *The Prelude* from reasoning despair to his poetic vocation as a prophet of nature who will teach others his vision; in Albion's awakening and self-sacrifice (following Los's example) in *Jerusalem*; in Prometheus's consolidation of internal rule and final turning from vengeful hatred to love at the end of act 1 of *Prometheus Unbound*; and in Keats's turning from dreams to visionary knowledge of human suffering in *The Fall of Hyperion*.

Romantic poets are convinced that what Blake calls the "Real Man"—the individual vision and its unique correspondent world—has to be revealed by the poet, and convinced also that this revelation will connect man with man because it enlarges the world in which we live. The single person turns toward his Real Man. If he is a poet, he reveals this Real Man to others: what he finds in himself, he reveals to others by teaching others to see, and in doing so, he enlarges the world of vision open to all. *Visions of the Daughters of Albion* is so constructed that Oothoon's vision of various worlds confronts "One Law" and denies its validity: the poem's effect is moral-political. In Coleridge's "Rime," the enlargement is moral-psychological, anticipated by the travel metaphor of a new sight: "We were the first that ever burst into that silent sea." In *The Prelude*, "in life's everyday appearances / I seemed . . . to gain clear sight of a new world" (13:368–70). In *Walden* (the first chapter) Thoreau requires "of every writer a simple and sincere account of his own life— some such account as he would send to his kindred from a distant land; for if he has lived sincerely, it must have been in a distant land to me." Even when the poet's stress, like Thoreau's, is on the uniqueness of the experience, the effect is that of enriching a single life shared by all mankind—the creation of community. In Thoreau the community is implied by the requirement of an "account" or communication, and by the idea of "kindred": others are unlike but kin, and we need—require, in fact—their accounts.

The poet as man aims at a society of independent thinkers, a democratic "republic," but on the smaller and more intensive scale of community. The poet as prophet seeks to create a community of prophets, a New Jerusalem. Both seek to awaken by example—the poet-man by the critical authority of an independent point of view, the poet-prophet by awakening the prophetic power in others: "Would to God that all the Lord's people were prophets."[11] Created by unique vision, and consisting of internal reality communicated to others, the new community would be a whole made up of distinct centers of value, an "identity-in-difference"— Truth-Osiris reintegrated and resurrected.[12] This community of unique souls is in Blake's terms "the Real Man the Imagination"; in Wordsworth's terms "the mind of man"; in Shelley's terms "the great poem" expressing the "one great mind" that is human culture. The Romantic belief that the person creates his own world is clearest in Blake; and for Blake, at least, the common world or community we *would* inhabit is not the common denominator of our unique worlds of experience but the ordered structure of their totality, seen simultaneously from all the unique perspectives that make it up.[13]

11. As the Old Testament prophets "listened to and obeyed a word and commission of Yahweh which came to them alone and which could not be transferred to anyone else, they became individuals, persons. They could say 'I' in a way never before heard in Israel" (Gerhard von Rad, *The Message of the Prophets*, p. 146).

12. In *Natural Supernaturalism*, Abrams speaks of "individuation in unity" and of "fragmenting community into an anarchy of unrelated parts" (p. 282). He further remarks that in the Snowdon vision of *The Prelude*, "the mature poetic mind" "has acquired self-consciousness, and is able to sustain the sense of its own identity as an individuation-in-unison with the objects it perceives" (p. 287).

13. Compare Leibniz's account of the heavenly city at the end of his "A Vindication of God's Justice" or the "Monadology," or his idea of monads mirroring the universe:

This connection of all created things with every single one of them and their adaptation to every single one, as well as the connection and adaptation of every single thing to all others, has the result that every single substance stands in relations which express all the others. Whence every single substance is a perpetual living mirror of the

*   *   *

Especially as it links identity with community, the spiral turning back to origin or other in Blake and Shelley has sources in Plato and the Bible. Both help us to see how Romantic poets recreate in individual or natural or revolutionary terms—as regeneration—an ancient ideal of community, classical or Christian: a symposium or a communion of saints. A turning back and to which seeks its end in its origin is described in Aristophanes' myth in the *Symposium,* where an original being's fall into division is followed by the "erotic" attempt at reunion with the other half of its divided self. Although Aristophanes' myth of erotic pursuit of our original oneness implies a circular turn back to the beginning, Socrates' later myth in the *Symposium* implies development or history: Eros as the mean between ignorance and knowledge, which leads finally to self-transcendence and knowledge of the Good. The symposium plot may be a simple bipolar movement that seeks to cure self-division, as in Aristophanes' myth, or a developed dialogue, as in Socrates' account of relations between lovers. *Developed* means "turned toward speech and community," as Socrates is. Relations between lovers prepare for symposium. The full symposium—the full diapason of voices and spectrum of points of view—is an image of many in one, of fully civilized community. (The term *symposium* for this form I take from Northrop Frye's *Anatomy of Criticism.*) Plato's Republic is perhaps such a community enlarged and systematized and hardened into an eternal city-state.

As Northrop Frye and M. H. Abrams (among others) have pointed out, a spiral plot is described also by the Bible's

universe.

Just as the same city regarded from different sides offers quite different aspects, and thus appears multiplied *by the perspective,* so it also happens that the infinite multitude of simple substances creates the appearance of as many different universes. Yet they are but perspectives of a single universe, varied according to the *points of view,* which differ in each monad.

(Paragraphs 56 and 57 of the "Monadology," in *Monadology and Other Essays,* p. 157.) Leibniz's view is not quite as "visualist" or passive as it seems here. He attributes activity to the monad in proportion as its perceptions are distinct, passivity in proportion as they are confused.

beginning in Genesis and ending in Apocalypse—by its progress from Creation through the Fall and expulsion from Eden, through exile, exodus, and history, to the regaining of a different Eden and a larger community in the New Jerusalem.[14] Though the spiral is greatly enlarged in the Bible, which "surveys the whole history of mankind, under the symbolic names of Adam and Israel,"[15] the restoration of Eden in the heavenly city yields a community roughly analogous to the erotic symposium. Under historical attack, this ideal of community may take theoretical and militant form as the City of God, Augustine's Christian analogue to Plato's Republic. Though one community is secular, the other sacred, one the goal of culture, the other the goal of history, both have emerged from an original one—the undivided sphere, or Adam. And both are bipolar or dialogical: the symposium turn toward or dialogue with the erotic other parallels the biblical turn toward or dialogue with God. In both cases, the dialogue tends to turn other—whether lover or God—into person. In the closest Christian analogy with symposium—the Last Supper—the disciples form a community with Christ only insofar as he is not wholly other: not only divine, but also person. And communicants in the Mass form a community only insofar as they see and converse with one another as equal persons. Blake's Christian idea of community, which is the most relevant here, strongly emphasizes the brotherhood and humanity of Christ and the brotherhood of the redeemed community. The vision of identity and community as one—as the two terms of a metaphor in which

14. See Frye's *Anatomy of Criticism*, 189–92 and 316–17. Abrams remarks in *Natural Supernaturalism*, "The design of Biblical history constitutes a sharply defined plot with a beginning, a middle, and an end" (p. 35). "The Biblical scheme is symmetrical. It begins with the creation of the heaven and the earth and ends with the creation of 'a new heaven and a new earth'; the history of man begins with his felicity in an earthly paradise and ends with his felicity in an equivalent paradise, first on earth, then in a heavenly city which will reproduce the conditions of Eden, including the 'river of water of life,' the 'tree of life,' and man's original innocence, for 'there shall be no more curse' (Revelation 22: 1–3). . . . And in this pattern it is the terminal and not the initial felicity which really matters, for the finish is also the goal, the *telos*, of the entire providential plan" (p. 37). See the whole section in *Natural Supernaturalism* on "The Design of Biblical History," pp. 32–36.

15. *The Educated Imagination*, p. 111.

each term retains its unique virtues—is strongest and clearest in Blake.[16]

The pagan and Christian ideas of community are of course not quite parallel, and neither is in any way convertible into the other. For our purposes, what is important is that such Romantic poets as Blake and Shelley tend to see community either in Christian or in pagan terms and to construct the plots of their poems accordingly. The biblical plot we may call a conversion plot after its major turn, or a redemption plot after its end. It begins in creation or fall or exile, and passes through conversion or revelation to end in brotherhood, with the Christian gospel having enlarged the original covenant promise. Augustine's *Confessions* is of course one of the great examples of a conversion plot. The symposium plot, whether Aristophanes' or Socrates', we may call an Eros plot. It passes through division or pursuit to end in reunion or ascent to knowledge of the Good. In the symposium's erotic state of self-division, the protagonist's pursuit of the original unity or of beauty may end in sexual reintegration, in knowledge of the Good, or in a community of lovers. *Candide,* for example, ends in sexual reintegration; *Prometheus Unbound* ends not only in sexual reintegration and knowledge of the Good, but also in a community of lovers and in the regaining of a more conscious Golden Age. In Socrates' Eros myth in the *Symposium* and in Shelley's *Prometheus Unbound,* brotherhood emerges from Eros. In Blake's plots, brotherhood must overcome Eros. Because Eden is neither Generation nor Beulah, in Blake's poetry Eros plots are often converted into or dominated by redemption plots, as in *The Four Zoas* and *Jerusalem.* This strategy is evidently Blake's deliberate attack on the persistence of pagan Eros forms in a Christian culture.

16. Owen Barfield, in *The Rediscovery of Meaning,* has essays that reproduce closely Blake's idea of community, though there is no sign that Barfield is thinking of Blake. Blake's "innocence," "experience," and "organized participation" appear in Barfield as "original participation," "isolation," and "final participation" (pp. 213–15). Barfield points out that uniqueness is distinct from equality-as-sameness, which makes "participation" impossible: "it is on the *in*equalities that participation in large measure depends" (p. 213). ("Inequalities" seems essentially to mean "differences.") Like Blake, Barfield wants us to see society as we see a work of art, where part and whole are identified. The identity of part and whole, in fact, is what he means by "participation." See especially the essays "Participation and Isolation: A Fresh Light on Present Discontents" and "Form and Art in Society."

Within a particular prophecy of Blake's, the progress from lament through Mental Fight to the fully human conversation of Eden often corresponds roughly to the turn from Eros plot to conversion or redemption plot. The lament, that is, is often a lament over erotic division. Eros and conversion plots in Blake's poetry have a further importance. The form of Blake's work as a whole (a form focused in *The Four Zoas*) is the fall and recovery of mankind, of Poetic Genius (in Los), and of poetry. For the last, the important myth is that of the stealing and perverting of the poetry of the Bible by heathens. "In Dantes Comedia," Blake observes in marginalia,

> Round Purgatory is Paradise & round Paradise is Vacuum or Limbo. so that Homer is the Center of All I mean the Poetry of the Heathen Stolen & Perverted from the Bible not by Chance but by design by the Kings of Persia and their Generals The Greek Heroes & lastly by The Romans. (E667–68/689).

Blake's prophecies begin in paganism and often seem pagan poems. (*The Marriage of Heaven and Hell* is the notable early exception.) Los is one of several pagan figures, but only he becomes a Christian, and as he does so he becomes the central figure in Blake's myth. Finding his way back to Christianity and the poetry of the Bible, he becomes a visionary Christian at the same time that he becomes a genuine poet (and artist). In Los, then, Blake shows the position from which the poet in a fallen world must start. Shelley in *Prometheus Unbound* uses a pagan Eros plot as a corrective to Christianity; Blake uses Los's rediscovery of Christianity— his conversion and his labors at the task of redemption—as a corrective to pagan Eros plots and the celebration of kings and heroes. The heathen corruption of poetry centers in its cosmogonies—the beginning in void or vacuum—and in the identification of God with kings. From these errors an inhuman One Law and the rule of pagan morality spring; and in Blake's view not even the most powerful Christian poets— Dante and Milton—are immune to them. God as king—"For God is only an allegory of kings," in Blake's satiric parody of Dr. Thornton's "Tory translation" of the Lord's Prayer—obviously implies hierarchy, and thus the destruction of the equal and free community that was Blake's vision of the origin and end of human being. Milton the revolutionary is criticized for making God in the image of a king.

The fall from and recovery of community for Blake, then, is as much a formal and poetic experience as a communitarian and religious experience. Beginning with *The Four Zoas,* it is a fall into division-error and a recovery of truth and unity in the poem, seen as a person. The person is Albion, so that the Zoas are sundered elements of a poem or book—a poem-gospel. Tharmas is the "Parent power" or speech-generating power of the tongue (and the primitive powers of touch and assimilation of food by the blood); Luvah is the energy of desire in the air-breathing nostrils; Urizen is the enlightened orb or eye of reason; Urthona is the upward-spiraling ear of imagination and the active, laboring hand and foot. Zoas separated from their Emanations—the power to reveal one's self to others—can no longer converse; their fall is a fall of speech into lament, lie, dissimulation, self-deceit, amnesia, paramnesia, struggle for rule and dominance. Tharmas and Luvah and Urizen, one after another, fall into a "serpent form," which begins as "nature" but ends as the "false tongue"—poetry so perverted that it can no longer envision or tell the truth of the fall and creation, or the fall into Satan. Finally, in Night VII of *The Four Zoas,* Los awakens as Christ and poet, and becomes creator and redeemer and enthusiastic artist. A later evangelist or "visionary of Jesus" like Paul— the focus of the evangelists' active power of vision—Los enacts both the purification of Old Testament poetry by the Gospels and a further purification made necessary by such errors as those of Dante and Milton. In doing so, he "acts" or imitates Christ; and the distinction between evangelist and Christ, the poet and the divine humanity he envisions, lessens. Finally, at the end of *Jerusalem,* Christ appears to Albion in the "likeness & similitude" of his friend Los, and Albion himself "acts" or imitates Christ by sacrificing himself for Los. The poet becomes what he beholds; the creator becomes his creation; the biblical poem comes to life. Blake, acting through Los, has turned back to and recreated the genuine poetry of the source, purifying it of pagan corruptions. We see then that Los's awakening as Christian poet-artist-prophet in Night VII of *The Four Zoas* is the decisive conversion, or turn toward redemption, in Blake's poetry as a whole. Both *Milton* and *Jerusalem* elaborate and intensify it until the human poem, in the person of Albion centered in Los, arises as Jehovah-Christ. Jehovah, the "he, who dwells in flaming fire" of *The Marriage of Heaven and Hell*, has learned humanity and brotherhood in Los-Jesus.

Other poets, especially Romantic poets, see the poet through an analogy with God. Blake sees (develops a vision of) God through the image and experience of the working poet, and in his major prophecies approaches and finally (in imagination) attains Jerusalem or Eden as Albion awakened in the ordered, active, "resurrected" poem. The risen poem at the end of *Jerusalem* is an Eden form of four rivers seen as four "nerves" or "senses" (in their fallen state, four elements) and as the four persons that are the four Zoas—the risen evangelists who are finally seen as enacting the life of Christ, each with his particular virtues or powers, each with his own vision. These different and unique sources and streams—whose sound is not "murmur" or "music" (as in Wordsworth and Coleridge) but the intelligent, and thunderous, speech of friends and equals—symbolize the variety and balanced wholeness of unique powers in the human poem.

Los's mode of regeneration and reordering in *The Four Zoas* and *Jerusalem* is not hierarchical, not an imposition from above, as Urizen's is in constructing the mundane shell, but a community in which each of the Zoas has his place: Tharmas as the power of generating speech and the feel of pencil and paper, copper plate and burin; Luvah as the spirited desire of generation (making beauty immortal, as in the *Symposium*); Los as the informing vision and active labor; Urizen as intellectual and systematizing order, writing down the poem on stone tablets, no longer usurping the work of creation. (Yahweh's gift to Man through Moses-Urizen on Sinai was the art of writing, as we are told in *Jerusalem*, pl. 3.)

As in Ezekiel's vision of the Zoas, any one of these four powers might at any instant take the lead and move the whole vehicle. If Los's order is not imposed by a head but emerges from the interplay of distinct powers, that is because in Los it is the work, or working, which dominates. In Blake's vision of a poem awakening as a "Mental Fight" and of a poem awakened as a "conversing . . . in Human Forms"

(*Jerusalem,* pl. 95), not only the whole poem but also its distinct elements are persons. Blake's cosmos is a person, and his smallest unit or atom-Adam is also a person—a reborn energy of visible, acting, creating speech: part of a communal dance or working or drama in which each dancer/worker/speaker composes his own part or work: "in Eternity the Four Arts: Poetry, Painting, Music, / And Architecture which is Science: are the Four Faces of Man" (*Milton* 27:55–56).

Among Romantic poets, Blake alone fully imagines human identity as active conversing in paradise—identifies men with one another and with God in the human form divine. The development of this identity-as-community through the work of Los is the task of all Blake's poetry.

*   *   *

This book treats Blake's poetry, not his illuminations. In doing that it admittedly omits a dimension of Blake's achievement. Furthermore, if Blake's "two contrary states of the human soul"—those presented in *Songs of Innocence and of Experience*—are day and night, I present the "day" side: I treat his myth, for all its struggles, sacrifice, and torture, as a divine comedy.[17] My approach to Blake is neither to analyze his problems nor to seek his sources or his tradition, but to stick closely to the terms and characters of his poetry in order to reveal the whole shape of his myth. My assumption is that the shape of any poetry, the whole mass of which gives the reader the strong impression that it all forms one body, is hard to see. I do not claim that I am making more perspicuous *the* form of Blake's myth, but *a* form—one around the figure of Los, an ellipse whose two foci are identity and community. My effort is speculative and is an attempt to see Blake's myth as he might have seen it—not as philosophy or psychology or criticism (though it contains these, largely in the form of Mental Fight), but as poetry. Blake's "holy forms of Thought" turn philosophy back into the poetry from which, in his view, it came—the primitive vision or "first principles of human perception," which precede analytic thought and the categories of knowledge used in libraries and universities.

17. David Wagenknecht, in *Blake's Night: William Blake and the Idea of Pastoral,* and Leopold Damrosch, Jr., in *Symbol and Truth in Blake's Myth,* offer two accounts of the "night"—the bitter and problematic—side of Blake.

2

Poetic Genius and Mental Fight

For Blake, true or essential humanity is a power of unlimited creative act that reveals itself as both a body of energy
and a speaking community—a community of men acting as
one, as in the one body of which we are members in 1 Corinthians 12. The individual characters or existences whose
speech and actions express the one forming, acting power
are *identities*.[1] The fall of man from this original identity-as-
community into division and conflict, and the regaining
(though with a difference) of the original state, is the subject
of Blake's poetry. Though it is implied in almost everything
Blake wrote, the original state is presented most clearly in the
regaining of Eden at the end of his last long poem, *Jerusalem*.
But the power of creative act survives in time, in the fallen
world, as Poetic Genius and is embodied in the figure of Los.
Mediating between the extremes of fall and redemption—
Satan and Christ—Los preserves identity and finds the way
back to community through the contest of visions Blake calls
"Mental Fight."

In this chapter, I intend to look at the divisions and root
integrity of Poetic Genius and at the action of Mental Fight

1. Compare Donald Ault's account of Blake's identity-in-community in
Visionary Physics: Blake's Response to Newton:

> The "identity" of Blake's Eternity consists in a principle of contrariety, of
> opposition and tension. The underlying constituents of Blake's Eternity,
> the "Minute Particulars" which Jesus, "the only General and Universal
> Form" "protects," "every one in their own identity" (E, p. 183, *Jer* 38:20–
> 23) are cells of energy in tension with one another. While, in terms of
> bodily preservation and cooperation, these cells live in "Perfect Har-
> mony," their drive toward individuation and differentiation is charac-
> terized by Blake as "Mental War." (p. 31)

I should also acknowledge at the outset that J. Middleton Murry's *William
Blake* also focuses on identity. My approach is less personal and auto-
biographical, less a matter of preaching Blake's Gospel, more a matter of
examining the structure of poems, but I have found Murry's account very
suggestive.

which seeks to regain that integrity in Blake's Tractates, *The French Revolution,* and *The Marriage of Heaven and Hell.* The first form of reasserted identity in a fallen world is Mental Fight; the achieved form is the community of Eden.

Blake's Tractates (the two series of principles entitled "There Is No Natural Religion" and the series entitled "All Religions Are One," engraved in 1788)[2] are among Blake's most elliptical and provocative statements. But since they prefigure the treatment of identity in the whole of Blake's later work, they are the inevitable beginning place. In the Tractates, as throughout Blake's work, we are identified by vision, by the forming power which shapes perception. True man is made what he is not by reason or sense experience but by Poetic Genius. As the "true Man," Poetic Genius is the power of immediate, unified, and active vision from which "the body or outward form of Man" is derived: the whole man acting or knowing. However, fallen Poetic Genius divides into separate organs of perception yielding a fallen body and the apparently separated outer world: the man reduced to isolated and shrunken senses. Thus the way we perceive men or ourselves is true or false according to whether the perceptive power is the one, active Poetic Genius—"the true faculty of knowing"—or the passive, divided five senses and the "Ratio" or sum of knowledge they give.

"All Religions Are One" begins with "the faculty which experiences," identified as Poetic Genius. "There Is No Natural Religion" (first series) begins by focusing on the limitations of our fallen senses and ends in the summary statement, "The desires & perceptions of man untaught by any thing but organs of sense, must be limited to objects of sense." But through the further implicit proposition that man's desires and perceptions are *not* limited to objects of sense, the second series arrives at a quite different "Conclusion": "If it were not for the Poetic or Prophetic character. the

2. It is now generally accepted that "All Religions Are One" was engraved before the "There Is No Natural Religion" series. This order, together with the ordering of the "No Natural Religion" plates proposed by Geoffrey Keynes in the notes for the Blake Trust facsimiles in 1971, means that we begin with "the faculty which experiences," and end with "Therefore God becomes as we are, that we may be as he is." See Erdman's 1982 edition of *The Complete Poetry and Prose of William Blake,* p. 789.

Philosophic & Experimental would soon be at the ratio of all things & stand still, unable to do other than repeat the same dull round over again." The Poetic Character and only the Poetic Character accounts for the new, for change, because it does not simply perceive, but creates.

Like much of Blake's poetry of the 1790s, the two "No Natural Religion" Tractates are ironic. In them Blake shifts the terms of the argument from the language of psychological atomism to the language of prophetic vision—from "organs of sense" to "spiritual sensation." A suppressed premise causes a leap in the sequence, so that we cannot get to the conclusion without assuming a different ground of experience: not the senses, but the one power behind the senses. Thus Blake moves from sense experience to its form or "first principle" (as Ezekiel calls it in *The Marriage of Heaven and Hell*). The plot or developing form of "There Is No Natural Religion" is the turning back from the explicit to the implicit, from the many to the one, from the separate and limited senses to the one and unlimited prolific principle at the root of creation and perception.

Responding point by point to the propositions of the first series, the "No Natural Religion" second series concentrates on the unbounded, the unlimited, and the "All." It arrives at the Infinite or God and at the identity of man and God, or the identity of men in God: "He who sees the Infinite in all things sees God. He who sees the Ratio only sees himself only. . . . Therefore God becomes as we are, that we may be as he is." The axiom—the last sentence in fact—contains the whole of Blake's prophetic myth and means to describe the whole of existence, the end turning back to its source in God. It puts both fall and redemption, the turning away and the turning back, in terms of perception: as we see the world, so we see ourselves; world and identity (or world and selfhood) correspond. It also puts fall and redemption in terms of despair and hope. God descends and becomes many, meets us in brotherhood, and by this act helps to release us from the despairing selfhood: he frees us into our genuine identity as many in one, a community of equals. Becoming as we are, the Infinite becomes a unique person: the whole becomes the individual. In this way God liberates us from the sense of being only an atom in an overwhelming universe and offers us the power to change—to redeem—the whole. The Tractates are of course not philosophic analysis but poetic prophecy, and "God becomes as we are . . ."—the last sentence of the Tractates—is the root metaphor of Blake's Christianity.

Characteristically, Blake uses a kind of logic to disarm logic, making human desire and intention overcome reason and external causation. His strategy in "No Natural Religion" is to appeal first to the fallen understanding, to the mind so divided into separate "organs of sense" that desire and perception seem "limited to objects of sense." But the division is not complete, and Blake's emphasis passes more and more to the surviving integrity and power of vision in Poetic Genius, which was announced as the central subject in "All Religions Are One": "That the Poetic Genius is the true Man. and that the body or outward form of Man is derived from the Poetic Genius." Poetic Genius is desire informed by perception—a kind of energetic perception. It is not an organ of perception but the source of perception, not the sum of sense data registering an outwardly located reality but a forming power, the active energy and vision of the whole man. Identity in this sense does not depend on memory, nor is it a kind of consciousness; though it is unique, it is less personal than impersonal.

Poetic Genius is the "true Man" in that it is a power to make forms based on a power to perceive form; and this perceived form is not an abstraction but the concrete and infinitely varied human form. Identity is many, yet one: the "infinite variety" of which a single forming power is capable. We leap in "No Natural Religion" from multitudes of men, all having divided senses and powers, to the one power that the senses and the body are "derived from": Poetic Genius. The one power implies one body. Moved by infinite desire, perception as forming power creates what will equal that desire: "The desire of Man being Infinite the possession is Infinite & himself Infinite." The "Infinite" is the totality of individual forms and perceptions given the universal form of perception—a communal body visible in each of its particular members. This is the body "identified" finally at the end of *Jerusalem*. In both the Tractates and *Jerusalem*, which span

Blake's poetic career, identity is in the polar equation of the individual member and the whole, the unique person and God.

"God becomes as we are" in the Poetic Genius. If we look at the roughly contemporaneous annotations, in which Blake speaks more directly than he does in the ironic argument of the Tractates, we can see more clearly that the Poetic Genius is not only "true Man" but God: "He who Loves feels love descend into him & if he has wisdom may percieve it is from the Poetic Genius which is the Lord" (Annotations to Swedenborg's *Divine Love and Divine Wisdom*/E592/603). As one and transcendent, God is Essence (as he is for Keats in the famous "Identical Soul" letter of 21 April 1819). As many and immanent, God is identity: "Essence is not Identity but from Essence proceeds Identity & from one Essence may proceed many Identities as from one Affection may proceed. many thoughts" (E593/604). "If the Essence was the same *as the* Identity there could be but one Identity. which is false" (E593/604). Blake agrees with Swedenborg that "there is but one Omnipotent Uncreate & God . . . but that there is but one Infinite I do not. for if all but God is not Infinite they shall come to an End which God forbid" (E593/604). Insofar as we are fallen, and our powers are divided and limited, we are creatures. But identity is the unique manifestation of an infinite power, and apparently for Blake it is uncreated: "Whatever can be Created can be Annihilated Forms cannot" (*Milton*, 32:36/E131/132). Mediating between Essence and Identity, Poetic Genius is our participation in the powers of God—is Christ. Since our body is derived from Poetic Genius, the form we perceive as man is an image of the creative power itself: "God is a man not because he is so percievd by man but because he is the creator of man" (*Divine Love* Annotations/E592/603).

*　　*　　*

Assuming that Blake's central mythic characters do much to determine the shape of the poetry, I want in this and the next chapter to look at Blake's prophecies of the 1790s as organized around the figures of Orc and Urizen, Los and Enitharmon, and to derive these figures, forerunners of the four Zoas, from the principles of the early Tractates. The Tractates imply not only Los—Poetic Genius—but also Urizen and Orc. Urizen in the Tractates appears as "Reason" and "the reasoning power," and Orc as "desire" and "the desires and perceptions of man," bound or "limited." Even Enitharmon can be inferred from the Tractates—as the object of desire implied in "If any could desire what he is incapable of possessing, despair must be his eternal lot." (And Enitharmon finally yields Enion and Tharmas—embodiments of "Pity" and "Parent power," and names which can be derived, in large part, from the letters in "Enitharmon."[3] The Tractates reintegrate man's fallen and divided powers by tracing them back to their one "source" in Poetic Genius, "the true Man." And from the Poetic Genius of the Tractates, Los emerges as Blake's source and unifying and saving figure. God descends and takes on human character and multiplicity in Los. "God becomes as we are, that we may be as he is"—becomes the human community of Eden—through Los. It is from Los that Urizen is divided in the fall, and the return first occurs in Los. Blake's Tractates reveal the person himself as a community of powers and recall the original many-in-one of the psyche from its fall into disorder. The poems which follow expand this recall and present it as universal dramatic act, as the universe awakening and speaking as act in Albion. The Tractates are the condensed form, the seed, of the whole of Blake's work. The whole work, like the Tractates, takes the form of a conversion plot—a redemptive turning back to the divine source.

Los as a principle, then, appears early in Blake, as do Urizen and Enitharmon and Orc. As a mythic figure, however, he is preceded by Urizen. Urizen appears early as Tiriel, the blind king who curses his offspring, in *Tiriel* (1789). He appears also, again without being named Urizen, in *The French Revolution* (1791) in the figures of Louis XVI and the Archbishop of Paris, and especially in the "aged form" who appears to the Archbishop in a vision. Orc and Los appear less distinctly in *The French Revolution*, but they are forcefully

---

3. John Beer notes that Enitharmon "contains within her name the names of [Tharmas and Enion]" (*Blake's Humanism*, p. 228).

implied. (Enitharmon is absent; the "female" is absent until later.) The king-priest of repressive reason who causes and opposes the outburst of revolution, then, appears strongly at the beginning of Blake's developing myth. He is followed by Orc—fiery rebel and dangerous son—who dominates *America* and "A Song of Liberty." Only then is the Eternal Prophet, Los, fully named and identified. The Prophet or Poetic Genius is the source, but Blake creates the source as person, Los-Urthona, only after creating the two figures into which he falls: tyrant and rebel, or angel and devil. (The name *Urthona*—as in "The Shadowy Daughter of Urthona" and "Urthona's dens" in "A Song of Liberty"—appears before the name *Los* does.) The rebel Orc appears as fiery "Devil"—his threat obvious and direct—and Urizen appears as snowy "Angel." But as the Angel Urizen is unmasked as the real Satan, and the fiery Orc emerges as victim, Los is identified as Prophet. Unmasking and identification go step by step, one impelling the other. When the Prophet unmasks Satan in himself (in Night VII of *The Four Zoas,* in *Milton* and *Jerusalem* and "For the Sexes") identity and selfhood have been sundered and clearly identified. But the sundering has simply carried out through the conflict of dramatic figures— through Mental Fight—the conflict of the psychological principles of reason, desire, and Poetic Genius in the Tractates. Even before Los appears as Los, wherever the poetry takes the form of Mental Fight he is implicitly present as the Eternal Prophet opposing the Eternal Priest, Urizen.

*   *   *

The first comprehensive statement of Blake's principles is the Tractates. His first really ambitious poem—an immense short poem with the word *epic* written in every line—is *The French Revolution.* The scale and deliberate march of the lines, some having more than twenty syllables, are as grandly epic as the giant forms—stars, clouds, mountains, and valleys—which emerge from the landscape as the rulers and people of France. *The French Revolution* is also Blake's first thoroughly political and contemporary poem and his first dramatized Mental Fight. In most of these ways, it prepares for the poetry to come, especially the political prophecies of the 1790s. And like most of the poems to come, it suggests in condensed symbolic form all of human history, from Fall-Creation through warfare to apocalypse. In the process, it implies Los, though Los has not yet been named.

Blake sees in revolutionary France the whole of human history come to a turning point. We begin (as in *The Waste Land*) with "The dead brood over Europe," with the king in a dream, unable "To awake from slumbers of five thousands years." At the end, "The enormous dead, lift up their pale fires and look over the rocky cliffs," awaiting the resurrection. The last words—"morning's beam"—imply the coming of the revolutionary sunrise Blake will later associate with Orc. The night is past. Like Blake's later prophecies—*The Song of Los*, for example—*The French Revolution* is a contest between death and life; and the change in the poem is the turn from one to the other. At the beginning, "Sick the mountains, and all their vineyards weep, in the eyes of the kingly mourner" (1:6/E283/286). "Again the loud voice of France cries to the morning, the morning prophesies to its clouds. / For the Commons convene in the Hall of the Nation" (2:15–16/E283/286). In this struggle between tears, mourning, woes, shadows, and clouds, on the one hand, and the morning on the other—between mourning and morning—Urizen and Orc are already implied and need only to emerge as persons from their images and elements.

With gathering energy we move from the opening laments of the mourning and dreaming king through the howling governor of the Bastille to the forceful visions of the Duke of Burgundy, the Archbishop of Paris, the Duke of Orleans, and the Abbé de Sièyes. For the Urizenic—but forceful and unweeping—Duke of Burgundy, the struggle is between heaven and earth. The heaven-palace is in danger of sinking into a clay cottage, the stars are about to be mowed and harvested:

> Shall this marble built heaven become a clay cottage . . . and
>   these mowers
> From the Atlantic mountains, mow down all this great starry
>   harvest of six thousand years? (5:89–90/E286/290).

Burgundy sees the ancient and established order of the universe itself as threatened by chaos:

> Till the power and dominion is rent from the pole, sword and
>   scepter from sun and moon,
> The law and gospel from fire and air, and eternal reason and
>   science
> From the deep and the solid, and man lay his faded head
>   down on the rock
> Of eternity, where the eternal lion and eagle remain to
>   devour? (6:94–97/E287/290)

For Burgundy, "One Law," as Blake later calls it, orders both
the universe and the State, and he sees the violation of this
hierarchical law as leading to the fall of the figure whom we
recognize as the forerunner of Albion, the "man [who lays]
his faded head down on the rock / Of eternity," divided by
internal warfare.

The contest of visions continues throughout the poem,
with Blake lending his own incomparable force of condensation even to error. At the center, roughly, the Archbishop of
Paris supports Burgundy. He tells of his vision of "An aged
form, white as snow, hov'ring in mist, weeping in the uncertain light," who laments (lament is often accusatory and
"priestly"):

> My groaning is heard in the abbeys, and God, so long
>   worshipp'd, departs as a lamp
> Without oil; for a curse is heard hoarse thro' the land, from a
>   godless race
> Descending to beasts; they look downward and labour and
>   forget my holy law;
> . . . .
> For the bars of Chaos are burst; her millions prepare their
>   fiery way
> Thro' the orbed abode of the holy dead, to root up and pull
>   down and remove,
> And Nobles and Clergy shall fail from before me, and my
>   cloud and vision be no more. (8:137–43/E288/292)

This is essentially Urizen's view of the "fiery" rebel Orc
bursting through the heaven inhabited by the "holy dead"
("the orbed abode of the holy dead" who "brood over Europe"), rooting up and pulling down. It is a lament for the
subversion of all ordered hierarchy, but especially the re-

ligious hierarchy in which the labor of the laboring man counts for nothing beside his submission and worship:

> They shall drop at the plough and faint at the harrow,
> unredeem'd, unconfess'd, unpardon'd;
> The priest rot in his surplice by the lawless lover, the holy
> beside the accursed,
> The King, frowning in purple, beside the grey plowman, and
> their worms embrace together. (8:148–50/E289/292)

The Archbishop's counsel is to "shut up this Assembly in their final home"—to put down this "city of rebels, that threaten to bathe their feet / In the blood of Nobility; trampling the heart and the head" (8–9:154–56/E289/293). To the Archbishop's bodily metaphor of the noble head and heart threatened by the ignoble feet, the Duke of Orleans counterposes a cosmic-bodily metaphor of the equal joys of function:

> Can the fires of Nobility ever be quench'd, or the stars by a
> stormy night?
> Is the body diseas'd when the members are healthful? can the
> man be bound in sorrow
> Whose ev'ry function is fill'd with its fiery desire? can the
> soul whose brain and heart
> Cast their rivers in equal tides thro' the great Paradise,
> languish because the feet
> Hands, head, bosom, and parts of love, follow their high
> breathing joy? (10:181–85/E290–91/294)

Bodily powers "follow[ing] their high breathing joy" imply the four Zoas—Los as "feet" and "hands," Urizen as "head," Tharmas as "bosom," Luvah as the "parts of love." They also imply Albion as the universe-body that contains paradise— the man who is the form and image of the nation, and the four Zoas as the four paradise rivers of the four senses at the end of *Jerusalem*:

> But go, merciless man! enter into the infinite labyrinth of
> another's brain,
> Ere thou measure the circle that he shall run. Go, thou cold
> recluse, into the fires
> Of another's high flaming rich bosom, and return
> unconsum'd, and write laws.

> If thou canst not do this, doubt thy theories, learn to consider
> all men as thy equals,
> Thy brethren, and not as thy foot or thy hand, unless thou
> first fearest to hurt them. (10:190–94/E291/294)

Here the parts of the body are equal, the state is a democracy, and the Zoas implied are not hierarchically ordered but equal brothers, as they will be at the end of *The Four Zoas* and *Jerusalem*. The Duke of Orleans speaks almost as Los-Urthona, remembering the former integrity of the whole body, especially the place in it of the laboring foot and hand.

The French Revolution is of course a structure of speeches, informed by rhetoric, in which a course of action is being debated and a decision is reached: to remove the army from Paris. The "art" of the poem, as Joyce might say, is oratory. But the rhetoric breaks into poetry, the speech into vision, and the decision is almost the millennium. So *The French Revolution* is not only a Great Consult modeled on Milton, but also a structure of voices in which fundamentally different or incommensurable constructions of the world and visions of human being decisively confront one another: a Mental Fight. It is won by the voice of the people speaking as the voice of the earth (Urthona as "earth owner," in David Erdman's translation of the name). Beginning by speaking of war, the Abbé de Sièyes as voice of the people—almost as Los—suggests the whole of Blake's later myth of the Fall-Creation and Apocalypse, especially in its political form of war yielding to peace:

> . . . the pale mother nourishes her child to the deadly
> slaughter.
> When the heavens were seal'd with a stone, and the terrible
> sun clos'd in an orb, and the moon
> Rent from the nations, and each star appointed for watchers
> of night,
> The millions of spirits immortal were bound in the ruins of
> sulphur heaven
> To wander inslav'd; black, deprest in dark ignorance, kept in
> awe with the whip,
> To worship terrors, bred from the blood of revenge and
> breath of desire,
> In beastial forms; or more terrible men, till the dawn of our
> peaceful morning,

. . . .

Till man raise his darken'd limbs out of the caves of night, his
    eyes and his heart
Expand: where is space! where O Sun is thy dwelling! where
    thy tent, O faint slumb'rous Moon.
Then the valleys of France shall cry to the soldier, throw
    down thy sword and musket,
And run and embrace the meek peasant. Her nobles shall
    hear and shall weep, and put off
The red robe of terror, the crown of oppression, the shoes of
    contempt, and unbuckle
The girdle of war from the desolate earth; then the Priest in
    his thund'rous cloud
Shall weep, bending to earth embracing the valleys, and
    putting his hand to the plow,
Shall say, no more I curse thee; but now I will bless thee: No
    more in deadly black
Devour thy labour. (11–12:210–26/E292/295–96)

When the "saw, and the hammer, the chisel, the pencil, the
pen, and the instruments / Of heavenly song sound in the
wilds once forbidden" (12:230–31/E293/296), the savage will
have been civilized, and the "city of rebels" and "rebellious
city" will have become "our peaceable city." Earth as the
"ruins of sulphur heaven"; the fall of "spirits immortal" into
the bodies of black African slaves; the sun and moon fled
from the limbs of the man who, like Albion, once contained
them; the priest who ceases to be a "devourer" in "deadly
black"—all form a condensed nuclear suggestion of the
whole history of man and the creation. The prevision of "A
Song of Liberty" is most obvious, but Los the laborer and
builder as well as Los the artist is implied in saw, hammer,
chisel, pencil, and pen. And the "peaceable city" man finally
enters predicts Golgonooza—the city of art and manufac-
ture—becoming Jerusalem in *The Four Zoas* and *Jerusalem.*

In *The French Revolution,* the form of Mental Fight slowly
emerges from lament and from a rather conventional epic
structure and moves toward increasing intensity of vision. In
The Marriage of Heaven and Hell, the form of Mental Fight is
achieved immediately and completely. Vision has been freed
from particular time and place: it has become not only the
mode but also the subject of the contest, and is given the

form of discontinuous, intensely energetic symbolic juxtaposition. The differences immediately suggest the direction in which Blake is moving. *The French Revolution* is
visionary politics; the *Marriage* is too. But it turns back
through a divisive political, economic, religious, and psychological conflict to a source in Poetic Genius from which, as in
the Tractates, everything human flows.

*   *   *

In the *Marriage*, the abstract terms of the Tractates are again
brought to dramatic life and become men, or classes of men.
Thus the opposition in the Tractates between Poetic Genius
and the "Ratio" or sum of the five senses becomes in the
Marriage the opposition between the Prophet and the Priest,
and from that opposition the poem takes the form of Mental
Fight. (Unlike *The French Revolution*, however, the *Marriage*
cloaks its contemporary political reference in timelessness
and recurrence.) Ezekiel's belief that "the Poetic Genius . . .
was the first principle and all the others merely derivative"
introduces one of Blake's many accounts in the *Marriage* of
the fall of creative power—God in us—into priestcraft. Isaiah and Ezekiel are carriers of Poetic Genius, seer-prophets,
whose "honest indignation" and "firm perswasion" result
from vision. The priests in the *Marriage*, on the other hand,
are "arbitrary dictators" rather than seers or prophets. "Every
honest man is a Prophet he utters his opinion both of private
& public matters Thus If you go on So the result is So He
never says such a thing shall happen let you do what you
will. a Prophet is a Seer not an Arbitrary Dictator" (Annotations to Bishop Watson's *An Apology for the Bible*/E607/617).
The result of seeing the prophet as arbitrary dictator is revealed by Ezekiel:

> . . . and we so loved our God. that we cursed in his name all the
> deities of surrounding nations, and asserted that they had re-
> belled; from these opinions the vulgar came to think that all
> nations would at last be subject to the jews. This . . . like all
> firm perswasions, is come to pass, for all nations believe the
> jews code and worship the jews god, and what greater subjec-
> tion can be. (pl.13/E38/39)

Here, as usual in the *Marriage*, the tone is ironic. If "god" is a jealous Nobodaddy or Urizen, he is himself a god who curses his progeny when he finds them unable to keep his iron laws. To love such a god necessarily involves cursing the deities of other nations. But if the god that Ezekiel speaks of is the Poetic Genius, the source of creation and of belief itself, then the cursing—if by that one means the convicting of error—is justified. However, it is almost bound to be mis-understood, so that other nations will love not Poetic Genius but something very like Urizen. Belief in anything but Poetic Genius or Imagination is for Blake a form of enslavement. The "firm perswasion" that in "ages of imagination" "re-moved mountains" is possible only when one creates one's own belief. To believe in the Jews' god as anything other than the power of imagination or prophecy that one knows in oneself and sees in others is not belief, then, but "subjec-tion": "For all nations came to worship the jews god and what greater subjection can be." The crucial question is belief *versus* unbelief. Belief that is not one's own creation, made in the fires of one's own genius—heart and mind, energy and desire—is not belief but subjection and violates one's iden-tity. Blake's *Marriage* attempts a purification—a return to the genuine source of the poetry of the Bible in the Poetic Genius of the Hebrew poets.

Beginning with the outcast figure of the Just Man and the division between Urizen and Orc, between the party of rea-son and the party of energetic desire, the *Marriage* turns back to seek identity in the source. Once it is found, the poem works through the source power ("he, who dwells in flaming fire") toward the reconstituting of the original many-in-one: identity regained in a community in which "every thing that lives is Holy." This turning back to the source identity and recreating from it a sacred community of life are the funda-mental actions of the poem.

The *Marriage*, however, is full of obscured, disguised, or misunderstood identities. Neither Milton nor the angel knows himself or realizes that he is of the devil's party. The restrainers and tormentors are not devils but angels, and the god of reason is shown to have misunderstood or deliber-ately perverted reason, so that it is no longer the bound or circumference of energy, but the restrainer of desire. Identity seems problematic, with names only masking identity and concealing from us our ignorance. In the "Argument," which is the pattern of the poem as a whole, the "just man" is revealed to be the formerly "meek" man who planted the desert, but who, having been forced out by the sneaking serpent, has become a man of wrath. The "just man," or prophet, has been cast out, which is a recurrent event, but the details of the fall are obscure.

They are even more obscure in the devil's account of *Paradise Lost*: "It indeed appear'd to Reason as if Desire was cast out, but the Devils account is, that the Messiah fell. & formed a heaven of what he stole from the Abyss" (5/E34/34–35). The devil here seems to say that desire was not cast out; rather reason, the Messiah, fell—apparently from the original ground, the condition of fire.[4] The proof is in the devil's citation of gospel, where the Messiah "prays to the Father to send the comforter or Desire that Reason may have Ideas to build on, the Jehovah of the Bible being no other than he, who dwells in flaming fire" (5/E35/35).

This account is like that in the Tractates. Without desire, reason would be a "Ratio of the five senses" and quite impotent—as (according to the devil) the Son is in *Paradise Lost*. The beginning of "A Song of Liberty" suggests a slightly different account of the fall, in which desire is cast out—"the fire, the fire is falling!"—and the casting out of desire leads to the fall of Messiah, "the Governor or Reason," the "starry king." This passage is compatible with the earlier one, but it refers more obviously to a king who casts out desire or active energy—the body of the body politic—and depends on pure restraint or pure "reason" to govern. The *Marriage* is a socio-religio-economic-political dramatization of the Tractates that becomes increasingly political as it moves from Genesis through *Paradise Lost* to the revolutionary situation of Blake's own times.

4. Compare John Beer's observation: "It appears to the Devil that the Messiah fell and to Reason as if Desire were cast out: and if the Devil has the better of it the only reason is that the Messiah fell further" (*Blake's Humanism*, p. 25).

Beneath the conflicting accounts one fact is undoubted: man has been divided. And from the division between reason and energy, head and body, a worse or more violent division has sprung: the division between good and evil, heaven and hell, angel and devil—divisions not to be found in the Tractates. In this division, good casts evil out. In "The Garden of Love" or "I saw a chapel" or "Earth's Answer," the division seems permanent, and the casting out an irrecoverable loss: "And the gates of this Chapel were shut" ("The Garden of Love"); "So I turnd into a sty / And laid me down among the swine" ("I saw a chapel"); "Prison'd on watry shore / Starry Jealousy does keep my den" ("Earth's Answer").[5] The *Marriage*, however, presents the conflict by which the outcasts may regain their position. Los-like figures of outcast energy and Poetic Genius—the devil, Jehovah, Jesus, Isaiah, Ezekiel, the Milton who is of the devil's party— keep appearing, in contest with elect figures of repressive reason. The *Marriage* envisions the regaining of identity

5. This is not true of all the "Songs of Experience." The prophetic energy of the seer in "London" implies behind the fallen, harlot city of London the regenerate and wholly human city, the bride, Jerusalem, so that "London," one of the biggest short poems in the language, is a kind of seed poem for Blake's longest completed epic, *Jerusalem*. I owe this view of "London" to Rosemary Deen.

"The Tyger" has a similar palimpsest structure. Behind the figures of Lamb and Tyger, Pity and Wrath (one could almost say Enitharmon and Orc), the poem's seer sees alternately a tyrant god of the starry heavens and a human creator figure—a Promethean Los at his forge. He sees God as Zeus-Urizen or as Los because he has both potentialities in himself—the Los vision predominating, but at the same time posing a threat. The speaker, that is, sees through the Genius of the tiger to the more conscious and single human power of Poetic Genius from which the tiger has fallen, and which it potentially *is*. But since he sees that power through the tiger, he sees it as demonic, freed of moral concern or limit, as in "A Divine Image," where the creative source is the human heart seen as the "hungry Gorge" of a sealed furnace. Just as "God becomes as we are" in the Poetic Genius, so he becomes as the tiger is in the Genius or marked nature of the tiger. This vision of immense and dangerous power restores an element of identity that had been ignored in "The Lamb" and denied by Urizen in *The Book of Urizen*— the fiery energy that destroys and creates. And the intensity of the vision implies what is never stated in "The Tyger," though it is argued in *The Marriage of Heaven and Hell*—the primacy of fire and of the Prometheus-Los figure over the Zeus-Urizen figure. It is the former that offers a way back to identity.

through a whole series of contests between Poetic Genius and the Selfhood, between the active prolific and the passive devouring who have "usurp[ed]" power and "govern the unwilling."

Identity, as Frye remarks, begins in confrontation, and such confrontations help to make the *Marriage* the most fundamentally polemical of Blake's works.[6] Blake's translation of Dr. Thornton's Tory Lord's Prayer begins "Our Father Augustus Caesar" and ends "For God is only an Allegory of Kings & nothing Else" (E659/669). That "God is only an Allegory of Kings" is precisely Shelley's opinion in *Prometheus Unbound* and Byron's in *The Vision of Judgment*. (As Byron's Satan says to Michael, "Our difference is political.") Blake arrived at the view before them (though it is not original with him) and goes to the root of the error in language and in vision. Convinced that Milton in *Paradise Lost* "wrote in fetters when he wrote of Angels & God" and "at liberty" when he wrote of "Devils & Hell," Blake wants to free himself of "God & his Priest & King" (From "The Chimney Sweeper" of *Songs of Experience*) and to unfix and dissolve the congealed vision or system of things that comes from their domination. He wants to replace the religion of kings with the politics and openly asserted identity of free men.[7]

Ultimately, Blake wants to find a set of terms that will bring religion and politics and the psyche together again, but in the devilish way rather than in the angelic way. The polar terms in the *Marriage*—heaven and hell, angel and devil, reason and energy, truth and error—are political and psychological terms as much as religious and poetic terms. And as religious terms, they are not terms of transcendence, but terms for carrying on the conflict of belief against the world. Blake

6. "Criticism, Visible and Invisible," in *The Stubborn Structure*, p. 74.

7. Mark Schorer's *William Blake: The Politics of Vision* is very good on the *Marriage* as political dialectic; see chapter VII, part vi, pp. 216–28. "Political institutions, like all conventions, are accidents, and Blake's search is for the cause. . . . Blake decreed an equalitarianism founded not on one energy but on man's total energies. Before a democracy is possible among all men, individual men must achieve a democracy of their faculties. It is as simple and as difficult as that" (p. 227). See also David Erdman's *Prophet Against Empire*, p. 392: "From his earliest interest in kings as accusers of adultery Blake looked upon psychology as a phase of politics and politics as an acting-out of mental strife."

seeks justice and wholeness in the *Marriage*, but he seeks it by divided ways. On the one hand, he accepts the necessity of conflict; on the other, he seeks the root or source that lies below division and will resolve the confusion about names.[8] Blake wants to construct an ideal politics that will merge into religion or vision so that divided identity will be integrated into a new whole. But (adapting himself to the Fall) he seeks this integration through conflict; and conflict most obviously dominates the poem.

Behind the separation of reason from desire, in the devil's view, is the unfallen Jehovah, "he, who dwells in flaming fire." Such a Jehovah would be a devil, to whom fire or energy is "Eternal Delight." "Know that after Christs death, he became Jehovah" would in the devilish interpretation mean that Christ after his death again took up his abode in flaming fire and became one with energy or desire. Reintegrated, Christ becomes not reason but Poetic Genius—Jehovah, he who dwells in flaming fire.[9] In the angelic view, Jehovah

8. Martin K. Nurmi, in *Blake's "Marriage of Heaven and Hell": A Critical Study*, emphasizes conflict very strongly, and his is the study on which most subsequent ones are based. Where I differ from Nurmi is in my emphasis on seeking the root or source, and on conversion, as the fundamental "actions" of the poem. The conversion of an angel to a devil implies that one's role as prolific or devourer, devil or angel, is not, as Nurmi suggests, identity, but party affiliation or state. Identity is, so to speak, below such divisions, though devils in the *Marriage* are closer to the one source than angels are.

9. "If the Son was truly human desire, and the Father, Desire removed from all incumbrances, then their identity in the resurrection of the human body is an identity of fire, of an implied desire flaming into that which delights in its own form" (Harold Bloom, *The Visionary Company*, p. 81). Compare Joseph Anthony Wittreich, Jr.: "The Devil's next observation is more enigmatic still: 'Know that after Christs death, he became Jehovah.' Here the Devil simply inverts the history to which Blake elsewhere subscribes. Christ undergoes Incarnation, journeys into the desert, to redeem the energy of which he has been emptied. He emerges a perfectly integrated personality, having cast aside the law of obedience for the gospel of love. After his death, he does indeed return to the Father; and the Father becomes like the Son rather than the Son's becoming like him; the God of Wrath, Jehovah, becomes a God of Mercy, Jesus. This is the history of God from an eternal perspective, but from another perspective this history has been inverted: God continues to be conceptualized as an angry, vengeful deity, and Christ, identified with him, has anger and vengeance imposed on his own character. This is the distorted view of history and the one the Devil expresses. The Devil, in other words, advances his critique from the perspective of history rather than eternity; and consequently what he says is historically, not eternally, true" (*Angel of Apocalypse: Blake's Idea of Milton*, pp. 211–12).

would of course be seen differently—as one who finds flaming fire torment. For Blake, this angelic view, the view that Milton meant to prevail in *Paradise Lost*, accommodates religion to the needs of Caesar, the state; and the angelic Jehovah is for Blake essentially the Urizen of *The Book of Urizen*, though the name is not used in the *Marriage*. In this reading, the Christ who after his death became Jehovah is the Christ who in the hands of the priesthood became Urizen, the arch priest, intellectual tyranny working through mystery. Jehovah as Urizen has his corresponding Satan, cast out and tormented. Jehovah as "he, who dwells in flaming fire" has *his* corresponding Messiah, the active Christ of burning energy or Poetic Genius; but the position of Satan as outcast disappears, and the position of antagonist is taken by an angel who is not cast out but, as the poem develops, converted.

Often using the devil as spokesman, the *Marriage* attacks the "religious" by revealing the humanity of the divine and the politics of theology. It does so not in order to reduce the divine to the human, but to exalt the human to the divine: to identify the human and the divine. "Some will say, Is not God alone the Prolific? I answer, God only Acts & Is, in existing beings or Men" (16/E39/40). The argument here is between belief in the unity and transcendence of God and the sinfulness of man, on the one hand, and belief in the immanence of God and the power of good in men on the other. And the claim of virtue or potency in men, of course, has political consequences. It denies both the king and the priest-lawgiver the right to rule as the vicar or representative of the "alone Prolific"; and it implies the opening of careers to talents and the opening of action and morality to individual judgment and conscience.

Similarly, in the contest between an angel and a devil over what Christ did and taught, the angel loses the illusion that he is the "only wise." To the devil's assertion that "The worship of God is. Honouring his gifts in other men each according to his genius. and loving the greatest men best" (22–23/E42/43), the angel replies that God is one and "visible in Jesus Christ," who has "given his sanction to the law of ten commandments and are not all other men fools, sinners, & nothings?" The devil counters that, on the contrary, Christ broke all the commandments: "I tell you, no virtue can exist without breaking these ten commandments: Jesus was all virtue, and acted from impulse: not from rules" (23–24/E42/43). At this revelation, the angel embraces the fire, is "consumed," and rises as Elijah; later, he becomes a devil with whom Blake reads the Bible "in its infernal . . . sense" (pl. 24). This conversion—this turning toward the Real Man—is the turning point of the action and implies that the power of prophecy is more devilish—more subversive of established powers—than angelic. Los himself later acts as "Elias"—Elijah.

And Christ too is closer to devil than to angel. That Christ has different roles or incarnations in history is implied by the phrase "Messiah or Satan or Tempter" (pl. 17), by the opposing definitions of Christ given by the angel and the devil, and by the devil's account of *Paradise Lost* and the Fall as a "history" which has been "adopted by both parties" (pl. 5). But the neglected elements of Christ are embodied now in Blake's devil. Angel and devil each sees only a portion of being or eternity and fancies that to be the whole, so that each is only a portion of Christ. But the devil makes the stronger claim, by power of injured truth. For Blake it is the devilish aspect of Christ that in 1790 (or 1793) needs to be preached, because it is the suppressed element of identity and closer to the source. Fire, not cloudy reason, is the elemental source of identity, and fire is the desire of the Tractates.

Though identity is divided in the *Marriage,* one portion remains closer to the source than the other, as Los in *The Book of Urizen* remains closer to identity than Urizen does. The inequality of "equal" portions of identity is seen not only in the division between devil and angel, energy and reason, but also in the division between soul and body (where the devil proves that he is not a materialist by giving the priority to soul), poet and priest, truth and error, the prolific and the devourer. Poets are associated with energy and genius, priests with reason, so that priests are derivative—having their source in poets. Truth is original, error derivative; the prolific is original, the devourer derivative.

The point of the *Marriage* (as of Shelley's later "Defence") is that poetry comes first and is the source of the culture that

makes us human. But in all the divisions in the *Marriage*—
between devils and angels, evil and good, body and soul,
energy and reason, truth and error—the poetry and truth
that are original and identifying have been lost sight of or
suppressed. The whole given by Poetic Genius has been superseded by its derivatives and abstracts, the power buried
by its products. The printing house in hell implies forces
buried in the mind, and implies also that energy converted
into thought or reason may turn against its source energies.
The result is the apparent enslavement of energy:

> The Giants who formed this world into its sensual existence
> and now seem to live in it in chains; are in truth. the causes of its
> life & the sources of all activity, but the chains are, the cunning
> of weak and tame minds. which have power to resist energy.
> according to the proverb, the weak in courage is strong in
> cunning.
>
> Thus one portion of being, is the Prolific. the other, the De-
> vouring: to the devourer it seems as if the producer was in his
> chains, but it is not so, he only takes portions of existence and
> fancies that the whole. (16/E39/40)

The prolific, having been so long cast out, see more of the
whole than the devouring do. Having suffered the attempted
domination of weak and tame minds, they know these minds
well, whereas for weak and tame minds, the energies of the
prolific are buried and unseen. The politics of dominant and
suppressed classes is familiar. But like revolutionary vol-
canoes, the "antidiluvians who are our energies" threaten an
outburst that would open the minds of the devourers and
reassert the powers that have been suppressed.

Blake's point is not the relativity of truth but its dynamic
reversibility. The denied aspect of a positive *will* assert itself,
violently if need be. Even if, having been too long denied, it
explodes, it does not annihilate its antagonist, but comes as a
radically new division or equalizing of forces, so that the
explosion furthers the progressive conflict of contraries.
"These two classes of men [the prolific and the devouring]
are always upon earth, & they should be enemies; whoever
tries to reconcile them seeks to destroy existence" (pls. 16–
17). But it is the classes, not men, that ought to be enemies.

God is the prolific, but "God alone" is not the prolific, so that the prolific are closer to God than the devourers. This would be compatible with their both being necessary to existence, and also with Blake's taking sides and joining the party of the prolific in their conflict with their enemies, the devourers. Life on earth is a warfare, and Blake does not want to reconcile prolific and devourer: he seeks victory, not reconciliation.

But victory would be the enemy's conversion, not his extinction or casting out. (In the terms Blake uses in *Milton*, the devourer sees himself as "Elect," but Blake sees him as "Redeemed"—capable of being saved.) Here, "Opposition is true Friendship," though only eventually; thus, the effect of the devourer's absorption of the productions of Genius might be the stimulation of latent prolific powers. Since one's class or state is not identity, it may be changed by conversion. Total conversion would presumably lead to the end of the present world, or to life upon earth, and this of course takes us beyond the explicit concern of *The Marriage of Heaven and Hell.* Nevertheless, like Milton in the *Areopagitica,* Blake envisions the superseding of politics by the rule of the saints—"all the Lord's people." *The Marriage of Heaven and Hell,* then, does not simply supplant the dominant heavenly doctrine with a hellish doctrine. The conversion-action and the dialectical structure of the poem present the conflict of divided parties, but they also suggest a new whole, a new identity in the whole community of men and in the action of all of man's psychic powers: the community suggested in the Tractates. In that community the warfare of good and evil, angel and devil, would be supplanted by the contest of contraries—the truth and error, reason and desire, body and soul of the Tractates.

Against abstraction or negation (the angel's denial of body), the devil speaks for the body—for the physical body and the psychological body, the body of needs and the body of desire. The contest repeats the disagreement between the Archbishop and the Duke of Orleans, in *The French Revolution,* about the body of the state. In speaking for the body, the devil speaks for embodied soul, and thus for the whole—for bodily-spiritual needs, or for the needs of the spiritual body, against the church's exclusively spiritual preachings. If one thinks of the bodily needs of the poor ignored by the church, Blake's point becomes familiar. In the organic metaphor of the body politic—such as we find in *The French Revolution*—he speaks for the body of the state as against its head, since they *will* be divided. But the separation of head from body destroys life in the body politic as much as it does in the individual. When angels become devils, they reunite themselves with the body and its energies and recreate the original community.

Out of the conflict emerges a new whole: "Empire is no more! and now the lion & wolf shall cease"; "For every thing that lives is Holy." The *Marriage* moves toward peace—a peace to follow the violence of revolution (or, more exactly, the violence of counterrevolution) implied in "A Song of Liberty." The force of "For every thing that lives is Holy," coming where it does, is that a new holiness has been established in which all are included. The peaceable city of the end of *The French Revolution* has been immensely enlarged and freed of time, but it is at least as much "vital" paradise as human community.

Having begun with an "Argument" in which the just man is cast out, the poem ends with a prophecy of a new paradise and a new community. The new whole in which no one is cast out is made possible because Christ is not One, as the angel asserts, but One-Many: identity in difference. Christ is many in that he is embodied in individuals: "All deities reside in the human breast" (pl. 11). He is one in that the Christ of the Gospels is an original embodiment, a whole which has later been divided, so that in later times identity has shown itself in portions and conflict, as it does in the *Marriage*, where Messiah and Satan, angel and devil, have parted Christ's garments among them. Christ as the human identity scarcely appears in the *Marriage*. He has descended and divided and adapted himself to the weaknesses of individual men, so that he is seen as many or one, as sanctioning the ten commandments or as all virtue and act and breaker of all the commandments. But Christ is infinite. Thus he contains all the specific identities or characters of the "Proverbs of Hell" and the unique identities of individual men.

The identities or characters in the "Proverbs of Hell" are "portions of Being," so that the proverbs, like the rest of the *Marriage,* are about partial or divided identities, or one's identity as a part, but the emphasis in the "Proverbs" is not on the conflict of parties but on the almost infinite variety of identity or character (as E. D. Hirsch has emphasized) and on the error of its suppression by "One Law."[10] As in the Tractates, this infinite variety stems from a single prolific and forming power, but this power is worlds apart from "One Law": "One Law for the Lion & Ox is Oppression." The proverb stands alone, introducing "A Song of Liberty." But it might very well come immediately after the "Proverbs of Hell," as summing up many of them. Particularly through the animals that appear in them, the "Proverbs of Hell" assert the difference and incommensurability of experience and of worlds. These worlds are closed from one another, and one must therefore imagine the difference: "How do you know but ev'ry Bird that cuts the airy way, / Is an immense world of delight, clos'd by your senses five?"; "For every thing that lives is Holy." The varieties of animal existence and perception in these proverbs are potentially human, the divided elements of the human form: they are "portions of Eternity." Although they are fragments, when totally revealed they are identified as human, as in the totally revealed and morally interconnected world of "Auguries of Innocence," in which one sees not the conflict of parts but the identity of whole and part. This is what Blake means by seeing the Infinite in all things—the prophetic vision of innocence, such as Isaiah or Ezekiel might have, rather than the lamb's vision of innocence.

In the prophetic vision of innocence, genius or conscience in one's self demands expression and must not be resisted: "the voice of honest indignation is the voice of God." In others it demands recognition: "The worship of God is. Honouring his gifts in other men each according to his genius. and loving the greatest men best." Here, more unequivocally than in "All deities reside in the human breast," and in "God

10. See the account of the "Proverbs of Hell" in E. D. Hirsch's *Innocence and Experience.*

only Acts & Is, in existing beings or Men," Blake identifies man with God: "those who envy or calumniate great men hate God, for there is no other God" (12/E38/38;22–23/ E42/43). God, then, is immanent in all the powers of men, and he is to be praised in all of them. God is "all in all." His creative powers, furthermore, are protean. The early parts of the *Marriage* are about the embodiment of energy or Poetic Genius.

The embodiment, however, is not a solidification (Urizen's error in *The Book of Urizen* and later), but a power of acting that may take other forms: the body may be transformed, and this world may be expanded into another. The later parts of the *Marriage* are about this transformed body, to be created or resurrected through the cleansing of the senses by fire—Isaiah's live coal—and through the "improvement of sensual enjoyment." The later parts of the poem show the bursting out of energy in the apocalyptic fire of revelation: "For the cherub with his flaming sword is hereby commanded to leave his guard at the tree of life"—the unfallen body and senses— "and when he does, the whole creation will be consumed, and appear infinite. and holy whereas it now appears finite & corrupt" (14/E38/39). Here the awakening of Albion is already implied. Body and universe, if not quite identified, at least correspond.

A power of active vision, identity is obscured by the binding down and shrinking of the body and by the closing in of the senses; and it is revealed by expansion and by the burning away of "apparent surfaces." The purifying fire is the fire of vision or of prophetic wrath. The divine body is a body of energy, and thus a body that takes constantly changing forms. In eternity, form is not corporeal but spiritual—energy as play and act and forming *power*—and is thus not restraint at all. And form is never final, so that the speaking and acting "visionary forms" (*Jerusalem* 98) in which the risen, spiritual body of Albion converses with itself in eternity are changing forms, continually created and destroyed—conversation brought to life and dramatic embodiment. Identity is not abstract or general, then, nor does it overpower the unique character of individuals: it expresses itself only through the unique. The giant Albion is made up of the concrete powers of individuals; and the forms of Albion, like the forms Poetic Genius may take in Blake's Tractates, are infinite.

*   *   *

The conversation in eternity of *Jerusalem* is foreshadowed by the principles of the Tractates and by the dialectic in time of *The Marriage of Heaven and Hell* (and *The French Revolution*). The argument of the *Marriage,* however, is conducted not only by the interplay between opposed voices but also by revelation through poetic worlds, which are frequently condensed into proverbs or sublime sentences. The "Proverbs of Hell" are introduced by "How do you know but ev'ry Bird that cuts the airy way, / Is an immense world of delight, clos'd by your senses five?" (pl. 7/E35/35). This has something of the antithetical structure of a couplet by Pope, with complex and even chiastic relations among "Bird," "clos'd by your senses five," "airy way," and "immense world of delight." If the bird is an immense world, then perhaps he contains the airy way through which he cuts. At any rate, he is not simply contained *by* it. The question remains open, but from the suggestion that the bird is its immense world, Blake causes a universe to expand in the "Proverbs of Hell"—various, concrete, living, ordinary, sublime. Here the *Marriage* proceeds both by argument and irony and gnomic point, on the one hand, and by revelation and immense suggestion on the other.

Truth is to be found or reaffirmed not only in conflict, but also by vision. At the same time, error or imposture is of course also revealed by vision, as in the magic show of mutual imposition in which Blake and an angel show one another their eternal lots. What is revealed in these worlds is not just intellectual error but sense error—misperception of world "owing to your metaphysics," as the angel says, or "Analytics," as Blake says. In the "Proverbs," Blake's four elements—and his birds, animals, insects, fish, and trees— make up a world to be perceived before it is reasoned. Unlike the monolithic one-sidedness of the "eternal lots," it is a world of complementary contraries and of unique points of view, much as, in "A Vision of the Last Judgment," the Last Judgment is "seen by the Imaginative Eye of Every one according to the situation he holds" (E544/554). Finally, the show of eternal lots, which is clearly opposed to the "immense world of delight" of Blake's seed sentence, is definitively condensed into two or three pithy sentences: "we impose on one another. . . ," "The man who never alters his opinion is like standing water, & breeds reptiles of the mind," and "Opposition is true Friendship." After the "Proverbs of Hell," proverbs continue to appear strategically, each proverb deriving from and giving intellectual point to a world of imagined sense experience, with the whole qualified by the ceaseless play of irony.

"The Memorable Fancy of a Printing House in Hell," for example, presents the creation of a world by expansion and reduction. Created in six psychocosmic chambers rather than days, it forecasts the "six days they shrunk up from existence / And on the seventh day they rested" of *The Book of Urizen.* Beginning with dragons clearing away the rubbish from a cave's mouth, the creation proceeds through adorning the cave with precious stones and making it infinite. Like the "immense world of delight" and the "airy way," the cave is neither internal nor external, but is the world which the perceiver is. When, after an immense expansion of the perceptive "cavern" and its "narrow chinks," the "unnam'd Forms" of the fifth chamber cast metals into the infinite expanse, they are "receiv'd by men," take the form of books, and are placed in libraries. The contraction is sudden and ambiguous. Books may be a source of delusion—as the angel's Bible and analytics are shown to be when Blake and the angel enter them for their trip through the seven houses of brick and the mill. But the dragon-men, the viper, the eagle-like men, and the lions that helped produce the books have charged them with energy—as the books of the Bible, for example, are potentially expansive and revolutionary. The angel's conversion to a devil in the *Marriage,* we remember, derives from a radically "virtuous" reading of the Gospel. And the *Marriage* itself consists of powerfully condensed and often cryptic world-visions.

*   *   *

Generating worlds from seed images and sentences, and condensing these worlds again into charged images—its expansive energy delineated by the reason of its proverbs and sublime sentences—*The Marriage of Heaven and Hell* carries on Mental Fight not only in the conflict of principles and clash of voices, but also in the active confrontation of possible worlds.[11] No other poem of Blake's seems so confident of revolution—a revolution in perception that will transform the political order by transforming the fallen world and vision. But its envisioned and immanent community remains a transformed natural world with its principle the holiness of life rather than a fully human community: it hovers between vital paradise and city. Though it has revealed the power by which that community or city might be created, it has not yet presented the community: it focuses on the moment and power of change. The energy of change is fire, Orc's element, and Orc is finally named in "A Song of Liberty." The vision of

11. In Wittreich's judgment, the *Marriage* is not entirely successful because "Blake sympathizes, but does not fully identify, with the principal voices in the prophecy; they represent two of the many prophetic gestures, all of which Blake the prophet comprehends, but the full array of these postures is not integrated within the prophecy itself." Blake has promised us a marriage, and though the "perspective of the Devil is fully developed," "the Angel is an incidental figure in the prophecy—one not acting but being acted upon, one whose perspective, rather than being developed as a contrary to the Devil's, is annihilated in the 'marriage' that occurs at the end of the prophecy when Devil and Angel meet in an embrace. . . . one perspective—the Devil's—is elaborated by the prophecy, and the other—the Angel's—is merely assumed of Blake's audience of prospective readers" (*Angel of Apocalypse*, p. 198).

To this one might reply that Blake is attributing the angelic view to the official morality and culture of his time, that it is perfectly familiar to his readers whether they share it or not—that it is to be found even in Milton, for example—and that it needs little development in Blake's poem. The marriage in Blake's poem *is* a marriage of unequal forces; it aims at restoring a lost balance by adding weight to the side whose claim has long been denied. Blake's poem is designed for its times: though it is prophetic—Wittreich's account of the *Marriage* as based on the sevenfold vision-commentary structure of the Book of Revelation is convincing—it is also political and satiric. Furthermore, marriage in Blake's poem points to a deeper unity in a source figure who does not fully appear in the poem: the figure of Los as he developed later in Blake's work. *The Marriage of Heaven and Hell* is as much revolutionary as it is prophetic and revelatory: its focus is on change, not final revelation; this Blake reserved for *Jerusalem*.

change is Los's; and though Los is not named (except as Urthona, again in "A Song of Liberty"), he is everywhere implied—distributed into the figures of the Christ who is all virtue, the Milton who is unconsciously of the devil's party, the "ancient Poets" Elijah, Isaiah, and Ezekiel—as the center toward which they point and the source from which they derive.

3

Los in the Lambeth Prophecies

Though the form of Mental Fight is complete in *The Marriage of Heaven and Hell,* Los has still not appeared under his own name. The devil and Jesus of the poem are as much Orc as they are Los. Since the idea of Los is present from the beginning in the Tractates, the puzzle is why it took so long for Blake to develop Los as a figure or character in his poetry. Partly, Blake seems to have been diverted by the French Revolution into concentrating on Orc and Urizen—on two-figure or two-party conflict. He turns to Los as the "true man"—the source—only, and in proportion as, revolution appears less overtly in his poetry. Los does not appear as a developed figure until *The Book of Urizen* in 1795, in Blake's first relatively full account of the fall. Los's gradual emerging from the matrix of short prophecies and the figures who dominate them is my subject here.

"A Song of Liberty" (appended to *The Marriage of Heaven and Hell*) forms with *Visions of the Daughters of Albion* and *America* a cluster of related revolutionary prophecies dominated by roughly the same three figures.[1] Derived from the Tractates, they later appear in *The Book of Urizen* as "parts" of Los. The three figures are a female and two males: a mother or object of desire; a youthful and desirous rebel; and an older figure of authority. Even in his most political prophecies, Blake's symbolism is sexual and generative. In "A Song of Liberty," Orc as the "newborn fire," born of the "Eternal Female," opposes snowy Urizen, "starry king" and priest,

1. W. J. T. Mitchell has noticed Blake's triad of "Individual, Spectre, and Emanation," and the "'Three Classes of Men' (*M* 4:4), the corrupt justice represented by the three 'Accusers of Theft, Adultery Murder' and 'Satans Holy Trinity, the Accuser, the Judge, and the Executioner' (Inscriptions to 'Our End is Come,' E660) . . . and the religious tyranny of the Christian trinity which consolidates all these other triads ('in Milton: the Father is Destiny, the Son, a Ratio of the Five Senses, & the Holy Ghost, Vacuum!' *MHH* 5, E35)" (*Blake's Composite Art,* pp. 203–4).

who "promulgat[es] his ten commands." Ruddy sexuality rebels against sexual restraint: "Nor pale religious letchery call that virginity, that wishes but acts not! For every thing that lives is Holy." Both these final sentences of "A Song" lead to *Visions of the Daughters* and *America*. The action of *America* begins with Orc's rape of the "Shadowy Daughter of Urthona" and passes to the struggle between Orc and "Albion's Angel," a Urizen figure.[2] *Visions* centers on Bromion's rape of Theotormon's beloved, Oothoon. Bromion is a figure of usurping reason; Theotormon is a kind of impotent Orc, desire so self-restrained that it has become the shadow of desire; Oothoon is an object of desire awakening into desire irrepressible.

The interrelationship of the major figures in *Visions* is further implied by the fact that the names of two can be derived from the third, so that the first two names seem elements of the third. All the letters of Oothoon, and all except the *B* and *i* of *Bromion*, are found in *Theotormon*. This suggests that Theotormon is the containing figure—like the later Albion—and that Bromion and Oothoon are his conflicting psychic elements. At the same time, *Theotormon* sounds oddly like *Enitharmon*. One might see the name *Theotormon*—and the word *torment*—as derived from *Enitharmon*, or the name *Theotormon* as changing or developing into *Enitharmon*. But looking back from the myth as it develops later, we see that Theotormon is a victim of Enitharmon. In *Europe*, Enitharmon delivers her message that "woman's love is sin" to her children Oothoon and Theotormon; and while Enitharmon is quite aware of what she is doing, Theotormon in *Visions* uncomprehendingly suffers his self-division. In *Visions*, both Bro-

2. Christine Gallant points out that the "sexuality of the 'Preludium' is incestuous, for Orc and the Daughter of Urthona are brother and sister, since Orc's father, Los, is the generated image on earth of Urthona" (*Blake and the Assimilation of Chaos*, p. 27). Both Ronald Schleifer and David Erdman stress the importance of the awakening into speech in *America*. Schleifer notes, "Prophecy creates a relationship between perception and speech, and this is why utterance is so important in *America*. . . . A human voice is necessary for prophecy." Only after Orc's embrace is the "Shadowy Daughter of Urthona" able to cry out ("Simile, Metaphor, and Vision," pp. 578–79). Erdman emphasizes the initial "silence": "Blake, working as a musician, first gives us silence, then the early emergence of articulate sound, and finally a conflagration of apocalyptic thunders and war-clarions" ("America: New Expanses," in *Blake's Visionary Forms Dramatic*, pp. 95–96.)

mion and Theotormon believe that woman's love is sin; but in Bromion, the belief causes the contemptuous rape that turns victim into harlot. Theotormon is tormented by this "law" and laments the metamorphosis of the virgin Oothoon into a harlot. The result is Theotormon's paralysis. (The answer to Theotormon's paralysis comes in "For the Sexes": "Every Harlot was a Virgin once.")

When bound, Oothoon is like Orc—one of the "gen'rous" who are kept "from experience till the ungenerous / Are unrestraind performers of the energies of nature," as Boston's angel puts it in *America* (11:8–9/E54/55). As generous desire, Oothoon bound back-to-back with Bromion as ungenerous rapist is a forceful image of marriage reversed and turned to enmity and lament, and is also a powerful expression of the crippling warfare between Law and Desire in the "caverned man," Bromion-Theotormon. (Bromion—Thunderer—is perhaps the forerunner of Blake's Jupiter as the "enemy of conjugal love" in a letter of 1804.) Oothoon as overflowing desire is not need but fullness, so that she is not an erotic figure in Plato's sense—not the child of poverty—but full of overflowing fire like Orc, and at the same time a visionary of bodily joys and the improvement of sensual enjoyment.

Oothoon in *Visions* and Orc in *America* are complementary figures who derive from the *Marriage*. Though Oothoon's apocalypse is one of the senses and desire, while Orc's comes through revolutionary war or Armageddon, Orc in *America* nevertheless speaks many of Oothoon's insights and sometimes sounds like Oothoon's champion, putting into revolutionary act what she has been able to express only as vision.[3] If we listen to Orc in *America*, we hear Oothoon's objection

3. If we can speak of an apocalypse in *America*, it is of course only foreshadowed. *Armageddon* is the word used by Erdman and others. And Minna Doskow sees Orc's effectiveness in *America* as limited: "While Blake does celebrate the terrible glory of the American Revolution, he simultaneously recognizes its limited nature and imminent betrayal. That Blake saw the revolution as betrayed first becomes apparent in the initial illustrations of *America*, the frontispiece and the title page, and in the 'Preludium' where the story of the American Revolution is related in its mythic dimension. The ominous notes sounded here later resound in both the text and illustrations and culminate in the final description and picture of the American Revolution on the last plate" ("William Blake's *America*, p. 168).

In "A Note on the Orc Cycle in *America*: New Expanses," David Erdman

to the doctrine of virginity as both repressive and hypocritical, and we hear Oothoon's preference—and that of the "Proverbs of Hell" and the "Song of Liberty" in the *Marriage*—for life and its energies. Orc says, "That stony law I stamp to dust: and scatter religion abroad / To the four winds as a torn book" (8:5–6/E53/54).

> That pale religious letchery, seeking Virginity,
> May find it in a harlot, and in coarse-clad honesty
> The undefil'd tho' ravish'd in her cradle night and morn:
> For every thing that lives is holy, life delights in life;
> Because the soul of sweet delight can never be defil'd. (8:10–
> 14/E53/54)

Oothoon's vision expands on the celebration of the variety and holiness of all life in the "Proverbs of Hell." "Enough! or Too much" is the central impulse of the poem. This "too much" is the source of joy and bliss, and the problem in *Visions* is of course the binding of joy and bliss—a binding whose source is traced to sexual prohibition, secrecy, hypocrisy, "modesty" demanded of women. In Bromion, joy is all but dead. Though he thunders, he is as much a pale fire as Theotormon or any of the dead in *The French Revolution*. In Oothoon, joy, though immodest, is virgin in that it is newly experienced. When Oothoon is bound and prevented from acting, desire spills over into the intensely felt associative overflow of "Prolific Vision." Sexual desire is the fountain, and each desire is an "infant" and a "moment"—an inexhaustible and ageless source. For Oothoon, every focus of desire or delight forms a world, so that there are as many worlds, or visions of the world, as there are desires or joys or loves. Each world is itself infinite, and each desirer is infinite, so that, as in the Tractates, "The desire of Man being Infinite the possession is Infinite & himself [the possessor] Infinite."

---

cautions us about misapplying the phrase "Orc cycle": "Northrop Frye wrote a brilliant mythopoeic chapter on the 'Orc cycle,' and the term is now so current that some people father it upon Blake (Frye, *Symmetry*, ch. 7, esp. pp. 206ff.). Frye ranges through the Lambeth works but with his focus on the *America* pattern. Recent criticism often focuses on the Napoleonic cycle, implying the corruption of revolutionary energy (equated with 'power') into tyrannic cruelty. To call this the 'Orc cycle' and then read that kind of corruption into *America* is to wander far astray" (*Visionary Forms Dramatic*, p. 112).

Oothoon is the "faculty which experiences" of the Tractates, celebrating the "infinite variety" of identity asserted in the Tractates. She images this variety through an almost Dickensian picture of the diverse occupations and obsessions of man and through a range of birds and animals that symbolize the inexhaustible variety of unique human identities. The wide field of experience touched on in *Visions* is that of the infinitely containing or perceptive mind; its order—as in the *Marriage*—is that of the psychological leap and the continuity given by force of feeling and conviction. (*The Book of Urizen* and *The Book of Los,* by contrast, are all narrow line and narrow focus—tunnel visions of the fall.) Even in her "wail," and even though she is physically bound, Oothoon remains "capable of possessing." The binding back-to-back of Oothoon and Bromion by Theotormon gives *Visions* the form of the "infinite desire" and "infinite possession" of the Tractates confronted by the incapability of possession: hope versus despair, seeing God versus seeing the self only. Oothoon's perceptions are clear, precise, vividly imaged and felt. Bromion's and Theotormon's are vague, weak, obscure. Taking our cue from Leibniz's *Monadology* (paragraph 49), we might say that Oothoon acts in that she has distinct perceptions; Bromion and Theotormon are passive in that they have confused perceptions.

Visions narrows to the point at which Theotormon and Bromion express their depressed and puzzled sense of diminished joys and narrowed senses, and expands into Oothoon's extraordinary flow of lamentation-celebration. The turn, the neck of the hourglass, is in this exchange between Bromion and Oothoon:

> And is there not one law for both the lion and the ox?
> And is there not eternal fire, and eternal chains?
> To bind the phantoms of existence from eternal life? (4:22–24/
>   E47/48)

To this Oothoon (the next morning) replies:

> O Urizen! Creator of men! mistaken Demon of heaven:
> Thy joys are tears! thy labour vain, to form men to thine
>   image.

> How can one joy absorb another? are not different joys
> Holy, eternal, infinite! and each joy is a Love. (5:3–6/E47/48)

In opposing Urizen directly, Oothoon seems a kind of Orc, as she also is in her emphasis on desire. But she is a very articulate and visionary Orc and becomes from this point on—from the "turn" in which she recognizes Urizen in Theotormon—a preliminary figure for Los. From Oothoon's recognition of Urizen, *Visions* becomes both a continuous expansion of the range and variety of sense experience imaginatively felt and defined, and a continuously intensifying excitement. In *The Book of Urizen, The Book of Ahania,* and *The Book of Los,* form reveals subject by the relative poverty of imagery, the constriction of line, the strictly relevant notation of events, and the dead end at which we arrive. *Visions,* by contrast, ends in a suspension of action and desire that is a flowering of vision (as in Yeats's "Among School Children"). The flower Oothoon plucked is a "soul of sweet delight [which] can never pass away."

If we look at "A Song of Liberty" and *Visions* and *America* as psychomachies as well as political prophecies, the dominant figures in them seem versions of the threefold psychology of the *Republic* turned toward revolutionary ends. Plato's "reason" appears in the "starry king" of "A Song of Liberty," in the Theotormon and Urizen of *Visions,* and in Albion's angel in *America.* Plato's "spirited part" appears in Orc in "A Song of Liberty" and *America* and *The Song of Los,* and in Oothoon in *Visions.* But the "passions"—Plato's potentially unruly mob—are missing. The Eternal Female and the Shadowy Daughter of Urthona and Oothoon (in Bromion's view) are not passions but objects of desire. Oothoon is the womb in which Bromion begets slave children and profits; she is the object only of distorted desire. But the Eternal Female and the Shadowy Daughter are the earth-womb in which Orc generates events. (In *Europe* that womb seems a fiery furnace.) The psychology of Blake's revolutionary prophecies pits the prolific power against its restraint. In *Visions,* of course, the marriage coupling is reversed, and Theotormon is self-hindered from fatherhood. Theotormon's binding back-to-back of Oothoon and Bromion may be seen as a moment in Adam's reaction to Eve's fall, with Oothoon as Eve, Bromion as Satan ("Satan as Desire, and hence one of the eternal contraries," as David Wagenknecht remarks), and Theotormon as Adam crippled by the accusation of sin. If Wagenknecht is right in seeing Bromion's questions as indicating that he is "on the verge of enlightenment," then we may see Theotormon as predicting the elect in *Milton*, while Bromion predicts the redeemed, and Oothoon the reprobate.[4]

Allegorically, one may see Theotormon as reason, Bromion as the desire which (after an outburst) he has bound, and Oothoon as the object of desire. Oothoon and Bromion bound back-to-back then seem an image of desire bound by reason and show the sinfulness—for reason—of woman's love. Or one may see Bromion as reason, Oothoon as desire, and Theotormon as the torment generated by their conflict. Blake's figures cannot be neatly translated because they are not simply allegorical: they are multivalent and in vital movement. What is clear is that Theotormon, though physically unfettered, is thoroughly bound because his manacles are forged in his own mind. The man has become his state, has become despair derived from the accusation of sin. In part, Blake envisions a harmony of powers or an alliance of two powers against a third, as Plato does in the psychology of the *Republic*. But he also sees the fallen man as becoming an inclusive state—becoming Theotormon or Urizen, becoming Bromion or Orc, becoming Oothoon as Los (as the condition of loss). At the end of *Visions*, the dominant or containing state is despair, desire incapable of possessing its object. Neither Bromion nor Theotormon is capable of possessing Oothoon, and both are images of reason tormented by desire, as Oothoon forcibly hindered from possessing her object is an image of desire tormented by reason. If we see the word *torment* in *Theotormon*, the name describes the state of all three figures, though in Oothoon it becomes ecstatic vision.

At the same time, Oothoon seems more complete—and more Orc-like—than Theotormon or Bromion because she is in touch with all four elements. Her element as "the soft soul

4. *Blake's Night,* pp. 184, 208.

of America" is presumably earth, but she is torn by Bromion's thunder (fire) and by "Theotormon's Eagles" (which
she addresses as "kings of the sounding air") and is associated with the waters of the Atlantic, which she crosses. Her
association with four elements suggests her participation in a
complete world of life, of which Theotormon and Bromion
know only parts. The experience of all four elements, which
might seem to immerse her thoroughly in "life's river," Generation, seems actually to help her see beyond it by seeing
through it. Oothoon experiences most of the kinds of madness named in the *Phaedrus*—not only the erotic but also the
prophetic or Apollonian and the enthusiastic/religious or Dionysian. The Muses of the poetic madness appear ironically
as the Daughters of Albion, Daughters of Memory who only
echo Oothoon's laments. Oothoon might best be seen as an
untaught ecstatic, her strongest furors erotic and Dionysian.
She is not a poet-prophet or visionary of Jesus—both of
which Los is to become—but visionary joy.

*   *   *

In Blake's psychology, imagination is not the ruler over
desire and reason but their source, and hence the balance
they achieve when the energy of desire has the initiative.
When the devil in the *Marriage* maintains that Messiah, or
the Son, prays to the Comforter, or desire, so that reason may
have ideas to build on, he implies that desire is prolific. In the
Marriage, fire-energy-desire, which issues from "[him] who
dwells in flaming fire," plays freely and finds reason as its
own bound or outward circumference. This balance is imagination, which envisions and creates its own object. Through
most of the Lambeth prophecies, however, desire and reason—Orc and Urizen—are in conflict. In *America*, the conflict bursts out as revolution. In *Visions*, it is contained in the
man and paralyzes him. This is to say that Los, or imagination, is absent from or inactive in these prophecies. They are
dominated by three figures: reason, desire, and the object of
desire. Los would be the fourth. With Los absent or at rest,
the prolific figure becomes Orc: imagination is supplanted by
desire, the imaginative prolific by the vital prolific. In Oothoon, however, the Eternal Female begins to desire as Orc

desires and to see as Los sees. The object of desire becomes desire and begins to awaken as imagination. When desire achieves its "natural" or sexual object, it becomes prolific, as in "A Song of Liberty" and *America*. When desire envisions or creates its object, it finds its own bound or outward circumference—reason—and becomes Los or imagination, as Oothoon almost does in *Visions*.[5] Desire bound in *Visions* may be able to awaken as imagination because it is not self-bound. But *Visions* remains a strange poem in Blake's canon. In later poems, desire bound still issues in lament, as it does in *Visions*, but not in such a flowering or overflow of vision.

* * *

In *Europe*, the cast of four interrelated characters who precede the four Zoas is for the first time complete: Los, Orc, Urizen, and Enitharmon.[6] To the figures of the earlier prophecies—always a female and two males—has been added a fourth and source male figure. (Milton's trio in the temptation in *Paradise Lost* is also a female and two males. If we read them as the Platonic psychic triad, Adam is of course reason, and Satan only a pretender to reason—really the spirited part in rebellion against reason and allying itself with the passions, Eve.) Los appears by name for the first time in *Europe*, and Urizen scarcely appears at all. For the most part, his place is taken by Enitharmon, who, as David Erdman suggests, is both Queen of Heaven and Marie Antoinette. Los's role, given Enitharmon's importance, is minimal, and the static dream form of the poem derives largely from his abdication of power—the complacency which allows Enitharmon to dream Europe for eighteen hundred years. She repeats the sleepiness of the king in *The French Revolution*,

5. Erdman, in "*America*: New Expanses," speaks of "the female in Promethean state" (*Blake's Visionary Forms Dramatic*, p. 109). This is a perfect description of Oothoon in *Visions of the Daughters*. Erdman's account of *Visions* in *Prophet Against Empire*, pp. 206–42, is the best we have, especially in linking Blake the engraver of book illustrations with Blake the poet and clarifying Blake's treatment of slavery and of attempts to abolish the slave trade.

6. For a detailed commentary on *Europe*, and especially its allusions to the Bible and to Milton's "On the Morning of Christ's Nativity," see Michael J. Tolley's "*Europe:* 'To Those Ychain'd in Sleep,'" in *Blake's Visionary Forms Dramatic*, pp. 115–45.

who knows that he should awaken after five thousand years but continues to dream.

This absence from reality is reinforced by Blake's presenting Europe as a heavenscape rather than a landscape—a fancy-dress ball of star-god kings and queens, "at sport beneath the solemn moon," ended by the outbreak of war. Only briefly, as in this condensed passage, do Europe's earth-dwellers appear:

> Enitharmon laugh'd in her sleep to see (O womans triumph)
> Every house a den, every man bound; the shadows are filld
> With spectres, and the windows wove over with curses of iron:
> Over the doors Thou shalt not; & over the chimneys Fear is written:
> With bands of iron round their necks fasten'd into the walls
> The citizens: in leaden gyves the inhabitants of suburbs
> Walk heavy: soft and bent are the bones of villagers. (12:25–31/E63/64)

If Enitharmon is indeed earth—"Earthona"—she has badly mistaken herself as Queen of Heaven. The mistake or topsy-turviness extends to "the nameless shadowy female," who, uprooted, complains that "My roots are brandish'd in the heavens. my fruits in earth beneath / . . . labour into life" (1:8–9/E59/60).

The stasis in *Europe,* like that in *Visions,* stems from sexual prohibition. But in *Europe,* it is laid at Enitharmon's door, for it is she who gives an essentially Urizenic message to Rintrah and Palamabron:

> Now comes the night of Enitharmons joy!
> Who shall I call? Who shall I send?
> That Woman, lovely Woman! may have dominion?
> Arise O Rintrah thee I call! & Palamabron thee!
> Go! tell the human race that Womans love is Sin!
> That an Eternal life awaits the worms of sixty winters
> In an allegorical abode where existence hath never come:
> Forbid all Joy, & from her childhood shall the little female
> Spread nets in every secret path. (5:1–10/E61/62)

Europe, however, does not end in this stasis. It ends in a coming action: Los calling his sons to "the strife of blood."

While Los was at rest—inattentive—Orc rebelled against Enitharmon's heaven or "crystal house." This is to say that Blake sees Europe as both the "giant form" Los and the family who have derived from him, as distinct psychological powers derive from Poetic Genius in the Tractates. Los is sleeping or carousing in Beulah, in his feminine state, Enitharmon. But Enitharmon's prohibition of act and putting off of desire—along with her provoking of Orc—lead to an explosion of violence finally embodied or given voice by Los.[7] In *Europe* Los suggests both the power of act—what is left of identity or the true man, Poetic Genius—and the containing figure whom Blake later calls Albion. Los-Albion dreams as Enitharmon and awakens in Orc, but the whole of Europe divided and at war is nevertheless moved by a single impulse, and this movement—a fall—Blake calls Los. If Orc's "thought-creating fires" (the phrase comes from *The Song of Los*) and Enitharmon's lamentation have awakened Los, this means in part that it was revolution which awakened Blake. Since Los's awakening is to a violent "strife of blood," Orc is still the moving force. (Contrast the peaceable victory of the people in *The French Revolution*.) Los as Los—named—has not yet become the champion of humanity in what deserves to be called Mental Fight rather than warfare.

*　　*　　*

After *The French Revolution*, revolution is less simply successful in Blake's poetry, and after *America* he may have

7. Michael Tolley identifies Los here with the "angel standing in the sun" of Revelation: "*Europe* ends with the twisting of an image from Revelation 19:

> Then Los arose his head he reard in snaky thunders clad:
> And with a cry that shook all nature to the utmost pole,
> Call'd all his sons to the strife of blood.

In Revelation 19:17–18 we have this equally macabre preparation: 'And I saw an angel standing in the sun; and he cried with a loud voice, . . . to all the fowls . . . come and gather yourselves unto the supper of the great God.'" Tolley points out that "Los . . . stands in the sun in *Milton* 21 as well as in the vision at Felpham recorded in Blake's letter of 22 November 1802 to Butts" ("'Ychain'd in Sleep,'" in *Blake's Visionary Forms Dramatic*, p. 144). Tolley reads the early epithet "possessor of the moon" as identifying Los with the sun (p. 126). If Tolley is right, Los's absence is the absence of the sun during Enitharmon's eighteen-hundred-year night.

ceased to believe that anything could come of the warfare between Orc and Urizen. At the same time, he apparently saw Los only in terms of fall and loss. After the apocalypses of "A Song of Liberty," *Visions of the Daughters,* and *America,* and after the suspension or stasis of *Europe,* most of the prophecies of the 1790s are falls. Some leap from fall to apocalypse, as *The Song of Los* does. In any case, in the Lambeth prophecies, history is missing or condensed into images of diamond pressure. As successful revolution disappears from Blake's poetry, his eye ascends to greater heights, and his ear turns toward remote times, taking in the whole range of time and space in condensed nucleus poems such as *Europe* and *The Song of Los.*

The fall poems present a narrowing of the senses and a one-line (straight or circular) plot, which is developed from a single point of view: One Law. Though they may contain a two-figure dance or action—like that between Los and Urizen in *The Book of Urizen* and *The Book of Los*—there is no Mental Fight, which requires vision. The narratives of fall tend to be called books—*The Book of Urizen, The Book of Ahania, The Book of Los*—and to be divided into short lines and numbered chapters and verses. They are unadorned, unprolific accounts, proceeding relatively evenly without the leaps from one character, time, or image to another that the apocalypse poems have. The straight-line or circular narrative and the single point of view of the books and "The Mental Traveller" imply "Single vision" and the fall into "Newtons sleep." Nevertheless, the fall poems are pregnant with change.

One of the recurrent images from the Tractates is that of the futile and repetitive circle of domination by One Law—the "same dull round even of a universe." It recurs in the Duke of Orleans's "Go . . . enter into the infinite labyrinth of another's brain / Ere thou measure the circle that he shall run" (*The French Revolution,* E291/294). It occurs also in *Visions of the Daughters,* in "they inclos'd my infinite brain into a narrow circle" and "To turn the wheel of false desire" (2:32/ E46/47; 5:27/E48/49) and in this remarkably condensed vision in *Europe:*

> Thought chang'd the infinite to a serpent; that which pitieth:
> To a devouring flame; and man fled from its face and hid

In forests of night; then all the eternal forests were divided
Into earths rolling in circles of space, that like an ocean
   rush'd
And overwhelmed all except this finite wall of flesh.
Then was the serpent temple form'd, image of infinite
Shut up in the finite revolutions, and man became an Angel;
Heaven a mighty circle turning; God a tyrant crown'd. (10:16–
   23/E62/63)

Along with the laments, images like this compressed metamorphosis of the universe are the controlling centers in
Blake's prophecies and the seeds from which the long poems
The Four Zoas, Milton, and *Jerusalem* finally spring. Even
when they are images of stasis, their density promises
change and unfolding, promises apocalypse.

The apocalypse poems present a Dionysian expanding of
the senses: the improvement, freeing, and increase of desire
and sensual enjoyment. *The Marriage of Heaven and Hell* (especially the "Proverbs of Hell") and *Visions of the Daughters*
multiply worlds of desire and perception and symbolize differences of sense and world through birds and plants and
animals: "With what sense does . . . ?" (*Visions*, 3:3/E46/47).
The apocalypses are sudden and revolutionary and tend to
be called songs—"A Song of Liberty," *The Song of Los*—or
they are named for countries or continents: *America* and the
"Africa" and "Asia" sections of *The Song of Los.* The apocalypse poems are further marked by constant change, pro-
liferating images, multiple points of view and "points of
desire," and they alternately expand from and contract to
seed images of concentrated power. *Europe* has three facets or
angles of vision—an introductory plate in which Blake cap-
tures a fairy who can show him "all alive / The world, when
every particle of dust breathes forth its joy" (iii:17–18/E59/60);
the "Preludium," which focuses on the lament of the Eternal
Female who seems all womb, bringing forth only the devouring and the devoured; and the "Prophecy," which shows the
world as alive but asleep, the prolific denied. In *Visions of the
Daughters,* the wide-ranging speculation and the heaping up
of more images and points of view and possibilities than can
be reduced to a single line imply the narrowness of One Law;

and the multiple points of view imply that every existence is a law unto itself, imply anarchy. This is the major implication of the "Proverbs of Hell," also, and is one of the major implications of the whole of the *Marriage*.

Though they have endings, most of the Lambeth prophecies are too short for the scale of their subjects. They lack middles, lack history or development. In this sense they are fragments and seem to be truncated efforts at writing something like the longer prophecies that came later. But their dense compactness makes them more like nuclei. *The Song of Los* is one of the best examples. To *America* and *Europe* it adds sections entitled "Africa" and "Asia," suggesting (as Erdman has observed) Blake's desire for geographical completeness. It is also complete in time. Perhaps because of his awakening at the end of *Europe,* Los sees all time. His mind is a nucleus or monad holding it all, as Moneta's mind does in *The Fall of Hyperion,* but holding it only as immensely compacted seed or as a focus of vision high above earth. At the same time, the song is immensely detached, and there is no sign that the singer takes sides or feels the decline of prophecy into error. Whether or not the whole of *The Song of Los* is sung by Eno, this removal or irony supports the impression one gets from most of the prophecies of the 1790s that Los has fallen silent.

Los's song begins with Adam and Noah, successive progenitors of mankind who are now reduced to "bleached bones" by the fall into error of the Eternal Prophet, and ends with an apocalyptic resurrection of these "bleached bones" through Orc's powers of awakening life. One of the first errors is Greek philosophy; a second one is the Gospel of Theotormon:

> Palamabron gave an abstract Law:
> To Pythagoras Socrates & Plato.
>
> Times rolled on o'er all the sons of Har, time after time
> Orc on Mount Atlas howld, chain'd down with the Chain of
>   Jealousy
> Then Oothoon hoverd over Judah & Jerusalem
> And Jesus heard her voice (a man of sorrows) he recievd
> A Gospel from wretched Theotormon. (3:18–24/E66/67)

Apparently Jesus received "A Gospel" (whether one of the four gospels or the gospel as a whole is not clear) from Theotormon rather than Oothoon. His being called "a man of sorrows" implies that he did not change it, but passed it on as he received it. Yet he "heard" Oothoon's "voice." If one of Jesus's voices is the Urizenic Theotormon who preaches One Law, another is Oothoon, who celebrates the liberation of desire. The vision which prevails is that of One Law. Later, when "a Philosophy of Five Senses" is "complete," and Urizen gives it to "Newton & Locke," the decline of prophecy seems almost total.

But this is only half the poem's movement. Like almost all Blake's early prophecies, *The Song of Los* is dialectical—a fight between Orc and kings. The "Kings of Asia" respond to "the thick-flaming, thought-creating fires of Orc" by crying "in bitterness of soul." What follows is an amazing satirical lament, which concludes:

> To restrain the child from the womb,
> To cut off the bread from the city,
> That the remnant may learn to obey.
>
> That the pride of the heart may fail;
> That the lust of the eyes may be quenched:
> That the delicate ear in its infancy
> May be dull'd; and the nostrils clos'd up;
> To teach mortal worms the path
> That leads from the gates of the Grave.
>
> Urizen heard them cry! (6:24; 7:1–9/E67–68/69)

Urizen's hovering over "Judea," over "his ancient place" and "Jerusalem," apparently reaffirms the death of Adam and Moses. But from "Adam, a mouldering skeleton," lying "bleach'd on the garden of Eden," and from "Noah as white as snow / On the mountains of Ararat" (7:20–23/E68/69), renewed life comes. Urizen's thunders are answered by an Orc who arises "like a pillar of fire," a "serpent of fiery flames," and the grave suddenly becomes a womb:

> Forth from the dead dust rattling bones to bones
> Join: shaking convuls'd the shivring clay breathes
> And all flesh naked stands: Fathers and Friends;
> Mothers & Infants; Kings & Warriors:
>
> The Grave shrieks with delight, & shakes

> Her hollow womb, & clasps the solid stem:
> Her bosom swells with wild desire. (7:31–37/E68/69)

The poem concludes with the words "Urizen Wept."

In *The Song of Los* Blake carries his symbolism to extremes of condensed opposition even for him: the contest between the grave and the womb and the turn from the grave at the start to the womb at the end present the whole of generation as life and death, death and life. (*The French Revolution*, similarly, begins with "The dead brood over Europe" and ends with the dead expecting resurrection.) When the grave becomes a womb at the end of *The Song of Los*, we see that the poem responds to and completes *The Book of Thel*, in the last section of which (probably a late addition) the womb is seen as a grave. And if we listen again to the bitter outcry of the Kings of Asia in *The Song of Los*, we hear almost the same voice as the one that emerges from Thel's grave pit—a voice which fears the lust of the eye, finds the ear too delicate, and wishes to close up the nostrils. The Kings of Asia want "To restrain the child from the womb." Thel *is* a child restrained or self-restrained from the womb, one who refused to enter the death of mortal birth or growth.[8] When the "eternal gates terrific porter lift[s] the northern bar," Thel has got as far as what the Kings of Asia call "the gates of the Grave." But she flees from those gates back to the "vales of Har." Oothoon in *Visions of the Daughters* completes the whole world of opposed choices implied in *The Book of Thel* by choosing differently from Thel. *The Song of Los* completes the grave image of *The Book of Thel* and at the same time traces Thel's fears to political repression by the Kings of Asia. Finally, we may note that the active power in *The Song of Los* is still not Los but Orc. Wherever the source of error is identified as kings, the awakener is Orc.

*   *   *

Europe and *The Song of Los* are tantalizing sketches or sym-

---

8. Thomas R. Frosch, in *The Awakening of Albion*, calls Thel a "wish," an "infant," and a "seed" that tries "to take root in the watery dreams of Beulah rather than the earth of Generation. That earth is the only means of access from Lower to Upper Beulah" (p. 166).

bolic condensations of Blake's whole myth of history as fall-apocalypse. *The Book of Urizen* gives a beginning to that myth and lays it out in what at first seems sequential narrative form. But the salient fact about *The Book of Urizen* is that, while Los is the source, Urizen, in the order of the poem, appears first. We begin with "a shadow of horror" who is soon identified as Urizen. But since he is later said to have been rent from Los's side, and since Enitharmon too springs from Los, we ought to speak of Los-as-Urizen, Los-as-Enitharmon, Los-as-Orc. If the Tractates reconstitute the "true man"—Poetic Genius—from the parts into which he has fallen, *The Book of Urizen* shows Urizen, Enitharmon, and Orc as the parts into which Los falls. If Urizen is reason, Enitharmon begins as pity and provokes jealousy. These are Urizen's emotions in Los, which turn Enitharmon into a forbidden object of desire. Orc, correspondingly, becomes desire bound or limited and turned to rage. Orc's generation is not only earthy but erotic, his rage derived from parental binding of the sexual impulse. The spirit of revolution is an Eros figure.

In Enitharmon and Orc, then, an original whole and integral power of action—identity—has fallen into self-divided conflict between pity and rage. There are, so to speak, two falls, Urizen's and Los's. First, reason (in the person of Urizen) asserts a self-conscious and secret and lawgiving existence; then Poetic Genius further divides into pity and rage. Once Urizen has been rent from Los, Los's share of reason begins to act separately within him, and Los the prophet, in the jealous fires with which he surrounds Enitharmon in a kind of fallen paradise, and in his binding of Orc, falls into priestcraft and almost becomes Urizen. But throughout, Los seems to act unconsciously.

In the fall with which the poem begins, Urizen separates himself from the other Eternals. First a "shadow," dividing times and spaces (as Los does later), Urizen becomes a landscape of "desolate mountains" and a "forsaken wilderness, / Of beast, bird, fish, serpent & element," and finally a voice uttering "Words articulate, bursting in thunders" (3:15–16, 4:4/E69–70/70–71). With articulate words, the first person singular pronoun appears in the poem:

> From the depths of dark solitude. From
> The eternal abode in my holiness,
> Hidden set apart in my stern counsels
> Reserv'd for the days of futurity,
> I have sought for a joy without pain,
> For a solid without fluctuation
> Why will you die O Eternals?
> Why live in unquenchable burnings? (4:6–13/E70/71)

From "a deep world within: / A void immense," Urizen creates "A wide world of solid obstruction" and composes books full of "secrets" and laws. The voice ends with

> One command, one joy, one desire,
> One curse, one weight, one measure
> One King, one God, one Law. (15:38–40/E71/72)

Urizen has separated himself from the other Eternals, who "live" (and change or die) "in unquenchable burnings"; he has begun to fight fire and its perpetual changes and to fear death. (It is Urizen, later, who teaches men the fear of death.) The emphasis on Urizen's solitude—"stretch'd o'er the void / I alone, even I" (4:8–19/E70/72)—implies that the fires that torment him come from the community of the Eternals and the Mental Fight they engage in. Though the fires burn, they are the fires of love. The little black boy of *Songs of Innocence* gladly received the heat and light of the sun, but Urizen turns away from the burning—from the confrontation of Mental Fight—and toward the solitary self. Since fire is not only love but also constant play and change of energy, Urizen's becoming the enemy of fire means that he seeks a congealed identity, a "solid without fluctuation" and a permanent joy. From the void and chaos his own separation brings into existence, he creates a world of "solid obstruction" and composes his books of secrecy and law. In fighting fire, of course, Urizen ceases to function simply as the bound or outward circumference of energy, or fire, and becomes the restrainer of fire. Ironically, he finds himself in a hell whose fires give no light. He has fallen into fires of eternal torment and is on the way to becoming the Satan of the Bard's Song of *Milton,* whose hell is his own creation.

The Book of Urizen is as much about the creation of Urizen and those who believe in him—in his "religion"—as it is about the creation of the world. The two, God and world, correspond and are indissolubly linked. Urizen and his worshippers form a sort of antiidentity—not the passions emanating in all their glory from intellect, but the passions denied (Orc is bound "Beneath Urizens deathful shadow"), not a community of equals but a tyrannical church. And this church has as its visible emblem the Egypt where the worshippers of Urizen "built / Tombs in the desolate places" (28:5–6/E82/83), and from which Fuzon—"first begotten, last born"—at the end leads the "remaining children of Urizen" (28:20/E82/83). Urizen is a twisted "Izrael."

Urizen, then, is the creator figure in *The Book of Urizen*. The "petrific" roof which he builds against the fires of eternity is "like a womb" and looks to the sons of eternity "Like a human heart strugling & beating" (5:36/E72/73). This heart is finally revealed to be the Egypt (Africa) from which Fuzon leads an exodus. And this in turn is the "pendulous earth." Urizen appears to be earth; his stony roof or beating heart is the ambiguous world Los is assigned to "keep watch" over, in order "to confine, / The obscure separation alone" (5:39–40/E72/73). But Los's creation or binding of Urizen's world-body continues to be initiated and moved by Urizen. And phrases such as "The eternal mind bounded," "In chains of the mind locked up," "inclos'd / In an orb, his fountain of thought" (10:19,25,33–34/E74/75) show that Los has fallen into Urizen and has become barely distinguishable from him. Nevertheless, Los, though fallen, is still one of those who "live in unquenchable burnings," and he is able to revive his fires when they seem to have died.

The fact that the name *Los* does not appear until after Urizen's separation from the Eternals implies that until Urizen's separation Los had no separate existence. Nevertheless, Los is primary, what is left of the source or first principle of the Tractates and the *Marriage*, and Urizen is rent from his side:

> Los wept howling around the dark Demon:
> And cursing his lot; for in anguish,
> Urizen was rent from his side. (6:2–4/E72/73–74)

Urizen is rent from Los as the priesthood is rent from the creative body of prophecy, or as the moral law is rent from the gospel. It is a creation in "dark visions of torment" (2:7/ E69/70), anguish, separation, and loss. Enitharmon is also rent from Los—the "first female now separate" (18:10/E77/78), an embodiment or splitting off of pity. She is both Urizen's reaction to Los and Los's reaction to Urizen. *The Book of Urizen* is a two-figure dialectic between Los and Urizen, initiated by Urizen's separation and changes, and it is from this masculine dialectic that a female comes into separate existence. (In "The Mental Traveller," a host-guest dialectic produces a female babe from the hearthfire.) When Los is "divided / Before the death-image of Urizen," Enitharmon separates from him as a "globe of life blood trembling" (15:1– 2, 13/E77/78). Life comes as a response to the image of death. One might say that in the creation-action of *The Book of Urizen*, death precedes life—but the *image* of death comes first. Los, Enitharmon, and Orc mirror Milton's Satan, Sin, and Death; but Orc is a figure of *life*.

Enitharmon is apparently earth, or earth-moon, as the letters in her name and the illumination showing her globelike birth from Los suggest; and Orc, who has been worm and serpent in the womb, is born "delving earth." That earth is pity is the perfect expression of Blake's view of the creation-fall. Urizen and Enitharmon, then, are two fallen faces of earth—the One Law of death, and pity. Urizen is earth as fetal skeleton in the illumination on plate 8. Enitharmon is earth as heart or womb—as pity. (Urizen as a fetal skeleton develops into Satan in Enitharmon's protective womb or tomb in the Bard's Song of *Milton*.)

In creating the body of Urizen, Los has been working as an artisan or demiurge, binding and dividing and riveting.[9] When Enitharmon appears, however, she is "fleshly"—as if she were an Eve grown spontaneously and unconsciously within Los-Adam. And when Los begets Orc on her, a generation or sexual action is added to the making action of the

9. In what follows, I often identify Los as *demiurge*. I am aware that Urizen is often identified as a kind of demiurge. As I use the word, however, I intend no implication of gnosticism: I take my use from the *Timaeus*. When I speak of Los as a demiurge, I mean that he has been appointed to watch over the fallen world, and that he is a workman who creates a world and embodies souls as a physical act.

poem. Los as worker is followed by Los as lover and progenitor. (Contrast the sequence in "The Mental Traveller" where the male as potent husbandman precedes the male as industrial worker, miner, metal worker, and so on.) The separation of Urizen and Enitharmon from Los, the begetting of Orc, and the growth of Los's chain of jealousy seem increasingly unconscious and driven actions. Poetic Genius has fallen into reason and generation—Los is more sexual force than force of vision—and generation has fallen into jealousy. Everything Los creates is an offspring of Urizen.[10] The Eternal Prophet has become the servant of the Eternal Priest, has become desire bound. The bound Orc is an image of Los's own desire bound, as Bromion (in one reading) is an image of Theotormon's desire bound. Los serving Urizen enacts the Theotormon of *Visions of the Daughters*, Enitharmon the Oothoon who is a forbidden object of desire, and Orc the bound Bromion.

Finally we see that Los has given form to a religion of sorrow, woe, and dismal torment generated from "the sorrows of Urizens soul" (25:17/E81/82). Called a "Female in embrio," it is a female form of Urizen: the "perverse and cruel delight" (19:12/E78/79) of Enitharmon's flight from Los is Urizen's. The Eternal Priest has arrived even before sexual division, so that he is there to forbid sexual delight before it exists. Urizen's priority or prevention is itself a bitter satire on the relation of One Law to the prophetic power in the book of Genesis, and *The Book of Urizen* as a whole is a long lament for the loss of prophetic power. That Urizen's worshippers "built tombs in the desolate places" obviously suggests a religion of death:

> Six days they shrunk up from existence
> And on the seventh day they rested
> ....
> And forgot their eternal life.

10. See W. J. T. Mitchell, "Poetic and Pictorial Imagination in Blake's *The Book of Urizen*," for Los's falling into "Urizenic" consciousness. For *The Book of Urizen* as based on the two creation accounts in Genesis, on the theme of division through jealousy in Genesis, and for Genesis and *Urizen* both showing the triumph of "Elohist" Justice over "Jahwistic" Mercy, see Leslie Tannenbaum, "Blake's Art of Crypsis."

"Bound down / To earth by their narrowing perceptions," they "left a noisom body / To the jaws of devouring darkness" (25:39–40, 41, 46–47;28:2–3/E82/83). All this suggests that the offspring of Urizen's religion is death. Los has apparently created his own antithesis or nemesis, all the while pitying him—as if Moses had made Yahweh, and made him as Frankenstein made his monster. No doubt each figure has contributed to creating the other, but the initiative is Urizen's and remains so in almost all of Blake's early accounts of the fall except for *The Book of Los.*

In giving permanent form and limit to Urizen's changes, Los is more demiurge than prophet. As demiurge, he serves the Eternals, and the creation action of *The Book of Urizen* seems more pagan than Christian. The fall is into pagan poetry. In showing Los as demiurge, Blake works as a primitive and pagan cosmogonist—like Hesiod or Anaxagoras or Empedocles, or like the Plato of the *Timaeus*. At the same time, the creation action of the poem parodies that of Yahweh-Elohim in the book of Genesis. For Blake, the poet is too much a pagan there also, and in parodying the book of Genesis, Blake works as Moses, giver of law.

In *The Book of Urizen* as in most of the short prophecies of the 1790s, then, there is little evidence of Blake's being a Christian. But as Los becomes increasingly visionary and conscious—becomes a visionary of Jesus—Blake's poetry becomes increasingly Christian. This is of course exactly what one would expect. But it is worth noting that Blake permits himself so little commentary on the action—he and Los so reflect one another—that in composing these prophecies Blake himself seems to recapitulate, like Los, the development of the poet-prophet in history. In Blake's prophecies as a whole, we begin with the fall into the pagan worship of a remote, heaven-dwelling lawgiver God at the limits of recorded human memory and end in the recovery of Christian and fully human prophecy in Milton and in Blake himself. Los, again, is the figure who contains the whole change of fall and recovery, though Blake is slow to develop him as a character.

The last of the short prophecies, in Erdman's ordering, are *The Book of Ahania* and *The Book of Los.* Both dwell on the fall.

We still have not regained the confident energy of Mental Fight in *The Marriage of Heaven and Hell*, which led to the revolutionary outburst of "A Song of Liberty." Los in these prophecies still means, primarily, loss; and *The Book of Ahania*, like *The Book of Thel* and *Visions of the Daughters of Albion*, is dominated by a climactic female lament—this one for a lost Beulah paradise. At the end of the fall into division, the only expression open to the isolated figure or psychic element is curse or lament. Laments are among the passages that reappear most often from one prophecy to another, and Ahania, formless and "weep[ing] on the verge / Of Non-entity" (4:53– 54/E87/88) in *The Book of Ahania*, prepares for both Ahania and Enion in *The Four Zoas*.

The Book of Ahania ends, "Where bones from the birth are buried / Before they see the light" (E89/90); it ends with the memory of loss. *The Book of Los* begins with the memory of loss—with Eno's lament for "times remote" when there was "Enough! or Too much." Oothoon has become Eno, and what for Oothoon is possibility is for Eno only the memory of past fullness. The lines "And Wantonness on his own true love / Begot a giant race" suggests a generation plot, which derives many figures from a single progenitor or pair of progenitors, like Hesiod's *Theogony*. But after this "too much," the action of the poem is all loss, even though it is also largely creation. We begin with "Raging furious . . . flames of desire" and the "Eternal Prophet," himself "bound in a chain / Compell'd to watch Urizens shadow," binding the "living flames / Intelligent, organiz'd: arm'd / With destruction & plagues . . . Into fiery spheres" (3:27–29, 31–32;4:2/E90/91). No more free than in *The Book of Urizen*, Los begins as Orc, bound in fire. But having separated the flames, leaving void, Los finds himself frozen in ice—"frozen amidst / The vast rock of eternity"— like Albion or Dante's Satan. And when his "Prophetic wrath" rends "the vast solid / With a crash from immense to immense," he falls like Albion or Urizen or Hephaestus: "Truth has bounds. Error none: falling, falling" (4:11–12, 16– 17, 30/E91/92).

"Indignant," Los "First in wrath threw his limbs, like the babe / New born into our world" (4:38–39/E91/92). The sequence is remarkably like Blake's other accounts of "bound" infancy and "infant sorrow." Los first appears "bound in a chain," thrusting out "his hands / And his feet," feeling "fury and hot indignation," the frozen fires binding in "his expanding clear senses" (3:31, 46–48;4:10/E90/91). But the fall through "vacuum" seems to generate "contemplative thoughts," and thoughts generate their organ: "Then aloft his head rear'd in the Abyss / And his downward-borne fall. chang'd oblique" (4:40–43/E90/92). The reference to falling "oblique" glances at atomism from Leucippus and Democritus, Epicurus and Lucretius, to Descartes and Newton. Los is apparently a falling infant-atom-Adam, becoming woeful reason, falling into intellectual error, a self-contemplating shadow or bodiless reason like the Descartes of the *Meditations* and the *Discourse on Method*. Thought leads to groans, and groans grow "finite inflexible organs": "Many ages of groans: till there grew / Branchy forms. organizing the Human / Into finite inflexible organs" (4:44–46/E91/92). Los has fallen from Orc into Urizen—and, as in *The Book of Urizen*, into the four elements, with a suggestion of the four Zoas:

> Incessant the falling Mind labour'd
> Organizing itself: till the Vacuum
> Became element, pliant to rise
> Or to fall, or to swim, or to fly:
> With ease searching the dire vacuity. (4:49–53/E92/92–93)

When Light appears, what Los first beholds is the backbone of Urizen, with the nerves ossified but pliant and perhaps serpentlike. That Los has developed a fallen body of his own before he begins the binding of Urizen, who until now has been a shadow, changes the account in *The Book of Urizen*, where Urizen had the priority in creation. The change seems more than simply a shift in point of view: Los in *The Book of Los* is making Urizen—God—in his own image.

After "Nine ages" the sun of the fallen world emerges from Los's hammer, and Los "the vast Spine of Urizen siez'd / And bound down to the glowing illusion / / But no light" (5:46–48/E93/94).[11] Urizen's spine bound to the orb of the sun is evi-

11. Donald Ault notes that Los's continual quenching of his globe of fire in the deeps echoes the same act by the demiurge in the *Timaeus*: "Los's final

dently the solar orbit and the planets, is time, and thus presumably the start of "The same dull round even of a universe." The sun is a "glowing illusion," and Urizen is himself a "Human Illusion." Not only the Yahweh of the Old Testament but also the sunrise of revolution itself may now be, in Blake's view, only a repeated cyclical "glowing illusion," part of the "revolutions" of day and night:

> But no light, for the Deep fled away
> On all sides, and left an unform'd
> Dark vacuity: here Urizen lay
> In fierce torments on his glowing bed
>
> Till his Brain in a rock, & his Heart
> In a fleshy slough formed four rivers. (5:48–53/E93–94/94)

If Los has begun as desire and Orc and as "he, who dwells in flaming fire" of the *Marriage,* he has turned light into a dark and fiery hell with four rivers, in which Urizen lies in torment like the Satan of the opening books of *Paradise Lost.* But Los's hell is only part of the world he is creating: "Siezing fires from the terrific Orbs / He heated the round Globe" (5:37–38/E93/94). When the "Sun / Stood self-balanc'd," "Los smild with joy" (5:44–45/E93/94). It is Los's first smile. His "Siezing" of the "fires" and his smiling—apparently at his work—suggest the artificer of Blake's Tyger. Most of the dominant images of "The Tyger"—fire, hands, feet, hammer, anvil, and chain—appear, and here it is plain that the artificer is himself chained. Read in the light of *The Book of Los,* the "fearful symmetry" of the tiger is in large part the correspondence of fallen orbs—fallen sun and stars with fallen eye. The stars in "The Tyger" "water'd heaven with their tears" because the stars are eyes. And the whole conception of stars created from the void is a "Human Illusion" of which Urizen is the embodiment.[12] The artificer in "The Tyger" is surely

error . . . is to bind down the globe to the Cartesian-Newtonian whirling cosmological chain of Urizen's spine. The continual quenching of the globe by Los has evaporated the water of the deeps (5:43–44); thus, there is nothing left but the void space, the hardened globe of fire, and the chain-spine of Urizen" (*Visionary Physics,* p. 153).

12. As Milton Percival observes, "The first diminution of light is indicated . . . by the star world. This world was created to keep the body of man from falling into the abyss, when both the sun and moon had failed" (*William Blake's Circle of Destiny,* p. 148). As Percival also notes, the "Mundane Shell" which Urizen causes to be built early in *The Four Zoas* is built "at the level of the stars" (pp. 154–55).

Los, but the whole creator figure envisioned there is Los-Urizen. One wishes that *The Book of Los* had gone at least as far with the myth of fall-creation as *The Book of Urizen* did. But with the figure of Los in *The Book of Los* Blake has derived a whole poem from the central and organizing "loss" figure of his postrevolutionary myth, and the development takes place at length in *The Four Zoas, Milton,* and *Jerusalem.*

* * *

Looking back a moment, we see that most of the figures of the short prophecies are gradually shown to be offspring of Los and Enitharmon (*Milton* is a major stage in this development), that the children sometimes appear before the parents do, revealing aspects of their parents we would not otherwise see, and that the figures often link unexpectedly with figures from pagan myth or the Bible or Blake's own developing myth, so that one prophecy mirrors or complements another.

Visions of the Daughters of Albion is an ecstatic (and static) prophecy that often seems to be slightly aside from Blake's main development. But it has a special relationship with the more Apollonian—or at least measured—*The Book of Urizen.* (*The Book of Urizen,* Blake's most rigidly divided and symmetrical poem, also contains his most expressionistic illuminations, arranged with the greatest symmetry.)[13] One poem complements the other. The opposites contained in *Visions* reflect a similar, more rigidly contained set of forces in *The Book of Urizen* (and *Europe*). Bromion, for example, looks as if he should be Dionysus ("Bromios" or "Bromius"). But he seems more like Zeus—thunderer—and Oothoon seems a Semele burnt by Zeus's thunderbolt, so the child that Bromion expects Oothoon to produce ought to be Dionysus. The child whom Enitharmon gives birth to in *The Book of Urizen* after she has almost been raped by Los in his Urizen-state is Orc, who is not only a fiery rebel but also a Dionysus figure, in some of Blake's illuminations to *America* seeming to be a vine. Even though Oothoon has no child, the effect of the

---

13. For the symmetry, see Robert E. Simmons, "*Urizen*: The Symmetry of Fear," in *Blake's Visionary Forms Dramatic,* pp. 136–73.

rape-in-thunder and of the attack by Theotormon's eagles that she invites in *Visions* is an ecstasy that might be described as Dionysian (as I have already suggested)—as if Oothoon-Semele had become a maenad follower of her son Dionysus (not yet born) in one of Blake's extreme condensations of pagan myth. Or perhaps the child she brings forth is Dionysian vision.

Although Blake in *Visions of the Daughters* seems to have led up to and stopped short of (or skipped) the birth of Dionysus, Oothoon's ecstatic vision not only forecasts Los's development into a visionary prophet; her fiery energy seems to make her Orc-Dionysus's sister or twin or feminine portion. (Bromion in raping Oothoon acts like Orc raping his sister, the Shadowy Daughter of Urthona, though slaveowner Bromion of course talks very differently from rebel Orc.) In surrounding us with allusions and approaches to Dionysus, Blake is creating two figures like Dionysus but different—Oothoon and Orc. And he is of course unfolding the character of Los.

The one who best forecasts the later Los is Oothoon, but Orc is a figure whom Los must "express" and later expel: Orc as fiery rebel enacts an early phase of Los's dance/embrace/struggle with Urizen. In the "Preludium" and plate 8 of *America*, Orc is a chthonic figure who enacts the myth in *Republic* X of iron/brass, silver, and gold men who have emerged from mother earth. In the "Preludium," Orc is "iron." In plate 8 he speaks:

> Fires inwrap the earthly globe, yet man is not consumd;
> Amidst the lustful fires he walks: his feet become like brass,
> His knees and thighs like silver, & his breast and head like
>   gold (8:15–17/E53/54)

The allusion is to the prophets in the fire in Daniel,[14] but it also suggests the fusion of Plato's three obedient classes into one figure of revolution. Blake's Orc seems not only fire and

---

14. Compare Ezekiel 22:20, where God addresses Jerusalem: "As they gather silver, and brass, and iron, and lead, and tin, into the midst of the furnace, to blow the fire upon it, to melt it; so will I gather you in mine anger and in my fury, and I will leaven you there and melt you" (quoted by David Wagenknecht in *Blake's Night*, p. 167).

metal worked in fire—the figure in "A Divine Image" and the figure created in "The Tyger"—but also the heart or core of earth-life opposed to Urizen's skeletal death-figure: a Dionysus both vegetable and mineral-metallic, whose fiery life, even when destructive, opposes a deathly Zeus-Urizen. Finally, Orc as "A Divine Image" of man as a furnace armed and armored reminds us of Mars, and it is as Mars that Los eventually rouses himself at the end of *Europe.*

The effect of these links and mirroring figures and events, then, is to show Los not only as Orc and Urizen—fire and snow, life and the image of death—but also as Bromion and Theotormon and Oothoon. The effect is also to show Oothoon and Theotormon as two faces of Enitharmon. As Los binds Orc, so Enitharmon reproves Oothoon's open sexual delight and generosity. Los and Enitharmon and their offspring are becoming a recognizable if somewhat polar and schematic family in which the child unfolds qualities in the psyche of the parent that the parent may repudiate. Furthermore, this psychic unfolding develops toward dialectic and Mental Fight. Blake is moving toward the family division in *Milton* of Los and Enitharmon into elect, redeemed, and reprobate: Satan, Palamabron, and Rintrah. (Northrop Frye suggests identifying them also as John, William, and Robert Blake.) As he increasingly links offspring with parents or subsumes them in their parents, Blake turns back from pagan toward Christian figures. As usual, he is seeking the source by reconstructing it in his own way.

Enitharmon, for example, suggests not only earth-mother; as jealous spouse and mother and sky-goddess, she also suggests Hera. The name *Enitharmon,* one notices, contains the name *Hera* as well as *earth* and *mother*; and in *Europe,* Enitharmon plays Hera/Juno to Los's Zeus/Jupiter (and Gertrude to Los's carousing Claudius and Orc's Hamlet). As containing and presiding female figure, Enitharmon contains the names—and is mother of—*Oothoon, Theotormon,* and *Bromion* (except for the *B*). When Tharmas and Enion appear in *The Four Zoas* as Enitharmon's parents or predecessors in the fall, her name contains theirs as a reminder of her line of descent, and also of her being the mother in the first of Blake's developed cosmogonies, *The Book of Urizen.* Enithar-

mon is both source and containing figure. Looking back on
her from the end, we see that, having begun as "mother earth
Enitharmon" and as the earth womb-tomb that contained the
fetal skeleton of Urizen in *The Book of Urizen*, she becomes
Satan's earth-heart-hearth in the Bard's Song of *Milton*
(Satan making his way to earth-as-hell in a revision of *Paradise Lost*). (In *Milton*, Urizen is still resisting life, as he does in
The Four Zoas, and entering his tomb.) Converted with Los in
The Four Zoas, she is finally linked very closely with generation as regeneration and the birth of Jerusalem and Jesus.
Enitharmon herself is of course Los's separated Emanation,
and thus an expression or distorted reflection of Los—forbidden desire or perhaps the desire that denies itself. One
again realizes that Bromion/Theotormon/Oothoon are unfoldings of Los. (That Los's "head" is "clad" in "snaky thunders" at the end of *Europe* and his "forehead" is "circled with
black bursting thunders" in *The Four Zoas* VII [96:20/E393/361]
associates him with both Zeus and Bromion.) Finally,
"Thunder of Thought, & flames of fierce desire" (*Jerusalem*
pl. 3/E144/145) associates Los both with thought and with
Jehovah (as Orc's "thought-creating fires" and Urizen's cloud
associate them with Jehovah).

That the Oothoon-Theotormon-Bromion triad is followed
and subsumed by the Enitharmon-Los-Orc triad—that *Visions of the Daughters* precedes *The Book of Urizen*—might be
taken to mean that Blake had abandoned the earlier group in
favor of the later (as he seems to have abandoned Urizen's
son Fuzon as a figure in his growing myth). No doubt Blake
is working things out as he goes. But in the emerging form of
his myth—and perhaps in working back, revising—he wants
in Oothoon to evoke Semele as mother of Dionysus, and then
to derive both figures from more primitive or original
sources in Los and Enitharmon. Los and Enitharmon are
revealed and changed by their children and the conflicts
among them, but Blake's emerging pattern is retrospective
and recovers the source even while the river branches out
into more and more distributary streams. As Los begins to
become a visionary of Jesus, it becomes clearer that the assertion in *The Song of Los* that Jesus heard Oothoon's voice
means that Oothoon is a Dionysian or ecstatic aspect of Mary

or Jerusalem—and thus of Jesus—that is usually suppressed. Blake is willing to take suppressed values where he finds them. Having found them, he wants increasingly to turn them back to their source in Poetic Genius and the Divine Vision or Everlasting Gospel; so that Dionysus, for example, "twice-born" and "vine of life," appears as a pagan reminiscence of Jesus and retains a lost value, countering the merely moral or "good only" vision of Jesus.

*   *   *

Blake's early prophecies are a clearing away; hence they are dominated by Urizen and Orc. But Blake does not know what to put in place of what is cleared away. What he offers most consistently is the "infinite Prolific" of the natural world and of Poetic Genius in the Tractates, *The Marriage of Heaven and Hell,* and *Visions of the Daughters of Albion.* Seen from the point of view of the later prophecies, it is clear that the key is Los, the faculty that experiences of the Tractates. One reason why it takes Los so long to emerge as a figure from his idea in the Tractates is that Los begins both with a large element of Orc in him and as a containing figure like the later Albion. Blake needs to distinguish Los as prophet from Orc as rebel, and Los as source figure or ancestor from containing form or nation—to distinguish the awakener, Los, from the awakened, Albion. None of these distinctions has quite occurred in the short prophecies of the 1790s. Los is still involved with Orc, and Albion as sleeping giant form of giant forms has not yet emerged.

Seen from the point of view of the later prophecies, what is also missing is Los's conversion. If Blake's revolution is American and French—philosophical and political, stemming from Paine and the American example, and from Voltaire and Rousseau—Los's conversion is to an English faith, to Bunyan and Milton and dissenting Christianity. As this happens, Blake begins to see Rousseau and Voltaire (and Locke) as Error. He becomes more and more English Blake and Christian dissenter Blake and working-class Blake; and *Milton* and *Jerusalem* become much more local than earlier prophecies, focusing on Felpham and London. Los's conversion to Christianity as forgiveness and self-annihilation occurs in Night VII of *The Four Zoas.* With this conversion,

Blake has transformed Mental Fight by the insight that Los can overcome Urizen only by self-annihilation, because Urizen is *within* Los. A corresponding change occurs in Blake's Jesus, who in *The Four Zoas* is much less impulsively antinomian than he is in the *Marriage,* where he is largely the Devil's Jesus—an Orc.

The change in Los can be seen clearly in the poems in letters to Thomas Butts on 2 October 1800 and 22 November 1802. It is a change toward greater humanity and toward a greater intimacy between Blake and Los—both of which make it possible for Blake to develop Los almost as a character in a novel might be developed. Many of the Lambeth prophecies are vitalist poems: "For every thing that lives is Holy," and "I will show you all alive / The world, when every particle of dust breathes forth its joy." In the first poem to Butts, dated 2 October 1800, the vitalism turns to a humanism in which all things are not only alive but also human. Every particle of light is "a Man / Human formd" and all the features of earth and sky "Are Men Seen Afar" (21–22, 32/ E683/712). Blake, having begun as primitive cosmogonist and "ancient Poet" who "animated all sensible objects," has gone on to the vision of all objects as human. More accurately, both visions appear in the poetry of the 1790s, with the merely vitalist vision gradually declining.

What is really interesting is the suggestion, once more, that Blake's poetry recapitulates the history of poetry or of Poetic Genius from the pagan Greeks and the Old Testament on. This is to say that the change is largely—as major changes in Blake's poems tend to be—a change in Blake's relations with Los, the image in which Blake sees himself and his task and powers enlarged and intensified:

> My Eyes more & more
> Like a Sea without shore
> Continue Expanding
> The Heavens commanding
> Till the Jewels of Light
> Heavenly Men beaming bright
> Appeard as One Man. (45–51/E683–84/713)

With "In his bosom sun bright / I remaind" ("Sun bright" can modify either "I" or "bosom"), Blake enters his own vision and sees himself and his wife as "shadows" in the "arms" of "lovely Felpham." Furthermore, Blake "remain[s] as a Child," with all he has known shining brightly before him (E684/713).

The Beulah threefold vision of the earlier poem to Butts is followed in the second poem, of 22 November 1802, by an Ulro-Eden vision. And Los as "guardian" of Blake's "infant" in the first poem is followed by Los "the terrible shade" and by a terrible Blake in the second, so that Blake and Los in both poems are correspondent or answering forms. Innocence, however, has given way to experience. After Blake's "Defiance" of Los as Sun, the sun trembles, the moon becomes "leprous & white as snow / And every Soul of men on the Earth / Felt affliction & sorrow & sickness & dearth" (74–76/ E693/722). "Terrible" Blake might seem to suffer delusions of omnipotence, but Mental Fight in Blake's poetry is always universal or cosmic, including all men. This battle occurs in air, as if the adversary were Satan. Los the "terrible shade," of whom Blake is "afraid," is, if not the "God of this world," at least the artificer or demiurge of this world—what Blake in *The Four Zoas* calls the "Spectre of Urthona"—and he appears in the sun and time and space of this world. The Los who, in *The Book of Los*, bound the spine of Urizen to the "glowing Illusion" of the sun's orb forged an almost indissoluble link between an inflexibly lawful solar system and God.

Though it is projected outward as a battle against sun and moon, the climactic Mental Fight is really internal: it is an overcoming of worldly fears and concerns and doubts, and a refusal to accept the "same dull round" even if it is "of a universe." Los the terrible shade helps Blake by stimulating him to Mental Fight, and through Mental Fight he achieves fourfold vision. Blake as infant in Beulah has in his own eyes suddenly grown up, though he has apparently not yet achieved the Mental Fight that is self-annihilation.

Los himself—or the sun—is changed, it seems, by the bows and arrows of Mental Fight. The image recalls Apollo smiting the Greeks before Troy with pestilence. But here Blake uses Apollo's weapons, bow and arrows, to smite

Apollo; the "Spiritual Sun" overcomes the "Corporeal Sun."[15]

> Los flamd in my path & the Sun was hot
> With the bows of my Mind & the Arrows of Thought
> My bowstring fierce with Ardour breathes
> My arrows glow in their golden sheaves. (77–80/E693/722)

This seems preparation for the epigraph poem to *Milton*, where the weapons are named as weapons of Mental Fight. The preparation consists partly in Blake's carrying on a Mental Fight against his own visionary creation, Los. The fight ends in a gain of consciousness, so that, after "The heavens drop with human gore," Blake turns from the vision to an account of it:

> Now I a fourfold vision see
> And a fourfold vision is given to me
> Tis fourfold in my supreme delight
> And three fold in soft Beulahs night
> And twofold Always. May God us keep
> From Single vision & Newtons sleep. (82–88/E693/722)

Since it is the "heavens"—not earth—which "drop with human gore," it is clear that Blake is describing "Spiritual Acts." Probably he is overcoming "Natural Fears" and "Natural Desires" and "the mere drudgery of business," as in the letter to Butts of 10 January 1803, where he writes, "I cannot live without doing my duty to lay up treasures in heaven," and describes his conviction that he is "under the direction of Messengers from Heaven Daily & Nightly." But "Temptations are on the right hand & left behind the sea of time & space roars & follows swiftly he who keeps not right onward is lost" (E688/724). The Los he overcomes in the second letter poem is the Los or sun of "the sea of time & space": "Thou measurest not the Time to me / Nor yet the Space that I do see" (67–68/E693/722).

15. Compare Blake's remark to Crabb Robinson: "I have conversed with the Spiritual Sun—I saw him on Primrose Hill. He said, 'Do you take me for the Greek Apollo?' 'No,' I said. 'That' (and Blake pointed to the sky)—'that is the Greek Apollo. He is Satan'" (Edith J. Morley, *Henry Crabb Robinson on Books and Their Writers*, 1:328).

But Los in this poem to Butts remains ambiguous: he seems to be not the sea of time and space and this-worldly fears and desires alone, nor the threats that come from the spiritual world alone, but a wavering between the two—Blake's indecision itself, until the decision has been reached:

> If we fear to do the dictates of our Angels & tremble at the Tasks set before us. if we refuse to do Spiritual Acts. because of Natural Fears or Natural Desires! Who can describe the dismal torments of such a state!—I too well remember the Threats I heard!—If you who are organized by Divine Providence for Spiritual communion. Refuse & bury your Talent in the Earth even tho you should want Natural Bread. Sorrow & Desperation pursues you thro life! & after death shame & confusion of face to eternity—Every one in Eternity will leave you aghast at the Man who was crownd with glory & honour by his brethren & betrayd their cause to their enemies. You will be calld the base Judas who betrayd his Friend!—Such words would make any Stout man tremble & how then could I be at ease? But I am now no longer in That State & now go on again with my Task Fearless. and tho my path is difficult. I have no fear of stumbling while I keep it. (10 January 1803/E688–89/724–25)

In the later poem to Butts, Blake's duty to his "brethren" in eternity wins out over his duty to his brothers and his father and his wife, over conflicting family voices and duties.

More important, in Blake's letter we hear precisely the voice Blake gives to the Los who appears in Nights VII and VIII of *The Four Zoas* and in *Milton* and *Jerusalem*, almost overcome by the task laid on him by Divine Providence. Los as he was appears to Blake in a vision, and Blake's Mental Fight with him turns him into the Los who appears in Blake's later poetry. The Los that Blake had known is changed into Los as he will henceforth be, certain of his course. The old Los is "what exists," the Los who bound and riveted the form of "the God of this world." The new Los is the one brought into existence in the later nights of *The Four Zoas*: "Spiritual Acts" and "Spiritual communion" with "brethren" in heaven, transforming this world.

The Los figures of the Butts poems—Los as guardian and Los as terrible shade—are both intimately related to Blake; they are his own Genius. This intimacy between Blake and

Los, which does not exist in the prophecies of the 1790s, forecasts or reflects the Los of Night VII of *The Four Zoas*, who is converted to loving parenthood and to Christian love. The Los overcome in Mental Fight at the end of the second letter poem ("With happiness stretchd across the hills") is the Los who becomes Blake's strength. The Mental Fight there is against a creation congealed or solidified, and the victory allows re-creation. The result is a new Los, capable of destroying the old heaven and earth and creating a new heaven and earth.

Both the guardian Los of the earlier letter poem and the terrible Los of the later one are projections of Blake's changing states of mind. The fears embodied in Los the terrible shade are the other side of Los the guardian. Both are the Los of the existent creation, and both visions overvalue this world. But in the later poem an eternal Los comes into existence in Blake; Los is what had been standing in Blake's way. That Los he comes to call the "Spectre of Urthona"; it is the Los who is twinned with Urizen and deeply involved in his fall. "With happiness stretchd across the hills" supports what one suspects from the Lambeth prophecies—that Los during this period is an ambiguous and threatening figure whom Blake associates with Urizen and a fallen creation. At the same time, Blake in "With happiness" triumphs over that figure and turns him into the Los who offers a recovery. It is, again, very close to the process by which a fictional character is said to come to life.

Blake's triumph over Los is a triumph over himself, a triumph over the Blake who in the prophecies after *The Marriage of Heaven and Hell* and *America* and *Visions of the Daughters of Albion* could only recreate the fall and recreate or re-embody the adversary Urizen. Before Los can change, he has to come closer to Urizen so that he can overcome him in Mental Fight. This is the psychic process Blake dramatizes in Los's confronting the Spectre of Urthona in Night VII of *The Four Zoas*. There Los overcomes himself in the figure of the Spectre of Urthona, much as the Blake of "With happiness" overcomes himself in the figure of Los. *The Four Zoas* is the first poem in which Los appears as—develops into—a fully human character.

*   *   *

Before turning to *The Four Zoas,* however, I want to discuss "The Mental Traveller," which was probably written during the long course of Blake's work on the *Zoas.* It is the negative counterpart of the second poem to Butts and clarifies the cycle of earthly duties, the "drudgery of business," and the swing between Natural Fears and Natural Desires, which overcome Mental Fight and blot out eternity. More important, it supplements the implicit four-Zoas psychology of the Lambeth prophecies—which derives from the Tractates—by the life of sexual division, of which it provides Blake's most condensed image. The Zoas and the sexes, along with Blake's late-developed Christian myth, make up the image of man in *The Four Zoas, Milton,* and *Jerusalem.* Although Blake's Christian myth is still absent from "The Mental Traveller," it is reflected or shadowed in the poem's Eros plot of division and pursuit.

4

Los's Deep Midnight in "The Mental Traveller"

"The Mental Traveller" is a poem of Christianity slipping back into pagan forms, condensed evidence of pagan poetry's survival into Christian times. Its central male figure evokes both the pagan hero and Christ, but the absence of both love and the creating Word—of speech of any kind—reduces him to a pagan fertility god endlessly reborn, a "Christ" little different from Adonis. Blake's source figure of the 1790s, who begat Urizen and Enitharmon and Orc and who fixed the forms of the fallen world, seems missing, or present only in those who have derived from him. Los's decline in "The Mental Traveller" leaves the creation as a turning mechanism, a repeating cycle, so that we have a study of the male hero in a "female space"—not human identity or the human prolific, but its lapse.

A poem of the postcreation, "The Mental Traveller" is in some ways the middle missing from the short prophecies of the 1790s—not the missing history, but the missing natural life, the cycle of male-female relations. Most of the prophecies are falls or apocalypses or both, and many focus on the Orc-Urizen battle. "The Mental Traveller" presents neither fall nor apocalypse, and it avoids warfare, revolutionary or not, entirely. Like the Tractates, it concerns perception: "the Eye altering alters all." But it is erotic perception, which sees the other as an object that can satisfy need. Beginning with a male figure "nail[ed] . . . down upon a rock" by a "Woman Old," "The Mental Traveller" presents "the faculty which experiences" (of the Tractates) "bound down to earth by . . . narrowing perceptions" (as in *The Book of Urizen*). Its male figure is like an utterly silent Oothoon who frees himself of his bonds but is unable to free tongue, ear, or imagination. Narrowed perceptions lead to necessary actions—a fatal track or preordained circumference. But narrowed perceptions evoke the Poetic Genius of the Tractates as their opposite. As I have already suggested, Blake's consolidation of the negative, of loss, in "The Mental Traveller" evokes its positive answer: the divine identity or creating Word from whom we have fallen, whose active remnant in the fallen world is Los.

"The Mental Traveller" seems to take its origin from—and give a circular form to—*The Book of Urizen,* in which Enitharmon divides from Los, they couple, and a male child, Orc, is born and bound down upon a mountain.[1] In *The Book of Urizen,* Enitharmon is generated by Los's interaction with Urizen. She embodies Los's pity for Urizen, the dialectical outcome of which is its opposite or counterpart: Orc's bound rage. In "The Mental Traveller," the initial figures are versions of Enitharmon and Orc, although the woman who binds the male babe down is "Old." The male babe matures into an "aged Host," after which the babe reappears through a kind of reversal of sexual generation that reduces the old man to infancy. "The Mental Traveller," even more than *The Book of Urizen,* focuses not on sexual generation but on what stops "increase"—on sexual division as unprolific. Thus, "The Mental Traveller" emphasizes more clearly what had

---

1. Like most writers on "The Mental Traveller," I am greatly indebted to Northrop Frye's account of the Orc cycle in *Fearful Symmetry,* pp. 207–35. I want, however, to see what the poem implies about Los.

The master of the revolutionary reading, as always, is David Erdman, in *Blake: Prophet Against Empire.* See also Morton Paley, who observes that in the male's pursuit of the maiden, "The revolutionary impulse represented by the Babe, having become an orthodoxy in its own right, grew progressively more enfeebled" ("The Female Babe and 'The Mental Traveller,'" pp. 102–3).

For a sexual reading of the poem, see Gerald Enscoe, "The Content of Vision," pp. 400–413.

John Beer sees the male in "The Mental Traveller" as "the Divine Image": "The Divine Image, unlike normal human babies, is begotten in woe and born in joy. But he is born into a world which has no place for him and fears the strength of his powers. So he is delivered to the Law, in order that he may be held in restraint" (*Blake's Humanism,* p. 90). Beer also remarks that the later fleeing maiden and pursuing aged Host "pass through the history of civilization. After the expulsion from paradise, man . . . passed through the pastoral state represented by Abel and then to the building of cities as initiated by Cain. So the presence of the lovers brings mankind through these stages in reverse" (p. 39). The great essay on "The Mental Traveller" is in Kathleen Raine's *Blake and Tradition,* 1:302–24.

already been suggested in *The Book of Urizen*: that Urizen is involved in Orc's birth and stops the progress of generation, "stops posterity." (*The Four Zoas* unfolds the link—and the blocking of "increase"—in detail.)

However desperate it may be, the two-figure dance or agon between Los and Urizen in *The Book of Urizen* (and also in *The Book of Los*) is a creation action, with Los binding and solidifying Urizen's successive changes. The two-figure dance in "The Mental Traveller" is not creation but frustrated generation and metamorphosis—a struggle between male and female in which the material of creation often slips out of reach. "The Mental Traveller" is a poem of Los's fall-division into Orc and Enitharmon: desire and its forbidden or impossible object, as in the Tractates. It is *The Book of Urizen* without Los's creation action and beginning not with Urizen but with Orc. One of the essential points about the poem is that both the male babe and the female babe are fatherless. (Both are motherless too, but the male is given to a surrogate mother.) *The Book of Urizen* gives us the whole of Blake's "This World" diagram of the globe (*Jerusalem*, pl. 54):

If in this scheme reason is Urizen, wrath is Los, desire is Orc, and pity is Enitharmon, "The Mental Traveller" gives us only three of the four figures: the babe as desire, the woman as pity, and the aged Host as reason. The missing figure and quadrant is Los as the wrath that generates Mental Fight. Mental Travelling is an evasion of Mental Fight.

As in *Europe*, Los's inactivity is Enitharmon's dominance. "The Mental Traveller" is not quite a "Song of Enitharmon," but it is a female vision of the subordination of male to female; hence it begins and ends with the male as infant. As circle, "The Mental Traveller" presents a version of Enitharmon's eighteen-hundred-year ahistorical dream of space in *Europe*, with both poems beginning and ending with the birth of an infant—Orc-Jesus. As in *Europe*, Enitharmon is the containing space, and the changes through which the male and female go are female states contained by Enitharmon. In the first, the containing female has become the torturer, Rahab. In the second, she is the Eternal Female or Shadowy Daughter of Urthona, raped by an Orc who "binds her down for his delight." In the third she is Eno, the prosperity and plenty enjoyed by the male, who has now become an aged Host, his "door" "for ever open." (See Eno's lament for lost plenty at the beginning of *The Book of Los.*) In the fourth and most ambiguous state, the hearthfire babe who "comes to the Man she loves" and casts out the Orc who has by now become an aged Urizen or impotent Theotormon, she is perhaps Oothoon. In the fifth, she is Leutha-Vala, the fugitive female pursued by the "aged Host" into his own second infancy. (Leutha is a Thel who has entered "this world" but nevertheless flees from experience.) In the sixth, the return of the Woman Old, she is Tirzah as the cruelties of sexual denial. Thus the feminine counterpart to the Orc-Urizen cycle, which has its source in Los, is the Rahab-Oothoon-Tirzah cycle, which is contained in Enitharmon. (Los as source figure and Enitharmon as containing figure are of course very different, since the first is a remnant of creative energy.) "The Mental Traveller" is certainly the most concentrated form of this cycle and illuminates the complexities of male-female conflict in the long prophecies. The poem is a history of Los fallen into Enitharmon—female space—as Orc-Urizen, contained in the female, inhabiting one female state after another, but always an infant because that is the form of male existence in a female space.

Encouraged by the absence of proper names to treat all the male figures as one and all the female figures as one, we see that "he binds her down for his delight," but "she" escapes, and though "She comes to the Man she loves," they do not close until the "aged Host" who had been driven out is reduced to infancy at the end of the poem. (It is as if Iocaste were being seen from the point of view of both Laius and Oedipus, father and son, and as if she saw husband and son as interchangeable.) Blake so drastically reduces persons to the class male or female, young or old, and his time-warps condense successive cycles so powerfully, that neither male nor female seems to be born until long after he or she has appeared in the poem. The mystery in "The Mental Traveller" is the mystery of generation, and Blake seems to present not vision but a study of mythology in which our given is the beginning of a story or mythos. The beginning of a story decides the end, and in this case it decides it rigidly and necessarily: the male babe in the hands of a Woman Old is both beginning and end. The time of the poem seems less consequential and successive than it is circular and simultaneous, and its cyclical form and time determine all its single events, making one event (and word) beget another and bending all of them back to earth.[2] (As a study of "mythological generation" or the generation of myths, "The Mental Traveller" again prepares for or condenses *The Four Zoas,* a poem which also assembles into a circular form the intermittent flashes we have of most myths.)

Strong verbs mark the stages of the narrative; and successive drastic actions imply, without comment, a surrealistically linked chain of causation—a cycle without human intention. The woman *nails* the babe down and *catches* his shrieks; she *cuts* his heart out of his side; she *eats* and *drinks,* and *grows* younger. The male *binds* her down and *plants* himself in all her nerves. The female babe *springs* from

---

2. Christine Gallant remarks that Blake, to describe "the beginning of the end," uses "the Yggdrasil, the World Tree of Norse mythology, which unites opposites with its roots in hell and its branches in the heavens. So Los:

> his vegetable hands
> Outstretchd his right hand branching out in fibrous Strength
> Siezd the Sun. His left hand like dark roots coverd the Moon
> And tore them down cracking the heavens across from immense to
> immense.

Los unifies the cosmic opposites of Sun and Moon, finally connecting them like the Yggdrasil with his 'fibrous' hands" (*Blake and the Assimilation of Chaos,* p. 96). In "The Mental Traveller," sun and moon shrink away and cannot be reached or torn down. In this way as in others, "The Mental Traveller" has the look of an indestructible narrative machine, closed back on itself in a circle which cannot be ended. "The Mental Traveller" shows Beulah turning into Ulro. Night IX of *The Four Zoas* shows Beulah turning into generation and regeneration and moving into Eden. The Beulah vision of "The Mental Traveller" can change only into Ulro because there is no real generation in the poem and no death. As Gallant remarks of "The Mental Traveller," "Death is not really accepted by either man or woman, for as each grows old each battens on the youth of the other" (p. 102).

the hearth (suggesting both energetic action and the arrival of spring); the eye *alters* all; sun, moon, and stars all *shrink* away; the male *embraces* and *pursues* a maiden, who, as he pursues, *beguiles* him to infancy. Having returned to the relative ages with which the poem began, male and female re-enact the opening action: "She nails him down upon the Rock, / And all is done as I have told."[3]

Presumably man in eternity—identified—contains and can act all ages at will, just as he changes his sexual garments at will. But in "The Mental Traveller" the protagonists utterly fail to achieve identity: they end as they began—in division of sex against sex, age against infancy. Blake's treatment of self-division nevertheless suggests a good deal about identity. Though the male protagonist seems at the mercy of nature and of naked erotic and economic need, his actions and passions evoke the primary and mythical identity figures of Oedipus (and the tragic protagonist more generally) and Christ.

Nailed down upon a rock by the Woman Old at both the beginning and the end of the poem, Blake's male protagonist reminds us of Oedipus, exposed as an infant, answering the riddle of a female sphinx whose fatality is carried on in the mother whom he marries, exiling himself from the city as he was once exposed on the mountain, and ending as a sacred figure who is taken to the gods in a sacred grove. Blake's male too is repeatedly exiled and ends as a sacred figure whom none but the Woman Old dares touch, and Blake's poem exaggerates the extent to which most of the female figures in *Oedipus Tyrannus*—mother, exposer, wife, queen—turn out to be the same figure. Blake's male protagonist reminds us also of Lear, cast out by Goneril and Regan, learn-

3. Compare Jacob Boehme: "Boehme left to philosophy a first principle which becomes creative by generating its own contrary, which it then proceeds to reconcile to itself. He left also the compelling vision of a fallen universe which is constituted throughout by an opposition of quasi-sexual contraries, at once mutually attractive and repulsive, whose momentary conciliations give way to renewed attempts at mastery by the opponent powers, in a tragic conflict which is at the same time the very essence of life and creativity. . . . The motion into which all things are thus compelled is a circular one, composing a design like that of the self-devouring serpent: 'For all things move onward until the end finds the beginning; then the beginning again swallows the end, and as it were eternally . . . (*Psychologia Vera* [1620], 74–78)" (M. H. Abrams, *Natural Supernaturalism*, p. 162).

ing need, humility, and suffering, bound on a wheel of fire. The wheel in all three poems, of course, turns from power and possession to need and weakness, but Blake's wheel begins, as Sophocles' does, with a male infant who achieves power and possession in spite of an unpromising beginning. Oedipus ends "blind & age-bent," as Blake describes his outcast protagonist about two-thirds of the way through his cycle. Lear's wheel turns further—back to the beginning—and Lear ends in the simplicity and naked need of old age as childhood, as Blake's figure does if we take his infancy as senility. But both old men, both Lear and Oedipus, end by being cared for by a daughter whose faithfulness has no counterpart in "The Mental Traveller." And both, unlike Blake's figure, have the power of speech and of conscious choice. The absence of these powers in Blake's figure shows his distance from identity and from Blake's source figure of identity, Los.

The lack of faithfulness, of speech, and of conscious choice in "The Mental Traveller" is a sign that the poem is more ironic—and more erotic—than tragic. The male figure in "The Mental Traveller" is a figure of need and of purely external action, or passion, without consciousness. (He undergoes what Kierkegaard calls external history: not ethically choosing himself as task but aesthetically seeking external possibility. And only external history, as Kierkegaard remarks, is capable of great condensation—such condensation, one might add, as we find in "The Mental Traveller.") If the just man in the "Argument" of *The Marriage of Heaven and Hell* has been cheated of paradise by the sneaking serpent, the male in "The Mental Traveller" has been left outside himself by sexual division and is thus a kind of anti-identity figure. Concentrating on fate as Eros—a frustrated external seeking for completion—"The Mental Traveller" reduces tragedy to irony, its point of view as distant as that of a star from the earth; and indeed its glimpses of turning cycles suggest that all is being shown from the vantage point of sun or moon, as if Blake's narrator were all-seeing Helios.

*   *   *

"The Mental Traveller" is not only Blake's most condensed nucleus poem and circle image, but also his definitive account of the Eros cycle, in which Mental Fight falls into sexual division and conflict. That cycle is of great importance in the three long prophecies. If the Lambeth prophecies end by revealing the failure of revolution, "The Mental Traveller" delineates the error of Eros or passion and presents history and revolution only under that form. It differs from most Eros plots in conventionalizing all the possible male-female relations as a sexual dance and showing them in metamorphic versions of only two figures:

old woman / male babe
fertile woman / potent male
old man / female babe
old man / maiden
old woman / male babe

(I shall argue later, however, that the female babe is twofold.)[4] The human mother/son and father/daughter relations are missing throughout.

Seen as pure Eros plot, "The Mental Traveller" seems to have adopted for its own purposes the erotic world of Andrew Marvell's "The Definition of Love." The male in "The Mental Traveller," like the speaker of "The Definition of Love," has an extended soul and is the victim of a separating Fate:

> For Fate with jealous eyes does see
> Two perfect loves, nor lets them close:
> Their union would her ruin be,
> And her tyrannic pow'r depose.
>
> And therefore her decrees of steel
> Us as the distant poles have plac'd,

---

4. Here I am indebted to Hazard Adams's view: "When the female [babe] appears she is . . . only potentially creative inspiration. She is . . . ambiguous, and seems at this point in the poem to split into two different figures: she is an inner image of spirit; the other, who gyres around the top of the wheel to become a maiden and crone again, the familiar Rahab-Tirzah" (*William Blake: A Reading of the Shorter Poems*, p. 93).

Donald Ault observes, "The Female has a range of potential choices for her lover which stretch beyond the perceptual scope of the poem. We are given two perspectives on the one choice the poem itself makes possible . . . the driving out of the aged Host is simply the opposite side of the Female choosing her lover, who, as we know, can be old. . . . What we have here is the division of the Male and Female each into opposing features and [this] is the schematic origin of the whole host of Male-Female and Female-Male hermaphrodites in Blake's later epics" (*Visionary Physics*, p. 189).

(Though love's whole world on us does wheel)
Not by themselves to be embrac'd

Unless the giddy heaven fall
And earth some new convulsion tear,
And, us to join, the world should all
Be cramp'd into a planisphere.

"The Mental Traveller," like "The Definition of Love," presents a world whose very structure and laws are erotic, so
that "love's whole world . . . wheel[s]" on the male and
female, and it presents that world not as rhetoric but as sober
vision. It apparently begins as a "planisphere" and moves
toward the brief convergence of male and female. But when
the "aged Shadow" pursues a maiden, "the flat Earth becomes a Ball," and the sun, moon, and stars all shrink away,
as the maiden does. It is the separation of old man and
maiden that rounds the world and, ironically, produces a
male infant we might describe, in Marvell's words, as "begotten by despair / Upon impossibility."

Behind love's absence from "The Mental Traveller" we may
see not only Marvell but also Shakespeare's "Venus and
Adonis." With its prolific "spring" and devouring "winter,"
Blake's poem follows a seasonal erotic rhythm like Shakespeare's, in which Adonis tells Venus, "'Love's gentle spring
doth always fresh remain, / Lust's winter comes ere summer
half be done'" (lines 801–2). Blake's poem is dominated by—
begins and ends in—"Lust's winter," a possessive devouring. First a Woman Old nails a male babe down upon a rock,
"number[s] every Nerve / Just as a Miser counts his gold,"
and "Catches his Shrieks in Cups of gold." When the male is
older, the female younger, he retaliates or imitates by "bind-
[ing] her down for his delight" and "plant[ing] himself in all
her Nerves." Love apparently enters with the birth or
"spring" of a female babe from the suddenly aged male's
hearthfire. She is like Shakespeare's Venus, whose "beauty
as the spring doth yearly grow" (line 141).[5] She comes as

5. She is like Fortuna or Vortumna, "she who turns the year." "Mutabilitie
is the aspect of the goddess Fortuna (probably from Vortumna, 'she who
turns the year'), as the controller of time. . . . She enters myth as a goddess,
and indeed, during the decadence of Rome and the early Middle Ages, she
was considered an omnipotent, though degraded, form of the universal
deity, more powerful even than Jove. Her appeal was then enormous.
Church thinkers from Lactantius to Aquinas countered it by attacking her

renewed and fearful energy, and none dares touch or swaddle her. She is one of two sacred forms in the poem—both babes, but of different sex—who may be threatening because, like Southwell's "Burning Babe," they do not come from earth.

"Love," Venus says, "is a spirit all compact of fire" (line 149). Blake's hearthfire babe too is "all of solid fire," and "She comes to the Man she loves." It is the poem's only mention of love without irony. But it is only at its spring that "Love is a spirit all compact of fire": afterwards it declines into lust as possession. As a whole, "The Mental Traveller" supports Adonis's accusation that "Love to heaven is fled" (line 793), leaving on earth the usurper Lust. Shakespeare's Venus is a lustful sexual aggressor who begins by pulling Adonis down on top of her. She is an "empty eagle . . . devouring all in haste" (lines 55, 57), one that Adonis, however, resists: "'Before I know myself, seek not to know me'" (line 325). In "The Mental Traveller," sexual knowledge is prematurely forced on the male babe and extracted from him by the Woman Old when "Her fingers number every Nerve" and she "Catches his Shrieks in Cups of gold." The second and final appearance of Woman Old and the male babe in Blake's poem, however, shows the cruelties not of love, but of refusal, as in *Jerusalem*: "to examine the Infants limbs / In cruelties of holiness: to refuse the joys of love" (68:58–59/E220/222).

If one sees "The Mental Traveller" as divided into two phases by the birth of the female babe, then both are phases of sexual torture or female will: aggressive sexual license, Venus-Rahab; and sexual denial, Diana-Tirzah.[6] Rahab is

worship as idolatry. . . . Yet she was omnipresent in the art, and her turning wheel summarized Everyman's shrug at the unfathomable flux of history and private life" (*The Mutabilitie Cantos*, ed. S. P. Zitner, pp. 50–51).

6. In this phase, "The Mental Traveller" incorporates Blake's manuscript poem "My Spectre around me night & day." The speaker in "My Spectre" threatens to annihilate the Emanation-Shadow on the "rocks" to "create" "another form" that "will be subservient to [his] Fate." What happens in "The Mental Traveller" is the reverse of this. The female hearthfire babe leaves the aged Host, and he, reduced finally to infancy, is "given to a Woman Old" who nails him down upon a rock. If the male figure has created in the hearthfire babe "another form" to be subservient to his fate, she fails to be subservient; instead, "She comes to the Man she loves." "The Mental Traveller" has neither the offered forgiveness nor the communion image which ends "My Spectre," but instead, parasitic devouring.

Natural Philosophy and sexual license. Tirzah is Natural Religion and sexual denial.[7] (Bromion and Theotormon of *Visions of the Daughters* seem the male forms of this double figure.) Seen this way, the two phases of "The Mental Traveller" correspond to the two days of "Venus and Adonis." The first phase in each poem is sexual aggression, the second denial and pursuit, though the sex of the pursuer differs. (In Adonis's parting from Venus at night, like a shooting star— "So glides he in the night from Venus' eye" [line 816]— Adonis is the unattainable object, and Venus's eye is frustrated like that of Blake's male when "Stars Sun Moon all shrink away" from it: "For the Eye altering alters all.") Adonis's hunt on the second day is introduced by his words, "'I know not love . . . nor will not know it, / Unless it be a bear and then I chase it'" (lines 409–10). In the corresponding second phase of "The Mental Traveller," the male hunts a fleeing maiden as "wild game," and the hunt generates "Boars" (and lions and wolves as well). The pursuit in both poems generates a landscape, with the "wild game," "wild Stag," "thicket wild," and "Lion Wolf & Boar" of "The Mental Traveller" reminding us of Venus's pursuit of Adonis's hunt.

Both Shakespeare's Venus and Blake's woman, then, are associated with, or assimilated to, earth; and both are at times prolific. But the scope and generosity of Venus's erotic landscape, though great, has its limits: she is an inviting but bounded "park" where Adonis as "deer" may roam, but not quite freely.[8] And in Blake's poem, as we shall see, female

7. The identifications of Rahab as Natural Philosophy and Tirzah as Natural Religion come from W. J. T. Mitchell's *Blake's Composite Art*, p. 188. David Erdman, in *Blake: Prophet Against Empire*, p. 325, identifies Rahab as sexual license and Tirzah as sexual denial. If "Rahab created Voltaire; Tirzah created Rousseau" (*Milton*, pl. 22), then Voltaire is to be associated not only with Natural Philosophy but also with sexual license—as in *Candide*—and Rousseau is to be associated not only with Natural Religion but with sexual denial or heroic restraint, as in *La Nouvelle Heloise*. Since "the Virgin Harlot Mother of War" is "Babylon the Great" (*Milton*, pl. 22), and Babylon is the convergence of Rahab and Tirzah, the suggestion is perhaps that the final appearance of the frowning male babe in "The Mental Traveller" is Mars, produced by the double influence of Rahab and Tirzah: Babylon.

8. Grasping Adonis's hand, Venus describes herself as an enclosing landscape:

earth herself has stringent limits. Both Venus and Blake's Woman Old seek mastery: Venus urges Adonis, "Be rul'd by me" (line 73); Blake's woman nails the babe down upon a rock. And in both poems the male is diminished. Adonis, refusing to "beget," pursues his own death and ends by "swallowing" himself as his own "grave," though Venus plucks him as a flower and places him in her bosom. Blake's male pursues a second infancy—as if he were Adonis reborn.

Both poems, finally, end in the fall or ruin of love. Defeated by the death of Adonis, Venus prophesies: "'Sorrow on love hereafter shall attend,'" and "'all love's pleasure shall not match his woe'" (lines 1136, 1140). In "The Mental Traveller," also, erotic joy is outweighed by woe. Venus's prophecy that love

> "shall be sparing and too full of riot,
> Teaching decrepit age to tread the measures;
> . . . .
> Pluck down the rich, enrich the poor with treasures" (lines
> 1147–50)

neatly fits the aging male in the second half of "The Mental Traveller." His grief becomes the joy of others, who riotously "make the roofs & walls to ring"; he is led a merry "dance" by a fugitive maiden; a rich man, he is "pluck[ed] down" while others are enriched.

Finally, Venus's prophecy that love shall "'Make the young old, the old become a child'" (line 1151) describes precisely and in order the fate of the male figure in the two half-cycles of "The Mental Traveller." Love first ages him, then reduces

---

"Fondling," she saith, "since I have hemm'd thee here
Within the circuit of this ivory pale,
I'll be a park, and thou shalt be my deer:
Feed where thou wilt, on mountain or in dale;
Graze on my lips, and if those hills be dry
Stray lower, where the pleasant fountains lie.

"Within this limits is relief enough,
Sweet bottom-grass and high delightful plain,
Round rising hillocks, brakes obscure and rough,
To shelter thee from tempest and from rain:
Then be my deer, since I am such a park." (lines 229–39)

him to infancy. The male babe who ends as an untouchable "frowning form" is a baffled Cupid or Eros who now shows his derivation not from plenty—as in his prolific phase, when the woman became his "Garden fruitful seventy fold"—but from poverty. Having lost all the gains he had earlier made through industry, he ends as naked as he began. He has entered the "freezing Age" of winter.[9]

Though it reflects "Venus and Adonis" especially well, "The Mental Traveller" presents a heightened model of the cycle of Eros as fate as it may appear in the poetry of almost any time or place. As the comparison with "Venus and Adonis" suggests, however, the object of frustrated Eros in "The Mental Traveller" is less woman than goddess of nature. The poem's larger subject is the effect of her dominance not only on the male figure, but also on the arts, on science, and on religion. Like Blake's painting "A Vision of the Last Judgment," "The Mental Traveller" is "a History of Art & Science . . . Which is Humanity itself" ("A Vision," p. 84/ E551/562). But the poem imbeds that history in the natural cycle, thus reducing it to the natural cycle:

> Every thing in Dantes Comedia shews That for Tyrannical Purposes he has made This World the Foundation of All & the

9. When Blake's Old Woman becomes the male's "Garden fruitful seventy fold," the outcome of sexual voracity appears to be prolific increase. And "increase" is what Shakespeare's Venus teaches:

> "Seeds spring from seeds and beauty breedeth beauty;
> Thou wast begot; to get it is thy duty.
> . . . .
> By law of nature thou art bound to breed." (lines 167–71)

The devourer as voracious female has her "prolific" time, but must wait for— or force—the male. In spite of the "law of nature," Venus finds Adonis unforceable: the law of breed is prevented by the law of death. Adonis, however, sees a different law of nature:

> "Who plucks the bud before one leaf put forth?
> If springing things be any jot diminish'd,
> They wither in their prime, prove nothing worth." (lines 416–18)

Blake's Old Woman, in enforcing the law of increase, violates the nature that Adonis appeals to. She drains the male's youth and forces his age, so that, having begotten, he immediately turns old. First his youth is devoured, then his possessions. Finally, he too becomes a devourer. Increase has become its opposite.

> Goddess Nature & not the Holy Ghost as Poor Churchill said
> Nature thou art my Goddess . . . & the Goddess Nature Mem-
> ory is his Inspirer & not Imagination the Holy Ghost. ("On
> Blake's Illustrations to Dante"/E667 –68/689)

If the Woman Old is earth as nature goddess, then the
poem begins with the winter birth of a male. It passes to
spring plowing and planting and autumn fruitfulness and
harvest, through the male's "winter," and through a spring
rebirth of nature or the year in the female babe's "springing"
from the fire on the hearth, and through a pursuit of the
fleeing year, which ends finally in the winter birth of a male
babe who is given to a Woman Old. The discrepancy between
male and female shows the maladjustment of humanity to
the natural world and the overwhelming or diverting of
human energy by natural necessity or process. The only roles
in "The Mental Traveller" are those of submission and dominance, host and parasite. The recurring structure is metamorphosis through powers in conflict with their opposites—
not progression through contraries, but a world turning on
grief and joy, which become one another or feed on one
another and which seem equally illusory. The birth of a
female babe from the fire on the hearth, however, both extends the illusion and exposes it. Her birth (or rebirth) and
departure (or apparent departure) are the major and most
ambiguous turn in the poem. One is driven to take it doubly
because seeing it singly—as either good or bad, truth or error, joy or woe—is unsatisfactory.

The hearthfire babe embodies both joy and woe, the two
defining emotions of the strange "Land of Men & Women
too" that the narrator sets out to describe. She is twofold,
begotten in the protagonist's grief, born in the joy of others:

> His grief is their eternal joy
> They make the roofs & walls to ring
> Till from the fire on the hearth
> A little Female Babe does spring. (lines 40 –43)

Springing from song, from the sound of joy, the hearthfire
babe seems an "infant joy" who leaves the protagonist and
"comes to the Man she loves." We are reminded of "She who
burns with youth" from *Visions of the Daughters*; here she

seems to escape from him who freezes with age, who "to allay his freezing Age" seeks a maiden.

Gerald Enscoe stresses the babe's goodness:

> she is the quintessence of energy, "all of solid fire." . . . The images associated with her are images of freedom, of lack of repression or confinement. . . . She and her lover must drive out the aged Host, for he represents the old repressive order. . . . The episode is an interlude to contrast that which is with that which might be.[10]

To me, the female babe has a double aspect of Emanation and Shadow, with the Shadow predominating. As Emanation, at the instant of creation, the female babe is the Host's word or gift. Frye's definition of Emanation is best here: the form of what a man loves and creates. But in fallen time the window into Eden is open only at the *moment* of creation, and the male appears only momentarily as Los exercising his creative powers. Afterwards, the form of "solid fire" leaves the furnace and her creator. "The Mental Traveller" focuses not on the babe and the man she loves—or at first seems not to focus on them—but on the fortunes and vision of the male figure. For him, the female babe remains grief and loss and the illusion of gain: the poverty of nature or this world, less Emanation than Shadow. For him, she has entered time; she shrinks from him and ages, and he avidly pursues her in others.

Blake's female figure embodies not only earth, but also the useful and earthly arts—husbandry, mining, metalworking, hunting, shepherding, and (distantly implied) city building. All are in danger of turning into false art or commerce. The hearthfire babe exposes this danger by leaving the aged Host for the man she loves. Insofar as she is Emanation rather than Shadow, the hearthfire babe leaves the poem. She is the true art who divides from and exposes false art. "No man can Embrace True Art till he has Explord & Cast out False Art . . . or he will be himself Cast out by those who have Already Embraced True Art" ("A Vision of the Last Judgment," p. 84/ E551/562). Having failed to cast out false art, and himself cast out by "those who have Already Embraced True Art," the

10. Enscoe, "The Content of Vision," p. 490.

male protagonist then continues to embrace or explore false art in the person of a maiden who is mistress of "various arts of Love & Hate." False art turns into fortune, embodied in a female figure of whom Blake says, "She alone is the Governor of Worldly Riches," or commerce:

> When Nations grow Old. The Arts grow Cold
> And Commerce settles on every Tree
> And the Poor & the Old can live upon Gold
> For all are Born Poor. Aged Sixty three. (Annotations to *The Works of Sir Joshua Reynolds,* Discourse I, p. 4/E631/642)

In this view, the arts have grown cold in the aged Shadow's desperate pursuit of a fleeing maiden, hoping "to allay his freezing Age." Deserted by Genius or a Daughter of Inspiration—Los as loss—he pursues a Daughter of Memory, a Shadow, until he is caught and bound down by her, and she catches his shrieks in cups of gold. His loss of identity seems complete.

As Shadow—as false art, fortune, or commerce—the feminine figure of "The Mental Traveller" is closely linked with economics—with labor, household management, and the exchange of material goods. She is an impoverished goddess who presides over a Malthusian economy of need and absolute limits. From this point of view, the two phases of the poem are those named in "To Tirzah": "The sexes rose to work and weep." When the male "binds [the female] down for his delight" and "she becomes his Garden fruitful seventy fold," sexuality shows itself to be prolific and is diverted into work: soon the aged male has filled a cottage with riches he has got by industry. But, as in the twofold Genesis curse alluded to in "To Tirzah," the second phase concerns not male work but female weeping. The maiden denies herself to the male—in the words of Shakespeare's Venus, she is a "Love-lacking vestal and self-loving nun" (line 853)—and we end with a Woman Old who is weeping. The field of work is slipping away.

Here too, what looks like progress has turned back to become the Tractates' "same dull round." Blake's male figure passes from infant to husbandman to industrious citizen (with a cottage full of gems and gold "which he by industry had got") to giver of gifts to merchant to infant again. In *Visions of the Daughters of Albion,* which I am quoting here, these character types, ignorant of each other's "pains" and "delights," go to make up a world. In "The Mental Traveller," the protagonist gains a "property," makes it part of himself, by mixing his labor with nature (as in Locke's economics) but loses it again. He gains "necessaries" and "accommodations" and "ornaments" (terms from Reynolds's account of progress in the *Discourses,* quoted in Blake's annotations), then loses them in turn. He has come into the world "naked . . . naked of natural things" (Blake applying the Book of Job to himself and his wife in a letter), and he prospers as well as suffers, but he ends as naked as he began. In "The Mental Traveller" as economic parable, sufferings are coined into wealth, into gems and gold; and what is gain for one agent becomes loss for another. Blake presents a Malthusian balance or "zero-sum game" (the anachronism is expressive here) in which what one gains—youth, food, pleasure, energy, potency—must be drawn from others, especially the opposing sex; and the host's loss is equivalent to the parasite's gain. Whatever creations they generate, actions in "The Mental Traveller" remain a matter of age feeding on youth, life living on life. The one exception, the aged Host's charitable feeding of others, becomes a parasitic diminishing of his own powers: the producer has become merchant of his own substance in a market where no one buys. Blake's own economics are the economics of the infinite inventive-creative capacity of the human imagination, in which, as in the Tractates, "The desire of Man being Infinite the possession is Infinite." In this view, there is no limit to goods because there is no limit to the creative power of imagination. But this possibility is closed off in "The Mental Traveller" by the female babe's departure, which leaves the male pursuing the goods of a strictly limited "Nature."

The babe, whether male or female, is a seed that gives new impetus to the cycle, but the cycle remains closed. The male's eros or need seems the moving force in the first phase, the female (especially her virginity) the moving force in the second. In the first phase, the male progresses from outcast suffering to wealth. In the second phase, he declines into poverty and frustration. In the first phase, the male appears after the initial binding-down to control and dominate earth or nature; in the second, the male-female relation is reversed: the female controls. In the first phase, the earth is flat, nature a field of work or of satisfied desire, the male's Emanation within reach. In the second, earth has become a ball; the sun, moon, and stars have become small and distant; and nature has become not a field of work but a withdrawn world of perception—a world outside, the Emanation perpetually fleeing: Ulro.

The aged Shadow's pursuit of a shadowy goddess of nature exposes not only false art and economy but (as I said earlier) false science and false religion. The aged Shadow's joys are tears, so that he embraces the maiden as Los embraces pity—Enitharmon—in *The Book of Urizen.* There the embrace shocks the Eternals into weaving the woof or roof of science to shut out the sight. In "The Mental Traveller," during the embrace-pursuit "the Senses roll themselves in fear," so that the flat earth becomes a ball, and the shrinking away of the heavenly bodies leaves the male figure in a vast desert, the desert of Descartian and Newtonian astrophysics. Seen this way, not only is the feminine figure space, but the male is her "masculine portion, death"—the "corporeal and Mortal Body," or the "Corporeal Vegetative Eye" as a synedoche for the mortal body given by a strictly rational-empirical science ("A Vision of the Last Judgment," pp. 91–92/E552–54/563). The poem has births but no deaths, then, because the male figure *is* the body of death and ultimate loss, imprisoned by the womb-as-tomb of this world. The aged Shadow's pity has given birth to an external nature or Enitharmon whose existence precedes and survives his and from whose womb he in turn is born, his reduction to infancy at the end being the triumph of this female space, the Genesis curse of painful childbirth denied: "For there the Babe is born in joy." (Compare the torturing females of *Jerusalem* [68:36–37/E220/222] who "bring forth under green trees / With pleasure.")

*   *   *

The greatest effects of Blake's goddess of nature are of course on religion and on the decline of vision into sense, myth into mythological tales, the prophetic artist into mere entertainer and maker of baubles. Once again, true art is cast out by false; but now we see the casting out not in economic but in mythological terms. Aphrodite or Venus remains the controlling figure, but both male and female suggest other mythical figures as well. Once again the crux of the poem is in the "fire birth" of a female babe: "Till from the fire on the hearth / A little Female Babe does spring" (lines 43–44).

Augustine helps us to understand the hearthfire birth in Blake's poem by noting that one of the many forms of the goddess of nature is the hearthfire. In his account in *The City of God*, for the pagan philosophers earth is Juno and at the same time Ceres or Vesta; and Vesta is the hearthfire thought to be necessary to the prosperity of home and city. If we see Blake's hearthfire babe as Vesta, her going to the man she loves and their casting out the aged Host helps to account for the failure of the male figure to found or even to enter a city. (If he suggests Cain or Romulus as city-founder, that role is truncated, and he remains an outcast.) Augustine maintains that Vesta is also Venus and may be virgin, harlot, or wife—like the maiden whom Blake's male pursues, one might add. Here is Augustine:

> Virgil [*Aeneid* 1.47] drew his inspiration, not from poetical fancies, but from the treatises of the philosophers, when he wrote: "Then the almighty Father, the ether, came down in fruitful rain, in the bosom of his joyful spouse" [*Georgics* 2.325,326] meaning, in the bosom of Tellus or Earth. Even here they see some difference in the earth itself. They think that Terra is one thing, Tellus another—Moreover, they also call this same Terra mother of the gods, so that one can have more patience with the reveries of the poets than with the sacred, but not poetical, books of the pagans, which make Juno not only "sister and spouse," but also mother, or Jupiter. They would also identify this same Earth with Ceres, and likewise with Vesta.
>
> More commonly, however, they believe that Vesta is but the fire that warms the hearth—failing which, there would be no city. Hence, the custom of dedicating virgins to its service, because nothing is born of fire, just as nothing is born of virgins. Surely, a stupid notion like this deserved to be banished and abolished by the One who was born of a virgin. Who can endure to see them paying to fire even the honor due to chastity, and

yet feeling no shame in giving the name Venus to Vesta? When they do this they make a mockery of the virginity which is honored in her servants. For, if Vesta is merely Venus, how could virgins minister to her without imitating Venus? Are there two Venuses; one a virgin and the other a wife? Or, rather, three—one Vesta for virgins, another for married women, and a third for harlots? To this last, the Phoenicians offered the gift of prostituting their daughters before they gave them husbands.[11]

Augustine's account of Vesta offers us the alternative figure of the Virgin. But there is no Annunciation in "The Mental Traveller," though there is perhaps the Virgin's conception without sin in the birth in fire, and even an Assumption in her apparent departure from the world of the poem. If we think of the association of Mary with the Church, and if we see the female as maiden or virgin—as Blake's pursuing male does—then she suggests the Virgin as Church. As Shadow rather than Emanation—as Emanation in flight—the female babe is both nature goddess and a "Female in embrio," the "Net of Religion" or the Church, born of the aged Shadow's pity and self-denial and then closing him out, renewing her virginity at his expense.[12] Blake's attitude toward a church that teaches the virtue of virginity is very different from Augustine's. For Blake, the virginity of such a church is her harlotry, is Babylon, the two states interdependent as opposites that define and require each other. And such a church, for Blake, is not at war with paganism and Natural Religion but is a manifestation of them.[13]

If Blake's female is virgin and Venus—wife, sister, and spouse of his male figure—then the male seems a pagan god, and Blake's male and female like the whole of the natural world, as in Augustine's account in *The City of God*:

11. *The City of God*, trans. by Gerald Walsh et al. (New York, 1958), book IV, chapter 10, pp. 91–92.

12. I am quoting from *The Book of Urizen*, 8:18, 22. In identifying Blake's female figure with the Church, I am following Blake's "A Vision of the Last Judgment" (where the female as Church is unfallen) and S. Foster Damon: "From the male's own hospitality (hearth . . .), an established code of conduct springs up: a Church, outward religion. This is the 'Female Babe,' so sacred that none dare touch her" (*William Blake: His Philosophy and Symbols*, p. 131).

13. "The Pope supposes Nature and the Virgin Mary to be the same allegorical personages, but the Protestant considers Nature as incapable of bearing a child" ("Annotations to Cellini (?)" E659/670).

. . . Let the learned pagans maintain all they please about Jove. Now, let him be the soul of this material world, filling and moving the vast structure of the universe, formed and compounded of four elements. . . . Again, let him be the ether embracing the underlying air, Juno. Now, let him be the entire sky and air together, and let him with fertile rains and seeds fecundate the earth—his wife and mother at the same time, for this is no scandal among the gods. . . . Let him be Jupiter in the ether, Juno in the air, Neptune in the sea, . . . Pluto in the earth . . . Vesta on domestic hearths, Vulcan in the forger's furnace, the sun, moon, and stars in the heavens. (bk. 4, chap. 11, p. 92)

"The Mental Traveller" divides male from female more than Augustine does in this account—it is the first principle of the poem—but it too shows female earth and male sky coupling and separating, with the male power shrinking or diminished. In presenting a "female" earth's relation to "male" sky, Blake shows earth as first drinking in heat and light, as in summer, then fleeing them, as in winter. In the birth of a female child of solid fire in the middle of the poem, which balances the Woman Old's "Cups of gold" at the beginning, female earth steals the male's vital heat or fire, as if she were a female Prometheus, and he is left vainly seeking to "allay his freezing Age." He has lost his prolific power to the female—to Enitharmon as earth/hearth/heart.

A male figure whose crucifixion at the beginning implies Christ begins with the appearance of fire to imply Prometheus and declines further into Hephaestus and his creature, Pandora. Vision declines into craft, and craftsmanship into mere begetting—a decline embodied more fully in Los than in any of Blake's other figures. There is no notable craftsman figure in the Bible, and the most striking fact about Los remains his derivation from pagan poetry and mythology. Read in the light of Hesiod and Homer and Virgil, "The Mental Traveller" shows the descent of heavenly male prolific fire to earth and yields a visionary satire on the progress of the culture-hero or artist-craftsman in "This World," where Los forgets that he is Urthona and cedes his power to Enitharmon.

The crucial points in "The Mental Traveller" read as Hesiod or Homer are the coming to female earth of heaven as a male babe—Ouranos, Kronos, Zeus, Hephaestus, Prometheus—from the sky. With the appearance of a sacred, untouchable female babe, the male ages and heaven withdraws ("The Stars Sun Moon all shrink away") to return at the end ("The Sun & Stars are nearer rolld") as the male is reborn. (His return is like a second and inconclusive, and therefore repetitive and debased, coming of the Christ child.) Put the other way around, earth first entraps and steals the male fire, then flees, to be pursued and caught as the Woman Old by the male babe who is entrapped by her. The poem's births are repeated births of the cosmos and of mankind-inhabited earth (or repeated mythological tales of that birth). But Blake emphasizes the triumph of earth over creation in fire, the female over the "he, who dwells in flaming fire" of *The Marriage of Heaven and Hell.* In "The Mental Traveller" as in the "Song of Liberty" at the end of the *Marriage,* "The fire, the fire is falling!"

We can begin with Zeus. Hidden as an infant by grandmother Earth in a Cretan cave, Zeus later gives motherless birth to Athena, from his head, and to Aphrodite, from the sperm-foam of his severed genitals—somewhat as "a little Female Babe . . . spring[s]" forth in the middle of "The Mental Traveller." That Blake's female springs from the hearthfire of an "Earthly Cot" means that she is of the earth, of the Cretan cave and the Cyprian foam, as much as of heaven, though she is "of solid fire" and spurns the earth (as Enitharmon does in her "crystal house" in *Europe*). Zeus's Emanations have escaped his control, but Zeus is not yet Blake's figure of fallen fire: Hephaestus is. "Stars Sun Moon all shrink away" when heavenly Zeus withdraws after begetting Hephaestus and when Hephaestus is thrown out of Olympus by Hera (or Zeus) for being misshapen (or for threatening his father).[14] Hephaestus is concealed for nine years, making

14. "The binding of Orc is not depicted in *The Book of Urizen,* but he is shown already bound in the first Preludium page of *America,* where the motif as a whole appears to refer to the chaining of Prometheus by Hephaestus, as depicted by Flaxman in his line engravings from Aeschylus of *Prometheus Unchained,* 1793. If Orc is Promethean, then a parallel between Los and Hephaestus is equally compelling. Hephaestus was, of course, a blacksmith, and Los riveting and soldering the form of Urizen recalls Hephaestus forging the armour of Achilles; Los's position as artist to the

jewelry in a cave, by Thetis and Eurýnomê (*Iliad* 18). The cave of course suggests Urthona's dens, but it is a "female" cave or womb, like Zeus's hideout, like the womb Enitharmon prepares for Satan in the Bard's Song in *Milton,* and like Vala's cave in *Jerusalem,* from which, as she maintains, she breathes forth the male.

It is especially ironic that the Hephaestus who makes jewelry and such devices as golden nets to catch and expose lovers (Ares with Aphrodite, Hephaestus's own wife or consort) also creates Pandora. The Pandora in "The Mental Traveller," since she is "of gold," seems to be assimilated to one of the gold "maids" or automata created by Hephaestus to serve him (*Iliad* 18). In "The Mental Traveller," she apparently escapes from and masters her master, or at least seduces him by her coyness. That Pandora is all of "gems" and "gold" and "solid fire" in Blake's poem emphasizes her nature and function: she is "all gifts" of the gods, sent by Zeus to punish mankind for the theft of fire. The Woman Old in the beginning, we remember, numbered the male's nerves "as a Miser counts his gold" and caught his shrieks in cups of gold. Hephaestus, who is strongly associated with gold in *Iliad* 18—gold is his prime material—has been charmed by his own creation, the fruits of his industry, and vainly pursues her or pursues her in others.

Eternals also recalls Hephaestus's role upon Olympus. Plate 21 [of *The Book of Urizen*] shows the fallen Los, bearded and tied by the Chain of Jealousy, resting his hammer upon the forge while he looks jealously upon the embracing Orc and Enitharmon. The motif is instantly recognizable as bearing a relationship to the common Renaissance subject of *Venus, Vulcan and Cupid at the Forge,* and it is sufficiently obvious to make it certain that the analogy between Blake and Hephaestus was made consciously" (David Bindman, *Blake as an Artist,* p. 93).

See also Erwin Panofsky, *Studies in Iconology,* p. 35: "The classical writers are unanimous in stating that Vulcan, or Hephaistos, was 'thrown down from Mount Olympus,' and was not readmitted to the Palace of the Gods before a considerable time. . . . According to some [traditions] he was ejected as a child, according to others as a man." For Blake, Hephaestus would be an outcast reprobate. Later, quoting Boccaccio's *Genealogia Deorum,* XII, Panofsky observes that Hephaestus has to be considered "not only as the 'smith of Jupiter' and the 'composer of all sorts of artificial things,' but also as the very founder of human civilization, inasmuch as the 'bringing up Vulcan,' that is, the purposeful keeping alive of fire, had led to the formation of the first social units, to the invention of speech, and to the erection of buildings" (p. 38). Boccaccio's source is Vitruvius's *De Architectura.*

If the motherless female babe in "The Mental Traveller" also suggests Athena, she too, as goddess of craftsmen and smiths, is closely associated with Hephaestus; and Hephaestus as rough midwife aided her birth by splitting Zeus's head with an axe. Hephaestus is given permission by Zeus to marry Athena. (His lack of success with her would no doubt increase his Eros state of "lovesick eye" and "akeing heart.") When Athena repulses him, his seed falls on the earth, which is made fertile—much as the maid's "fear" in "The Mental Traveller" "plants" "many a thicket wild" and "Labyrinths of wayward Love / Where roams the Lion Wolf & Boar"—and bears a male child, Erichthonius, whom Athena shuts into a chest with snakes and gives to the daughters of Cecrops to keep; after opening the forbidden chest, they throw themselves from the Acropolis. With Earth giving birth to a male child, and with a male child being given to a woman or women, the cycle has once more come back to the beginning. Blake's poem seems to have an infinite power of condensation.

But with Hephaestus we have begun to see Blake's male as a kind of Los. If we compare Hephaestus with what Los becomes, we see Hephaestus as a source figure for the artist-craftsman, but we note that Hephaestus contents himself with making jewelry and curious devices and armor and marvelous representations of mortal life on the shield of Achilles. The male in "The Mental Traveller" is, like Hephaestus, a mere craftsman who feeds his consumers or devourers with gold and gems; and his industry degenerates into mere pursuit of unwilling maiden or separated Emanation. It scarcely needs to be added that Athena, Aphrodite, and Pandora would for Blake be dim memories—pagan perversions—of the Emanation as the form of what a man loves and creates.

The pursuit is of course a round, and for Blake the round is apparently a pagan poetic form:

> In Dantes Comedia . . . Round Purgatory is Paradise & round Paradise is Vacuum or Limbo. so that Homer is the Center of All I mean the Poetry of the Heathen Stolen & Perverted from the Bible not by Chance but by design by the Kings of Persia and

their Generals The Greek Heroes & lastly by The Romans. ("On Blake's Illustrations to Dante" E667–68/689)

If Dante's universe in Blake's view is a series of concentric spheres within which Dante's own movement is spiral, "The Mental Traveller" is a double round or spiral. As Blake's hero moves outward and ages in a purgatorial ascent from the satanic center toward a vanishing paradise, his end is vacuum; as he moves inward in a brief spiral toward infancy, his end is the satanic rock and center—Homer. Correspondingly, the female figure in the first phase is an earthly fertility figure, the "nameless shadowy female" of the Lambeth prophecies. In the second phase she is the "queen of heaven" of the Old Testament—in Blake's scheme a denier of sexuality, as Enitharmon is in *Europe.* (Queen of Heaven—*Regina Coeli*—is of course an epithet for the Virgin, in the Church and in Dante.) As the first, her elements are evidently earth and water; as the second, they are fire and air.

If the female hearthfire babe in the center of "The Mental Traveller," all of "solid fire," suggests the change of the Common Aphrodite (Aphrodite *Pandemou*) into the Uranian Aphrodite of the *Symposium*—a female figure who becomes less and less attainable—this in turn suggests the Eros element in Dante's Beatrice: when we last see her smiling down on Dante from the third circle from the highest, and then turning toward the "eternal fountain" (*Paradiso* 31), she has become a Uranian Aphrodite. Blake's interest, as always, is in the pagan infection of Christian or biblical poetry; and his system is in large part a condensed, selective, reordered history of poetry.

If Blake's fallen form is the round (as in "Round Purgatory is Paradise & Round Paradise is Vacuum"), to see the male babe as Hephaestus is also to see how the ciruclar form of "The Mental Traveller" echoes that of the shield Hephaestus makes for Achilles: concentric circles with sun, moon, and stars in the center, surrounded by earth, surrounded by ocean stream (as the shield is often read). Both the shield and Blake's poem have sun, moon, and stars, along with cities, fertile farmland, rich pastures, and a dance of man and woman or men and maidens. (On the shield, almost all are done in gold.) Perhaps the nameless "Land of Men & Women too" where "The Mental Traveller" takes place is the dancing floor represented on the shield. In any case, Homer's description of the dancing floor emphasizes once more the circles of the shield:

> They circled there with ease
> The way a potter sitting at a wheel
> Will give it a practice twirl between his palms to see it run.
> (Fitzgerald translation)

The potter's wheel is also of course an Old Testament prophetic metaphor, but here it suggests an entire cyclical cosmos and its mover; and the whole of the shield of Achilles seems a triumph of art as imitation rather than as prophetic vision—the essence of pagan poetry as opposed to the poetry of the Bible.

> *   *   *

In the center of the poem we seem to have left the opening crucifixion behind, and Hephaestus cannot be seen as the object of that opening crucifixion without forcing. But Prometheus *can* be seen in that way, and the importance of fire and of craftsmanship in "The Mental Traveller" also fits Prometheus. Blake's disordering or rearranging of time so that it no longer has an apparently causal or consequential form appears now in his beginning with Prometheus's punishment and moving from that to the Promethean gift of fire and Zeus's hiding of fire from man. The fire is personified or animated in the babe who is also the Pandora through whom Zeus punishes mankind. Through sheer compactness of implication, the female babe of gems and solid fire forms an image of diamond brilliance in the center of the poem. Here the Prometheus (Forethinker) who in one tradition created Pandora evidently turns into the Epimetheus (Afterthinker) who married her. (Her box has effects like that of the not-to-be-opened chest Athena gave to Cecrops's daughters.) When we think of Pandora's "gift" of afflictions, the males in "The Mental Traveller" seem to show mankind punished by the gods working through female agents or messengers. From Olympic god to Titan we pass to a mankind created or ruined in the first woman, Pandora. Such a creation looks very much like Blake's Shadow. The Promethean male has learned to make something—gems and gold, food and joy for others—of his suffering. But if he is a god or Titan, he is a fallen one, and his art is fallen: crucified or bound down, he lacks vision; forethought has diminished to afterthought.

In "The Grey Monk" (also in the Pickering Manuscript) suffering can be turned to vision because it *is* fallen vision:

> For a Tear is an Intellectual Thing
> And a Sigh is the Sword of an Angel King
> And the bitter groan of the Martyrs woe
> Is an Arrow from the Almighties Bow.

Blake might agree, reluctantly, that in a fallen world the artist must begin in suffering, but if suffering is fallen vision, the male in "The Mental Traveller" creates an eroticized form in which he never achieves vision or Mental Fight:

> And these are the gems of the Human Soul
> The rubies & pearls of a lovesick eye
> The countless gold of the akeing heart
> The martyrs groan & the lovers sigh.

The "martyrs groan"—like the "Human Soul"—is here overwhelmed by its erotic context of "lovesick eye," "akeing heart," and "lovers sigh," and by the erotic pursuit that follows in the poem. The male by now has declined from Christ through Prometheus to Epimetheus or Hephaestus.

The binding down of the male babe in "The Mental Traveller" is the Los-Enitharmon binding-down-of-Orc phase of *The Book of Urizen,* in which Los as Zeus binds Prometheus. Both Urizen and Orc, Zeus and Prometheus, are aspects—self-divisions—of Los. The punishing agent in "The Mental Traveller," however, is the female, the male's "feminine portion" as Ololon calls it in *Milton.* The "sky-god"—Ouranos, Kronos, Zeus, Yahweh—is absent, as are all the son-sacrificing, son-consuming, and father-castrating horrors of Hesiod's *Theogony* and *Works and Days.* Heaven, the source of fiery heat and light, is present only by implication, as is male "making." Having begun with a female earth, our perceptions remain bound down to earth, and Prometheus, the male prolific power of making, is overwhelmed by mother earth. In short, "The Mental Traveller" shows Los in his limited form, before he turns visionary.

We begin with a child "begotten" in "dire woe" and a sowing in "bitter tears." We have begun in suffering, a crucifixion-punishment-torture (which is joy for others) in which the heart is "cut . . . out at his side" and made to feel, to suffer; and beginnings are decisive. The Woman Old has "sown" gold, which, as in usury, "begets" more gold and her own rejuvenation in the male's suffering and aging. But she has also begotten a balancing or responsive action in which he grows young while she grows old. The whole poem, in fact, can be seen as the "begetting" "in dire woe" of the male babe who appears at the end (or of the female babe who appears in the center, but then the begetting is in joy). The prolific power is apparently male, as in the primitive Greek idea of the female as mere incubator of male seed, so that we are apparently to take literally the words "He plants himself in all her Nerves." The male plants himself: the poem's final fruit is the male babe come again, fruitlessly it seems. The more inclusive view, however, sees that each has planted himself/herself in the other. If "Her fingers number every Nerve," he, in turn, "plants himself in all her Nerves." They are mutually bound; each is soil for the other.

In the balancing and mirroring movement of the poem, the "aged Shadow" whose "Cot" is "full filled all with gems & gold" seems at first to repeat the miserliness of the Woman Old. But unlike the Woman Old, he feeds his gold and gems to others and becomes what he had earlier fed and entertained—a "Beggar" and "Poor Man." Having been a generous or pitying Dives, he becomes Lazarus; or he lives the experience of Job. The alternative possibilities and doubles in the poem are for the most part both realized. The two seed or topic sentences describe female actions: she "nails him down upon a rock," and "She comes to the Man she loves." The second one divides the poem in half, and the second half reverses the male's state and growth in the first half just as it reverses the female's state and growth in the first half: chiastic structure dominates the whole as well as the part. When

the Woman Old "grows young," she shows what will happen
to the male. Each is prophetic or proleptic for the other: in
each the other could read his/her outcome. The balance is
almost perfect. The male becomes a child for the Woman
Old; the female becomes a "Virgin bright" and "maiden"—
like Athena—for the young male and the aged Shadow; the
female babe "comes to the Man she loves."

The female as the male's "dwelling place" shifts with a
rapidity that dazzles the eye from "rock" to "Garden" to
"Earthly Cot." But even as he "wander[s] round an Earthly
Cot" filled with the gems and gold of his "industry," the male
"fades" as an "aged Shadow." The female hearthfire babe
seems to consolidate the gems, gold, and cottage—roof,
walls, door, hearth, and fire—into one burning form of
"solid fire" (as if she were Enitharmon as the heart or hearthfire of the earth), and they disappear from the poem, to be
replaced by an earth no longer "flat" but a "Ball"; a sun,
moon, and stars which shrink away; a "dark" (and later
"vast") "desart"; thickets; "Labyrinths" "Where roams the
Lion Wolf & Boar"; "many a City"; and "many a pleasant
Shepherds home." The "dwelling places" change so rapidly
that they begin to seem desert mirages. The "sand," which
(in "Mock on Mock on") becomes a "Gem" when it is "Reflected in the beams divine," has, with the departure of light,
become mere sand and a "dark desart," though light returns
when the "Sun & Stars are nearer rolld." But woman as
"dwelling place" becomes overwhelming, and however
much the male "wander[s] round," he remains bound to the
female—in place. The places in the poem are all erotic—
topoi in erotic poetry also—and Eros perception does not
progress beyond erotic art.

Perhaps both male and female are seeking the "original
oneness" of Aristophanes' myth in the *Symposium.* If so,
the "sweet Extacy" of erotic touch is first exacerbated beyond
the threshold of pain in "her fingers number every Nerve";
then touch is forbidden and Eros shifted from touch to sight,
to "roving Eye" and "Eye altering." If touch was fire—as in "I
strove to sieze the inmost Form / With ardor fierce & hands of
flame" in "The Crystal Cabinet"—fire has become light, and
touch sight; and the object has become correspondingly dis-

tant. Gems and fire and gold, the apparently tangible meat and drink that the aged Host feeds to others—the devourer—disappear about midway through the poem, replaced by the food of female charms on which the aged Host grows young. If the Woman Old is nourished by shrieks and cries until she is reborn gems and gold, the male is renewed by "the honey of her Infant lips," "the bread & wine of her sweet smile," and her "various arts of Love & Hate."

The female made prolific by male attention and suffering, and the male seeking food of female charms, is the male-female balance that makes up the whole of the erotic poem. Together, male suffering and female charms plant or beget the "gold" or perfected form of the erotic poem, and the poem as female offspring takes on what Susanne Langer calls a "virtual life" of its own. The deprived poet (or Cellini) has begotten his poem or work on the unattainable female. (Homer's description of the shield of Achilles, though not an erotic poem, gives us the definitive representation of the made object taking on virtual life, as if Hephaestus making the shield were the demiurge making earth and human souls.) The female takes the coined sufferings of the male as dowry to the "Man she loves," who appears in final and perfected erotic female form at the end of the poem as man reduced to infant, as if Eros were the victim of his own dart. In "The Mental Traveller," neither Beulah nor Generation gets anywhere. Though the female of gems and gold and solid fire at first looks unchanging and immortal and perfect, she grows old and has her life renewed by the shrieks and cries of mortals—by human sacrifice. Blake seems to see male suffering in erotic poetry, the "akeing heart" and "lovesick eye," as a trivialized recall of the human sacrifice once aimed at renewing the immortal life of a cyclical fertility goddess.

The generations in "The Mental Traveller" are inhuman or perverse in a different way than the pagan poets' mother-son and brother-sister pairings, which lead to normal birth. In Blake's poem the female is never identified as mother or sister or daughter, nor the male as father or brother or son. The female babe seems a case of autogenesis; feeding is perverse ("She lives upon his shrieks and cries," "The bread & wine of her sweet smile"); and though the male babe is said to have been born, the poem proceeds to show his birth as the progressive reduction to infancy of the aged Shadow or aged Host. Its sexual Contraries are negations; there is no progression. Generation has left its proper realm and entered the realm of making, where it becomes mere repetition; and real birth, the birth of the new and unique person, has stopped. This is to say that history has stopped—or, in pagan poetry, never begun.

For Blake, the unique person who gives form and meaning to history is of course Christ. If in "Auguries of Innocence"

> God Appears & God is light
> To those poor Souls who dwell in Night
> But does a Human Form Display
> To those who Dwell in Realms of day,

"The Mental Traveller" shows an approach to and wavering between the two forms of God. the Woman Old's catching the shrieks of a male babe in cups of gold suggests earth capturing the waxing light of the male sun, reborn at the winter solstice, so that the two phases of the poem are a turning first toward, then away from the sun—an increase and a waning of light.[15] (The protagonist's waxing and waning earthly light is of course very different from the "clear, unchanged, and universal light" in which the narrator of the poem seems to stand.)[16] The birth into this world of a male of

15. My indebtedness to Northrop Frye here will be obvious. "Mythologies are full of young gods or heroes who go through various successful adventures and then are deserted or betrayed and killed, and then come back to life again, suggesting in their story the movement of the sun across the sky into the dark or the progression of seasons through winter and spring. . . . Usually there is a female figure in the story. Some . . . critics . . . suggest that these stories go back to a single mythical story. . . . In [Robert] Graves' version of the one story, the heroine is a 'white goddess,' a female figure associated with the moon, who is sometimes a maiden, sometimes a wife, sometimes a beautiful but treacherous witch or siren, sometimes a sinister old woman or hag belonging to the lower world." Frye himself sees Graves's story as part of a still larger story, the story of the loss and regaining of identity between ourselves and our world (*The Educated Imagination,* pp. 50–51). Later, Frye remarks, "The Classical myths give us, much more clearly than the Bible, the main episodes of the central myth of the hero whose mysterious birth, triumph and marriage, death and betrayal and eventual rebirth follow the rhythm of the sun and the seasons" (p. 112).

16. Morton Paley speaks of "the distance . . . between our apprehension of the poem as symbolic in mode and cyclical in structure and the narrator's presentation of it as if it were literal and linear" (*Energy and the Imagination,* p. 131). Hazard Adams says of the narrator that "His position is eternal and his eye contains the fallen world" (*William Blake,* p. 99).

waxing and waning earthly light is apparently the subject of "The Crystal Cabinet" (also in the Pickering Manuscript). "The Crystal Cabinet" shows the male figure—light as power of seeing—imprisoned and confused by the fallen eye, the crystal cabinet. When he bursts the cabinet, he is born as a weeping infant or tear. (In "the Eye / Which was Born in a Night to perish in a Night / When the Soul Slept in Beams of Light," we have the action of "The Crystal Cabinet" condensed. In "Every Tear from every Eye / Becomes a Babe in Eternity," we have the same action reversed. Both passages are from "Auguries of Innocence," in the Pickering Manuscript.) The babe and the "Weeping Woman pale reclind" of "The Crystal Cabinet" have passed from threefold Beulah into twofold Generation—into the world of "The Mental Traveller." In both poems the male babe seems a Christ treated ironically: the light that came into the world as an infant, overwhelmed and distorted by this world. Oedipus and Lear, Eros and Mars, Hephaestus and Prometheus, are pagan figures contained within their source extremes: Christ and Satan. For Blake, extremes in this world generate their opposites. "The Mental Traveller" is a kind of "Satanic mill," turning without end.

*   *   *

If at the beginning and the end of "The Mental Traveller" we have the birth of a male babe at the winter solstice, the event inevitably recalls Christ's birth at the winter solstice.[17] It recalls the light that came into the world of John's Gospel and the divine birth in Milton's "On the Morning of Christ's Nativity": "It was no season then for her [nature] / To wanton with the Sun, her lusty paramour." Both poems begin and end with the male babe and woman. Milton's begins with the male babe's intrusion into nature and ends with Mary and the resting babe: "But see! the Virgin blest / Hath laid the Babe to rest." In "The Mental Traveller," we begin and end with the male babe in the power of a Woman Old who seems

17. "Orc is born when Jesus is born, in the dark frozen terror of the winter solstice, when all things seem to be gathering together for a plunge into an abyss of annihilation, the sun reduced to a cold and weak light unable to bring any more life from the earth" (*Fearful Symmetry,* p. 220).

the equivalent of Milton's nature with "guilty front" and "foul deformities." Reborn in winter, when earth is old, the sun causes rebirth of the earth in spring and makes it fruitful in summer and autumn. Winter Ulro passes into spring Generation and summer Beulah, and might pass into autumn Eden—the final harvest (as at the end of *The Four Zoas*)—if the cycle were brought to an end. Instead, the sphere turns back to fall Generation and winter Ulro. Though all flee Blake's frowning babe at the end of the poem as the pagan gods flee the birth of Christ—a greater sun than the sun—in the "Nativity Ode," Blake's male is nevertheless more a pagan fertility god than a Christ. Milton adapts pagan myth and insight to Christian truth. Blake's immensely detached ironic vision shows Christ falling back into something like Augustine's Jove, Neptune, Pluto, or Vulcan.

Blake has taken the biblical paradise, wilderness, and heavenly city and presented them in pagan erotic terms, so that behind the Eros plot we see outlines of Genesis, Christ's temptation in the wilderness, his crucifixion and resurrection, and the apocalypse.[18] The wilderness is not only eastward from Eden, but is also the wilderness of the exodus from Egypt and the New Testament flight into Egypt and the temptation. The protagonist suggests Adam and Moses and Christ, the Woman Old a satanic Eve, Pharaoh, Herod, and finally the Church. Founded on Peter's rock, the rock of cru-

18. The apocalyptic implications of "The Mental Traveller" have of course not been overlooked and may have been exaggerated. Martin K. Nurmi, for example, points out that near the end of the poem, when the trees "bring forth sweet Extacy" and cities are being built, the "moment when man may return to Eden is at hand, and everything is fruitful and productive. A Second Coming has arrived, if only mankind knew it." But mankind is "frightened by the babe, who to them is a 'frowning form.'" "His fearfulness, like the female babe's and the Tyger's, is mostly in the eye of the unregenerate beholder." Fallen man "does not recognize that the animals 'howling flee' to make room for the civilized human society of Eden, that the trees shed their fruit as an aspect of an apocalyptic last harvest and vintage, and that arms are withered which touch the babe because everything material will be withered and transformed as man beholds a new world. But again the chance is missed, and once more the babe is given to a 'woman old,' who once more starts the cycle" ("Joy, Love, and Innocence in Blake's 'The Mental Traveller,'" 115–16). My difference with Nurmi is that I see the poem as more ironic than he does—as emphasizing the absence or failure of the hero whose coming is evoked. To put it differently, Nurmi supplies more of what is absent from the poem than I do.

cifixion, the fallen Church in the Mass catches the shrieks of a crucified "vegetable" Christ in cups of gold, and the gold cup assimilates the Church to the Whore of Babylon. Though she is a separated Emanation, a fallen outer world, a fallen Church, and (as Morton Paley remarks) a reborn Natural Religion, the Woman Old is nevertheless potentially a community: Babylon is a shadow of Jerusalem. That community is never realized in the poem, however, only named in "Till many a City there is Built, / And many a pleasant Shepherds home."

Cottage and city both suggest a settling down from wandering—Vesta in pagan terms, Jerusalem as end in biblical terms. If the male entered into it, the city would be Jerusalem, and "The Mental Traveller" alludes to Hosea and Jeremiah and Ezekiel and the Book of Revelation as much as it does to Genesis and Exodus and the flight into Egypt. The final male form—the frowning babe—suggests not only Oedipus first exposed on the mountain and later self-exiled from the city, but also the symbolic male infants in Hosea and Isaiah and the male child who is to rule all nations with a rod of iron from the Book of Revelation. And the fleeing maiden suggests the pregnant woman clothed with the sun in Revelation 2: "a woman clothed with the sun, and the moon under her feet, and upon her head a crown of twelve stars," threatened by a dragon whose tail sweeps down a third part of the stars. "She brought forth a male child, who was to rule all nations with a rod of iron." But "her child was caught up unto God, and to his throne. And the woman fled into the wilderness, where she hath a place prepared of God, that they should feed her there a thousand two hundred and threescore days." When the aged Shadow in "The Mental Traveller" embraces a maiden to allay his freezing age, the sun, moon, and stars all shrink away (as a woman, one might add, but virgin rather than pregnant); and the maiden he pursues flees into the wilderness that her own flight generates.

In short, sun, moon, stars, and wilderness in "The Mental Traveller" as in Revelation are associated with a female figure. But the woman in Revelation is Mary-Jerusalem. The woman in Blake's poem is more like the "queen of heaven" whose worship is denounced by the prophets. She is nature and a fallen Church, which teaches Natural Religion; and her flight, together with the male's pursuit, generates the thickets, lions, and boars of generation.[19] Instead of the male child's being taken up to heaven, and instead of the final descent of Jerusalem out of heaven, so that God's city and temple—and God himself as the temple—dwell among men, the female babe born of the hearthfire goes to the man she loves, and they expel the aged Shadow. He, in pursuit of a maiden, is "beguiled" to a second infancy. Though what seems a pagan Eros cycle has begun to evoke Genesis, Christ's temptation in the wilderness, his crucifixion, and the final apocalypse, the suggestions are all suspended, as if we were reading an Old Testament prophecy like that of the suffering servant. The woman clothed with the sun is not yet ready to appear in glory. The male child is not snatched up to the throne of God. Satan the dragon has not yet revealed himself; the end of history—fallen into fertility cycles—has not yet come.

"The Mental Traveller" begins in desert wilderness (signified by the rock on which the male babe is bound down), progresses to an erotic garden, and—in "full filled all with gems & gold / Which he by industry had got"—to what seems a very industrious artisan's or shepherd's cottage and to the cottager's Job-like charitable acts: "He feeds the Beggar and the Poor / For ever open is his door." But the cottager is turned out of his cottage, and with the trees that once brought forth "sweet Extacy" having "shed" their fruit, he

19. The thickets, lions, wolves, and boars of generation suggest Artemis: "Artemis represented to the Greeks the old goddess in her aspect as mother of the wild beasts and guardian of the untamed wild lands." Artemis had a "reputation for having demanded human sacrifice in the past," as in the "sacrifice by Agamemnon of his daughter Iphigenia." At Sardis, Artemis "is more than the Greek Artemis. She is also Aphrodite, great goddess of Asia . . . that being upon whose footsteps the wolves and panthers of Ida fawned, and whose lion of miraculous birth was carried in procession round the Lydian citadel" (Vincent Scully, *The Earth, the Temple, and the Gods,* pp. 80, 85, 93). Scully remarks that it is not "inappropriate to link the virgin goddess Artemis with Aphrodite, the goddess of love," because "it is clear from Greek myth that they were in part two sides of the same coin" (p. 93). Blake evidently also links two female phases, which might be named Aphrodite and Artemis, in the two phases of "The Mental Traveller."

reverts, like the Rechabites, to a nomadic life in the wilderness and ends where he began:

> . . . for Jonadab the son of Rechab our father commanded us saying, Ye shall drink no wine, neither ye, nor your sons for ever: neither shall ye build house, nor sow seed, nor plant vineyard, nor have any; but all your days ye shall dwell in tents; that ye may live many days in the land where ye be strangers. (Jeremiah 35:6–7)

Blake's male is just such a stranger in the changing world of the poem: desert, wilderness, garden, and (briefly named) city—for the most part, Generation and Beulah.

Voltaire's *Candide* turns in much the same way as Blake's poem, generating similar worlds through a similar male-female dance, ending in a similar state of suspension, not end but cessation. Candide is expelled at the beginning from a garden made paradise by the presence of Cunegonde. He pursues her through the "Egypt" or "Babylon" of Europe and the "wilderness" of sea and new world. As in "The Mental Traveller," his pursuit itself seems to generate the spherical world. From the farthest reach of his journey, the heavenly golden city of reason, El Dorado, Candide turns away and returns to the world with enormous wealth, which he loses innocently and spends recklessly in pursuit of Cunegonde. Blake's figure is also momentarily and generously wealthy, his cottage filled with gems and gold, and he too is carried past cities in his pursuit of a maiden. Candide's pursuit having ended in a garden inhabited by a Cunegonde-Eve and a Woman Old, he submits to a laborious tilling of the soil, as in Genesis, and to satisfaction with a great deal "less than all," as Blake puts it in the Tractates. The male figure in "The Mental Traveller," exposing what Blake evidently saw as the real form of Candide's relation to both Cunegonde and the garden, ends bound down by a Woman Old, the natural world.

Voltaire in *Candide* has accepted the expulsion from Eden as a permanent expulsion and turned it into an ironic Eros plot. What is real in *Candide* is not Eden or the heavenly city El Dorado (which is at best a satiric norm), but the exile, the wilderness, the diminished garden, and the repeated im-

plication (made explicit in the late fable of his majesty's ignorance of the fate of the rats in the hold of the ship he sends to
Egypt) that the Supreme Being has turned away from the
world. If Candide suggests Adam, he also suggests the second Adam, Christ—a Christ unable not only to change the
nature of this world, but unable even to comprehend it,
though finally he settles down in it. Voltaire in *Candide* turns
a plot of expulsion from Eden and of expected redemption
into an Eros plot, and one of diminished expectation. With a
further turn of ironic consciousness, Blake in "The Mental
Traveller" has done the same, giving us the essential form of
Candide (even to Voltaire's repeated "resurrections" of his
figures after their apparent death) and of most Eros plots.

*   *   *

The female figure in "The Mental Traveller" contains almost all the implications that Emanation and Shadow have
elsewhere in Blake' poetry—of vision, of artistic creation, of
community fallen into a tyrannical church, of separation into
male and into female will, and into observer and outer world.
Many of these implications are to be found in Voltaire's *Candide*, in the Vesta-Venus-Ceres-Juno of the pagan philosophers in Augustine's account of them, in the *Theogony*, and
in a poem of despairing or doomed Eros like "The Definition
of Love" or "Venus and Adonis." In the more distant background, however, Milton's "Nativity Ode," Genesis, Exodus,
Kings, the Prophets, the Gospels, and the Book of Revelation
loom up, suggesting behind the Eros plot a conversion and
redemption plot, and behind erotic division, identity.

In *The Four Zoas, Milton,* and *Jerusalem,* a Christian conversion or redemption plot overcomes the Eros plot. In "The
Mental Traveller," the polar and erotic opposition of male
and female generates a world of cyclical reincarnation rather
than human history. Identity is not regained; Eros remains
triumphant. The triumph of sexual division prevents the return to or emergence of a full humanity that is neither male
nor female, but the human identity—not sexuality but brotherhood, not the Other presented as object of outward worship, but the human. Los remains fallen.

In Blake's divisions generally, the friend with whom we carry on the inner dialogue of thought and speech that keeps us human after our fall from the original community, and that is continuous with life and consciousness,[20] separates first into external object of desire or knowledge and then into Adversary—into Vala or Rahab or Satan. "The Mental Traveller" gives us only the speechless stage of this division, in which speech as thought is absent. In this primitive narrative, the speech we carry on with the separated Emanation or the Adversary has not yet arisen. Until it does—before speech has even become the false tongue—there is no hope of redemption and no hope of recovering identity.

The situation in Blake's *The Four Zoas* is of course very different. In *The Four Zoas,* action gives rise to speech; eros yields to agape or brotherhood; and erotic division yields to identity. The figure in whom these changes occur is of course Los, who begins as pagan demiurge and ends as Christian artist and poet. And for the first time the name *Los* begins to remind us of *Logos,* creative word or speech. Los's great turn from demiurge to redeemer and from pagan eros to Christian faith in *The Four Zoas* gives Blake's prophecies as a whole the form of a conversion plot. Since the symposium or eros community is an exclusive and aristocratic one, that turn is necessary for Blake's final community, in which all mankind are brothers. In some ways it is a recovery of the community envisioned in *The Marriage of Heaven and Hell,* but it is a more fully human and less vitalist community than that in the *Marriage.*

---

20. Hannah Arendt, *The Life of the Mind,* vol. 1, *Thinking, passim.*

5

Priest and Poet, Serpent and Human Form, in *The Four Zoas*

In the much enlarged and complicated epic-prophetic-novelistic form of *The Four Zoas*, we arrive at the centrality and dominance of Los only after a preparatory history of the fall into error, confusion, incompatible points of view, and deceit. The slow emergence of Los as the dominant figure in *The Four Zoas* parallels that in the earlier prophecies and also coincides with a shift from mythic figure toward human—even novelistic—character: from the presenting of outward act (as in "The Mental Traveller") toward increasing inwardness and sympathy of treatment. Los grows with Blake's own experience and understanding, but Los is not alone. Blake's initial and major characters—Los, Urizen, Enitharmon, and Orc—are implied as early as the Tractates; and the whole form of fall-creation ending in apocalypse and entrance into a peaceable city is implied as early as *The French Revolution*.

But only when Blake's characters have developed a fairly long history and internal experience can they form a community of the kind suggested at the end of *The Four Zoas* and flowering at the end of *Jerusalem*, when the Zoas and their Emanations pass from earthly to transcendent life. Los needs to be father and to have companions or counterparts before he can turn from fatherhood to brotherhood; and paradise regained can emerge only after a complex development. The great turn in *The Four Zoas* occurs in Night VII. If the Orc, Enitharmon, Spectre of Urthona, and Los who are the dramatis personae of Night VII are essentially the original four figures of the Tractates and *The Book of Urizen*, the essential change in Night VII from the earlier pattern is that the Spectre of Urthona, though a Urizen figure, is enough a part of Los to make Los's "Self-Annihilation" possible.

The action of *The Four Zoas* occurs within the body of Albion, the universal man, who is identified with the world as Eden. His fall from this identity is thus the fall of the cosmos—the fall of Eden from human form into the sea of time and space in Tharmas and Enion, and into serpent form in Vala, Luvah-Orc, and Urizen. The fall is also from brotherly love through sexuality into warfare. For most of its course *The Four Zoas* is a poem of Beulah, Generation, and Ulro, a poem of love and war. In presenting the ultimate human degradation as warfare and tracing warfare to its roots in sexual jealousy, Blake alludes to the great poem of war, the *Iliad,* as if it were an account of the fall. Many of his speakers believe the fall was caused by a quarrel between two "heroes"—Albion and Luvah—over a woman. This sexual quarrel is like Agamemnon and Achilles' quarrel over a female prize, Briseis, a quarrel which reflects the sexual cause, in the rape of Helen and in Aphrodite's earlier sexual bribing of Paris, of the war in which they are engaged.

In Blake's own account, *The Four Zoas* is about "The torments of Love & Jealousy in / The Death and Judgement / of Albion the Ancient Man" (title page/E296/300). The serpent— the worm—is the ultimate form of this torment, and the serpent, according to "the voice of Luvah from the furnaces of Urizen," derives from Vala: Vala has been earthworm, serpent, dragon, and infant as well as mother (Night II, pp. 26–27/E311/317). She is apparently Eve as serpent, speaking for Satan as priest: Urizen. This serpent emerges later in Luvah-Orc and finally becomes the comprehensive form of the Adversary in *The Four Zoas.* The action of the poem is to separate serpent form from the triumphant human form. (In *The Book of Urizen* Orc in the womb is first worm, then serpent, before he emerges as infant.)

When Urizen reassumes human form in Night IX, Vala-Urizen—the negating power of Ulro—has been overcome by Enitharmon-Los, who are the power of Generation to become Regeneration or Beulah, and ultimately Eden. As in the Lambeth prophecies, the Mental Fight takes place between the primeval priest and Poetic Genius. Urizen is a mathematical god, an atomist philosopher and a Malthusian prince of limit, who effectively opposes Luvah's sexual-generative power and seriously confuses his mind. Luvah as victim of Urizen—the "voice of Luvah from the furnaces of Urizen"—expresses the nadir of hope and belief as intellectual-emotional confusion:

> we all go to Eternal Death
> To our Primeval Chaos in fortuitous concourse of incoherent
> Discordant principles of Love & Hate I suffer affliction
> Because I love. for I was love but hatred awakes in me
> And Urizen who was Faith & Certainty is changd to Doubt.
> (II/27:11–15/E311/318)

But Urizen is unable to overcome Los's prolific Poetic Genius or Los and Enitharmon's instinctive fostering of "the human form divine." The "great red dragon"—Urizen-Luvah-Vala—fails to "devour" the "child" of "the woman clothed with the sun" (Revelation 12:1–4). The child is finally Jesus; the woman is Enitharmon, who becomes Mary and Jersualem.

The Fall

Blake refuses to give us a single truth of the fall in *The Four Zoas*, and accounts of it remain legendary and confused and self-deceived.[1] As usual in Blake's accounts, the beginning is blurred by his characters' self-involvement and distorted memory. One recurrent account is that it was brought about by a falling out between two conspirators against Albion: Urizen and Luvah.

In the masculine account of the fall, Urizen and Luvah exchange functions and powers (Luvah's wine of life and darkness for Urizen's horses and chariot of light) and fall into confusion and enmity. In Urizen's words,

> Because thou gavest Urizen the wine of the Almighty
> For steeds of Light that they might run in thy golden chariot
>   of pride
> I gave to thee the Steeds I pourd the stolen wine

---

1. Brian Wilkie and Mary Lynn Johnson, in appendix B of *Blake's Four Zoas*, summarize fourteen accounts of the fall in *The Four Zoas*.

> And drunken with the immortal draught fell from my throne
> sublime. (V/65:5–8/E337/344)

Urizen's great confession-lament in the center of the poem, from which this is taken, offers perhaps the clearest account. His speech is rational—he retains memory and a measure of personal identity—and his remorse suggests the possibility of recovery, though his story is still self-absorbed and single-perspectived:

> O Fool could I forget the light that filled my bright spheres
> Was a reflection of his face who called me from the deep
>
> I well remember for I heard the mild & holy voice
> Saying O light spring up & shine . . .
> . . . .
> . . . Go forth & guide my Son who wanders on the ocean
> I went not forth. I hid myself in black clouds of my wrath
> I calld the stars around my feet in the night of councils dark
> The stars threw down their spears & fled naked away
> We fell. I siezd thee dark Urthona In my left hand falling
> I siezd thee beauteous Luvah. (V/64:19–29/E337/344)

The body that with difficulty assembles itself from the shattering effects of this fall is the watery, chaotic body of Tharmas, who seems here to come into existence only at the fall:

> from the smoke
> Of Urizen dashed in pieces from his precipitant fall
> Tharmas reard up his hands & stood on the affrighted Ocean
> . . . .
> Crying. Fury in my limbs. destruction in my bones & marrow
> My skull riven into filaments. my eyes into sea jellies
> Floating upon the tide wander bubbling & bubbling
> Uttering my lamentations & begetting little monsters.
> (III/44:19–26/E323/330)

In contrast with Urizen's speech, Tharmas's cry here is speech at the limit of fall, expressive but incoherent—"Discordant principles of Love & Hate," as Luvah says. Nevertheless, Tharmas deserves the epithet "Parent power" because he attempts to reorganize himself as "Man," whereas Luvah, speaking "from the furnaces of Urizen" in a voice only half his own, says that he "blotted out / That Human delusion to deliver all the sons of God / From bondage of the Human form" (II/27:16–18/E311/318). In almost every account, the blame continues to rest with Urizen and Luvah (and Vala), who accuse one another and themselves.

In the feminine version, the fall is a falling-out caused largely by sexual jealousy and is a form of idolatry. When Albion speaks "idolatrous" to his own Shadow or projected self, loosely identified as Vala but associated also with Luvah and Urizen, he falls under the influence of Urizen, who is essentially the "primeval Priest" of *The Book of Urizen*.[2] The Shadow contains Luvah (whose Emanation Vala is), and Luvah and Albion fight over Vala until Albion, under Urizen's influence, curses Luvah: "Go & die the Death of Man for Vala the sweet wanderer" (III/42:1/E321/328). The powers of love and life (Luvah and Vala) and light (Urizen) have fallen asunder in Albion. Each has turned into its opposite (Urizen to dark secrecy, Luvah to hate, and Vala toward death), and each seeks dominion. Urizen has devised the worship of an obscure and shadowy deity—himself—against which Luvah becomes a rebel. (In *The Marriage of Heaven and Hell*, pl. 13, Ezekiel says, "And we so loved our God that we cursed in his name the deities of surrounding nations, and asserted that they had rebelled.") In Blake's running allusion to *Paradise Lost*, it is as if Milton's Messiah—Blake's Urizen—had provoked the battle in heaven and then cast out his enemy Satan-Luvah; and at the same time, as if Messiah as judge had cursed Adam-Luvah for following the lead of Eve, the "sweet wanderer." Blake here assimilates the fall in heaven in *Paradise Lost* to the fall in paradise, and derives both from an idolatry that has a strong sexual component

2. When Albion speaks "idolatrous" to his own Shadow, he addresses the God of the second account of Creation in Genesis—the one who "formed man of the dust of the ground, and breathed into his nostrils the breath of life." But Albion sees himself as "nothing" without this breath. He says, "I am nothing & to nothing must return again / If thou withdraw thy breath, behold I am oblivion" (III/40:17–18/E321/327). Urthona's Spectre similarly is "nothing" in his own view—mere breath of Enion's nostrils. And to the Angel in *The Marriage of Heaven and Hell*, men are also "nothings."

from which only Urizen is immune, or which only Urizen, the first priest, condemns.

When Urizen in Albion condemns Luvah to "die the Death of Man," he condemns both Luvah and Vala as "spirits of Love and Pity" who have "absorbed the man." They have flown from Albion's loins to his brain—Urizen's place—and Urizen-Albion expels them. Like an Adam and Eve cast out of a bodily Eden, they

> Went down the Human Heart where Paradise & its joys abounded
> In jealous fears in fury & rage, & flames roll'd round their fervid feet
> And the vast form of Nature like a Serpent play'd before them. (III/42:11–13/E321/328)

Vala shrinks from Luvah and remains in the "Human Heart," which is Enitharmon's heart as well as Albion's, while Luvah falls through it. Remaining in Enitharmon's heart, Vala turns Enitharmon toward the "female will," which seeks dominance over the male. If paradise is in the "Human Heart," Vala is a kind of Eve who remains in paradise after the fall of Luvah-Adam through the heart "far as the east & west." As a result, "the vast form of Nature like a Serpent roll'd between" them (III/42:17/E322/328). Tharmas elsewhere sees Urthona's body fall like a "raging serpent" (I/22:29/E308/312), and Albion describes the fallen body as serpentlike. The falling body "draws out" a serpent form or path of nature; the fallen time of nature *is* the serpent. When the serpent later becomes the satanic form of warfare, nature is revealed as a state of war derived largely from sexual jealousy.

When the Luvah-Vala-Urizen account of the fall is told to Urizen (as if he hadn't heard it before) by his own Emanation, Ahania, Urizen reacts violently, perhaps because the story implies his own weakness: Albion's "wearied intellect." He asserts, "Am I not God," and condemns Ahania as "the feminine indolent bliss. the indulgent self of weariness" that reflects "all my indolence my weakness & my death." Complaining that Ahania has "become like Vala," he casts her out (III/43:5–6/E322/328). Immediately, he falls, bringing to ruin the Mundane Shell he had caused to be built as the Zoa put in charge by the faltering Albion. If we see Urizen's brief elevation as a parody of the exaltation of the Son in *Paradise Lost* and of his creation of the world following the war in heaven, then the casting out of Ahania-desire leads to the fall of Messiah and of his creation (as in *The Marriage of Heaven and Hell*).[3] The emphasis on Tharmas's watery flood as the outcome of the fall of Urzen's Mundane Shell conflates this fall with the flood. And the flood is followed by a second creation, when Tharmas commands Los to rebuild the shattered ruins of Urizen's Mundane Shell. Urizen has enacted a parody of the angry God of Genesis, who destroys in the Flood most of the life his Creation had generated. In casting out his Emanation-creation Ahania, Urizen as God blames his creatures rather than himself—much as, in *The Book of Urizen*, he saw that mankind was incapable of keeping his iron laws. In Blake there is no omnipotent God, only the false claim to omnipotence. Blake sees the absolute God of the Old Testament and *Paradise Lost* psychologically and in his weaknesses as the recurrent fearful impulse toward idolatry and self-protection that destroys life.

In the version of the fall told by the Shadow of Enitharmon in Night VII, Albion begets on Vala a "prince of light," "first born of generation," named Urizen. Vala then appears as a double form Luvah-Vala. Not only are Luvah and Vala dark to Urizen's light—the primal division of darkness from light—but in them is forecast the power of generation: the "love" and "life" of Albion's speech in Night III (41/E321/327). But to Urizen they appear as sin and death, and this they will eventually become, under his manipulation: Vala will become sin (and Luvah's "robes of blood"), Luvah the death that results from sin. Urizen is the head from which they spring. But Urizen does no begetting; Blake always separates the prolific power from the devourer. In themselves, Vala and Luvah are not sin and death, but the power of Generation, and this is what Urizen casts out as sin. All Urizen's actions

---

3. Wilkie and Johnson point out that Tharmas's command to Los, "Go forth Rebuild his Universe . . . A Universe of Death & Decay" "parodies the Father's charge to the Son to create the universe in compensation for the damage done by Satan and his followers" (*Blake's Four Zoas*, p. 85).

stem from and follow out the obscure, ambiguous prophecy
he utters about Luvah and Los:

> O bright Ahania a Boy is born of the dark Ocean
> Whom Urizen doth serve, with Light replenishing his
> darkness
> . . . .
> . . . I must serve & that Prophetic boy
> Must grow up to command his Prince but hear my determind
> Decree
> Vala shall become a Worm in Enitharmons Womb
> Laying her seed upon the fibres soon to issue forth
> And Luvah in the loins of Los a dark & furious death
> Alas for me! what will become of me at that dread time?
> (III/38:2–11/E319–20/326)

The fear of "futurity" and of "that Prophetic boy"—elsewhere a "terrible boy"—dominates all Urizen's actions. He
attempts to stop birth.

In *The Book of Ahania*, Urizen has a son, Fuzon, who attacks him—his genitals—and whom he crucifies:

> The corse of his first begotten
> On the accursed Tree of MYSTERY:
> On the topmost stem of this Tree
> Urizen nail'd Fuzons corse. (pl. 4/E86/87)

This foretells what is to happen in the later books of *The Four
Zoas*. It is as if Urizen were to turn Orc—Los's offspring—
into Fuzon, giving him his own serpent form, and then were
to crucify him.

*   *   *

With this account as context, we can now turn to the story
of Los and Enitharmon, who were once man and Emanation,
Urthona and Enitharmon, but who are reborn as male and
female children into Urizen's ongoing struggle against Generation, and who as man and wife make choices that decide
the history and end of the struggle in the birth of Jesus and in
the final apocalyptic renewal of heaven and earth. They are
children who grow up to become parents and who create
humanity—the human family, brotherhood, and human
powers of creation. Insofar as it focuses on Los and Enithar-

mon, *The Four Zoas* is the history of a marriage, its internal conflict, and the determined opposition it suffers. It is a succession of births that leads finally to rebirth.

Children into Parents

At the fall, the Zoas divide into male Spectre and female Shadow, and the male Spectre enters into a womb or world-space dominated by the female Shadow. When Urthona falls, the Shadow of Enitharmon flees to Tharmas; Urthona's Spectre flees to Enion. Enion accuses Tharmas of infidelity with Enitharmon; Tharmas accuses Enion of the accusation of sin. In mutual accusation they fall or "die" into the Shadow of Enion and the Spectre of Tharmas—the ocean-space-chaos which forms the indefinite exteriors of Albion. The Shadow of Enion as midwife draws the Spectre from Tharmas in a kind of male childbirth. (The delivered Spectre is described as "weeping in wayward infancy & sullen youth" [I/6:2/E299/303], somewhat as in "The Crystal Cabinet.") She mates with the Spectre and gives forth Enitharmon and Los (almost like the appearance of female hearthfire babe and male babe in "The Mental Traveller"). If the Spectre of Tharmas contained the Shadow of Enitharmon, and the Shadow of Enion contained the Spectre of Urthona—Spectre containing Shadow and Shadow containing Spectre—the birth of Los and Enitharmon aligns them with the fallen Tharmas and Enion and stems from sexual jealousy.

Their birth is also a two-stage entering into a new world of which the parents are the space-time dimensions. Although these dimensions are thoroughly sexual and jealous—time male, space female—they are also protective and caring. The Spectre of Tharmas and the Shadow of Enion form a nine-day-and-night Ulro Circle of Destiny that confines almost the whole action of the poem to Ulro; but within this sphere, the Shadow of Enitharmon and the Spectre of Urthona form a protective Beulah world.

When Los and Enitharmon are born into this world as new beings or identities, the task they unconsciously begin to carry out is to turn creation into the human form from which it fell. The fall was into a serpent form of jealousy; the resurrection will be into the human form of brotherhood, the mediating term between Ulro and Eden being sexuality and the human family: Generation and Beulah.

Born as Enion's "sorrow & woe," Los and Enitharmon drink up all her "spectrous life" and push her into "Non-Entity." (Enion seems a female "aged Host" cast out, as in "The Mental Traveller.") They are marvelous, heartless children, prematurely sexy, shamed (as if brother and sister) and jealous:

> A male & female naked & ruddy as the pride of summer
> Alternate Love & Hate his breast; hers Scorn & Jealousy
> In embryon passions. they kiss'd not nor embrac'd for shame
>   & fear
> His head beamd light & in his vigorous voice was prophecy
> He could controll the times & seasons, & the days & years
> She could controll the spaces, regions, desart, flood & forest
> But had no power to weave a Veil of covering for her Sins[4]
> She drave the Females all away from Los
> And Los drave all the Males from her away
> . . . .
> Conversing with the visions of Beulah in dark slumberous
>   bliss. (I/9:23–33/E300–301/305)

Though fallen, Los and Enitharmon have considerable powers, which apparently derive from Eno's "soft affections / To Enion & her children." Eno, who speaks the opening of *The Book of Los*, has made the world they delight in:

> Then Eno a daughter of Beulah took a Moment of Time
> And drew it out to Seven thousand years with much care &
>   affliction

4. With "weave a Veil of covering for [Enitharmon's] sins," contrast the Son judging Adam and Eve in *Paradise Lost* and clothing their nakedness with skins. Their "inward nakedness" he covers "with his Robe of righteousness"—"cover'd from his Father's sight" (10.220—23). Los's powerlessness to weave such a veil for Enitharmon leaves her as Vala unveiled—speaking what she feels—and implies that Los and Enitharmon are already fallen, though further on in *The Four Zoas* (in Night VII) we find Los accepting the apple from Enitharmon and eating it. At the end of Night VII, "Female Forms" are created by Los and Enitharmon, "Mortal & not as Enitharmon without a covering veil" (E357/363). Here the covering veil seems to be Vala as the mortal body.

And many tears & in Every year made windows into Eden
She also took an atom of space & opend its center
Into Infinitude & ornamented it with wondrous art. (I/9:9–13/
  E300/304–5)

This is the world of which the Shadow of Enitharmon and
the Spectre of Urthona form the space and time limits. The
Shadow of Enitharmon is the center opened into infinitude
that comes to life as Jerusalem in Night VII, and the Spectre
of Urthona is the moment drawn out to seven thousand
years. Enion's Ulro Circle of Destiny reaches into all nine
nights of *The Four Zoas*; Eno's Beulah world takes up seven
nights: II through VIII. Enion is not only a womb, but, as the
messengers from Beulah see it, a "bosom" in which Enitharmon—heart—is "embalmed" for a "moment" of seven thousand years: the moment of fallen life, earth as womb and as
tomb, as Beulah and Ulro, with the life of Generation between. In Night IX, all the Zoas, but Tharmas and Enion last,
are drawn back through Eno's seven-thousand-year atom-
moment, and both the time-space world and the indefinite
exteriors of Albion that furnished the matter of the Circle of
Destiny are converted into Beulah around Eden. Enitharmon's embalmment (as her Shadow) in Enion's bosom has
been only a moment, but in that seven-thousand-year moment Enitharmon becomes Jerusalem.

In spite of their marvelous space-time or world-wielding
powers, Los and Enitharmon at first live a fallen life that we
learn to identify with Vala, the worm-serpent-dragon state of
sexual warfare. The clearest evidence of this life is the birth of
Orc. That Orc is Luvah has been revealed prophetically by
Urizen: "And Luvah in the loins of Los a dark & furious
death" (III/38:10/E320/326). And Orc was conceived in the af-
termath of a violent Luvah-Vala quarrel between Los and
Enitharmon. After Enitharmon has sung Los a "song of
Vala"—"The joy of Woman is the death of her most best
beloved"—Los smites her. Urizen, who is often found nearby
during sexual quarrels, descends in response to Enitharmon's request. His assertion, "I am God the terrible destroyer and not the Saviour," is apparently a refusal to
intervene or redeem, a continuation of the quarrel, and it
immediately puts the issue in ultimate terms. It is as if the

Father—not the Son, as Milton has it—had appeared in response to the fallen quarrel between Adam and Eve and had immediately separated himself as "God the . . . destroyer" from the "Saviour." Los defies Urizen, pities Enitharmon, repents his blow, and embraces her wounded loins: "They eat the fleshly bread, they drank the nervous wine" (I/12:44/ E303/307). In making and trying to heal a wound, Los has apparently opened a loins-gate into Beulah. (Enitharmon's heart-gate into Beulah remains closed until later, when Vala is born, and the brain-gate opened is the final change of mind and vision that recreates Eden, but gates in the body already assimilate body to city, to Babylon or Jerusalem.) With demons singing obscure prophecies of Orc's birth and binding, Los and Enitharmon are married. In due course, Orc is born of Enitharmon's obdurate heart.[5] He is Luvah, but not recognized or identified. Like Los and Enitharmon, he has undergone a bodily and psychic transformation in which identity is all but lost. The major events in *The Four Zoas* are births and rebirths, and Orc's birth works great changes in Los and Enitharmon, as Vala's birth later will.

At Orc's birth, Los is in a Urizenic state because he has been binding Urizen after Urizen's fall. He begins building Golgonooza—a bower for Enitharmon and perhaps a creation to rival Enitharmon's motherhood. When Los perceives that Orc, at age fourteen, lusts after his mother and plots his father's death, he and Enitharmon take Orc a nine-days' journey outside Golgonooza and bind him to a rock. Los then leads Enitharmon into his labyrinth in the deeps and leaves the Spectre of Urthona to watch over Orc. Los and Enitharmon have fallen still further into sexual jealousy. Los's labyrinth suggests the brain of jealousy become a secret and hidden labyrinth, or the labyrinthine serpent form of the umbilical cord in the womb, as if Los had put mother Enithar-

5. "The birth of Orc is not merely set against the incarnation of Urizen but is an inevitable outgrowth of it, indeed virtually the same event. Providing Urizen with the organs of sense and the means of emotion inevitably means the erupting and expression of these senses and emotions—in short, the appearance of Orc. That eruption, in turn, demands an equal and opposite reaction in the form of a renewed effort at control by intellect; therefore it is inevitable that Urizen be awakened, as he in fact now is—by the pulsations of Orc" (Wilkie and Johnson, *Blake's Four Zoas*, pp. 111–12).

mon into a womb of his own. (Since Orc is like a bull and the bulls of Luvah are mentioned in Night VII [77:16/E346/353], the labyrinth suggests that Los is both Minos and Dedalus, and that hiding Enitharmon-Pasiphaë in the labyrinth is designed to prevent her coupling with the bull Luvah-Orc and conceiving and bearing the Minotaur—as if Los half-remembered and meant to prevent Minos's fate.)

If the labyrinth is built to defend both Enitharmon and Golgonooza (which is built "Upon the limit of Translucence" [V/60:4/E333/340]), then Golgonooza is already the city as woman. That Orc is imprisoned a nine-days' journey from Golgonooza implies very deep defenses, an Ulro-hell in the loins, nine-days' journey from the heart—Generation suspended in raging desire, Luvah bound and divided from Vala. If so, Orc's binding repeats or shows from a different point of view Vala's shrinking from Luvah, so that he falls from her bosom "far as the east & west," with the "vast form of Nature" rolling "as a serpent between." The serpent is the umbilical cord or serpent-worm of Generation-and-death—Generation become Ulro—which Orc himself eventually becomes, showing that he is Vala's offspring as much as Enitharmon's. (Since Vala remains in Enitharmon's heart—Albion's heart—until her birth in Night VII, Enitharmon and Albion remain in what Blake will later call the "state" Vala until Night VII.) The irony here is that "the voice of Luvah from the furnaces of Urizen" claims to recall a time when he "carried [Vala] in my bosom as a man carries a lamb." "I hid her in soft gardens & in secret bowers of Summer / Weaving mazes of delight along the sunny Paradise / Inextricable labyrinths" (II/27:3–7/E311/317). Blake's labyrinths are usually "jealous."

Los finds that in following Tharmas's command to rebuild Urizen's ruins and bind the Eternal Mind he is also binding Enitharmon. And he finds, after the birth of Orc, that he has forged of his own flesh and blood—of his bosom—a chain of jealousy, with which he and Enitharmon bind Orc. Beginning by binding Urizen, Los has ended by binding Orc—who is Luvah—in a chain of jealousy. Urizen has slipped free. Though he set out to bind the mind, Los has bound energy: he works against Generation and delays the birth of Jesus, which will turn Generation into Regeneration. In doing so, he serves, however inadvertently, Urizen. Urizen as "first born of Generation" fears the birth of "that Prophetic boy": evidently Urizen wants to be Albion's only begotten son. In any case, like Kronos or Pharaoh or Herod, Urizen wants to stop, to bind, Generation. In his enmity to a male and female capable of Generation, Urizen is the limiting necessity of Malthus's vision; he is a Malthusian deity, with Orc being the prolific power he must restrain.[6] Albion's "Urizenic" cursing of Luvah—"Go and die the Death of Man for Vala the sweet wanderer"—means "cease to be," "have no offspring," "stop posterity." In this curse, Urizen speaking as "God the terrible destroyer" begins to turn Luvah into the Satan-serpent who owes a death. (See Los-Urthona's account in Night VIII [115/ E366/381] of the successive Eyes of God who refuse to die for Satan.) At the same time, Albion's Urizen-curse prepares for Jesus's "willingly" dying for Satan in "Luvah's robes of blood." Orc bound outside Golgotha-Golgonooza—which will become Jerusalem—is a type of Christ crucified.

6. The kind or form of Orc's prolific power derives in large part from Tharmas, one of his forebears. When Tharmas (like all the Zoas at one time or another) makes his claim to be God, he appears as a god of subhuman oceanic life. Urizen, as mathematician god and Malthusian limiter of mankind's geometrically multiplying prolific power, advocates "Compell[ing] the poor to live upon a crust of bread" because "there are enough / Born even thus too many & our Earth will be overrun / Without these arts" (VII/80:9, 12–14/E348/355). In momentary alliance with Urizen, Tharmas proposes a despairing pact in which Urizen is to withhold light from him, while he withholds food from Urizen. But the epithet "Parent power" shows Tharmas's fundamental opposition to Urizen. The double character of the fallen Tharmas—one face toward Urizen the destroyer, another toward Los the rebuilder—is seen in his command to Los to rebuild the Mundane Shell: "renew thou I will destroy" (IV/48:7/E325/332). At the same time, if Urizen's building of the Mundane Shell suggests God's creation of the firmament of heaven on the second day, Tharmas's reign suggests the gathering together into one place of the waters on the third day. Los and Enitharmon appear as the "dry land Earth," also on the third day: Tharmas sees them "Emerge / In strength & brightness from the Abyss" (IV/47:2–3/E324/331). Here they also suggest Deucalion and Pyrrha. On the fourth day, rebuilding the Mundane Shell, Los creates the sun, moon, and stars, to rule over day and night: he creates time. Night IV evidently corresponds to day four of the Creation. Finally, Tharmas's momentary "raping" of Enitharmon from Los's left side and bringing her back on a wave suggests not only the inundation of Enitharmon-earth during the flood, but also the second creation in Genesis, in which God creates Eve from one of Adam's ribs.

Los, Enitharmon, and Orc repeat the Urizen-Vala-Luvah pattern of the Shadow of Enitharmon's story of the fall in Night VII. Los is like the Kronos who succeeds Ouranos, or the Zeus who succeeds Kronos, in Hesiod's *Theogony*. That is, Los is now the Urizen figure who fears overthrow—he fears the "terrible boy"—and Orc and Enitharmon enact the Luvah-Vala parts of dangerous sexual energy, complicated now by the incest problem. The Urizen-Luvah-Vala pattern is developing toward the human family, a development that is intensified when Los and Enitharmon begin (and they begin almost immediately) to regret their treatment of Orc. (Los is even willing to give up his own life, but when they return to Orc, they are unable to free him.) Urizen, when he was given power by Albion in Night II, was told to pity Luvah. He did not, and Luvah suffered terribly in Urizen's furnaces. But Los and Enitharmon *do* pity Luvah as Orc. He is, after all, their offspring. Having begun as heavenly and spoiled children, Los and Enitharmon have become earthly parents. In feeling parental sorrow, they shift from living the life of Luvah and Vala to living the life of Tharmas and Enion, who seek reunion, Tharmas hoping for the rebirth of Enion. (That the name *Enitharmon* contains part of the name *Tharmas* and all of *Enion* reminds us that they are forebears of the fallen Enitharmon, though Enitharmon arrived first in Blake's myth.) The larger struggle, then, is between Tharmas and Urizen, and Tharmas's most significant epithet is still "Parent power." Los begins to feel a parental love like Tharmas's, and later he "fosters" children.

It may be that the birth and binding of Orc has freed Los of the Luvah in him. (It suggests the binding of Satan in the Book of Revelation.) The later birth of Vala, also from or through Enitharmon's heart—breaking her heart-gate and softening her heart—frees Enitharmon of the Vala in her. Los and Enitharmon, then, are both freed from sexual warfare. Vala seems to have been using Enitharmon for her own purpose, either to bring down Urizen in a fall or to enable Urizen-Satan to invade earth. In any case, when Los and Enitharmon are "drawn down by their desires . . . To plant divisions in the Soul of Urizen & Ahania" (II/34:1–3/ E316/322), it is Vala's doing. It leads to Ahania's telling Urizen a Vala-tale of the fall, for which Urizen throws Ahania out and falls. Vala and/or Urizen have also used Los and Enitharmon to assure Vala's birth into Los and Enitharmon's world, fulfilling Urizen's prophecy that "Vala shall become a Worm in Enitharmon's womb."

Vala's birth into Los's world brings the last of the eight Zoas and Emanations into Los's world and leads not only to an intensified confrontation of adversaries, but also to the conversion of Los and Enitharmon. At about the time of Vala's birth, the central action of the poem begins to become Christian.

Vala as sin, followed by hordes of the dead, enters Los and Enitharmon's world through Enitharmon's broken heart-gate. (Judging by the letters in her name, Enitharmon is on-earth or Earthona, and the dead enter earth/heart.) The cloud of Spectres who follow Vala become humanity condemned to death; but sin and death (in Blake's revision of Milton) prepare a way for Jerusalem, for Mary and Joseph and Jesus. Jerusalem has been sleeping outside Enitharmon's closed gates since the end of Night I. Now that Enitharmon's heart-gate is broken—and it is Albion's heart-gate as well—Jerusalem is able to enter Los and Enitharmon's world, and Enitharmon can become the Emanation Jerusalem, but this change occurs silently. Los-Enitharmon as "Tharmic" "Parent power[s]" are building Golgonooza, which becomes the city Jerusalem, preparing for the birth and crucifixion of Jesus. Los was prematurely called "visionary of Jesus" by Urizen in Night I (long before the finger of God touched his seventh furnace at the end of Night IV). He now begins to earn the epithet and to play an independent, though still largely instinctive, part. Blake is apparently giving us a history of the Christian poet-prophet who is also an artist. In proportion as Los becomes a Christian visionary prophetic artist and poet (all five words are essential), he plays an increasingly dominant and decisive role in *The Four Zoas*.

The adversary emerging after Vala herself has become Orc's guardian and fallen into his control is the Satan-serpent of formless war—"Energy enslaved" by Urizen's religion, war as a Malthusian power of limit. By then, Urizen too has become a serpent, Rintrah and Palamabron, prophetic powers, having been drawn away from his war (which they were part of in *Europe*). Vala's serpent seed, the sexual binding of Luvah-Orc, has borne its fruit. Blake assimilates the serpent—"the great red dragon" of Revelation 12, waiting to "devour" the child—to the Malthusian view of sexuality as a necessity, but a necessity which must be restrained or bound. (David Erdman points out that it is uncertain whether Blake knew Malthus, but that Malthusian ideas were everywhere.)[7]

The serpent heritage which Luvah in the furnaces ascribes to Vala, but which is as much Urizen's as Vala's and which goes through Orc and Urizen to Satan, has to be separated from the procreative-regenerative strain in Tharmas and Enion, Los and Enitharmon.

The turning of Generation into Regeneration in Los and Enitharmon, which balances the turning of Generation into Ulro in Orc, is the action that now needs to be treated in some detail. It begins with the fearful and guilty Spectre of Urthona. Los-Enitharmon's double conversion to humanity and to Christianity begins unpromisingly in fear and guilt and temptation.

Conversion

The offspring of the Spectre of Urthona's "conferrings" with the Shadow of Enitharmon among the branches of the tree of mystery is Vala. Urthona's Spectre is terrified by the Spectres of the dead who follow her. He puts Vala in charge of Orc and flees: "Then took the tree of Mystery root in the World of Los" (VII/85:23/E353/367). Most important, the Spectre enters Los's bosom. The Spectre is Los and Enitharmon's growing awareness of death and their horrified vision (like Adam and Eve's) of the death of all the generations to come. But the fear of death—the Spectre—will be shown to have brought its own cure in Los and Enitharmon's reaction to it.[8]

---

7. *Blake: Prophet Against Empire*, p. 342.
8. Blake's Spectres are those "who through fear of death were all their lifetime subject to bondage" (Hebrews 2:15) (quoted in Wilkie and Johnson, *Blake's Four Zoas*, p. 152). In delivering them, Los is acting as Christ.

The Spectre of Urthona has earlier told Enitharmon's Shadow a tale of his own birth, hers, and Los's. The Spectre of Urthona is jealous: "now a Spectre wandering / The deeps of Los the Slave of that Creation I created" (VII/84:30–31/ E352/359). Though he is Los's creator, he insists that he has become Los's slave. He tells Enitharmon, "I view futurity in thee," and promises, "I will bring down soft Vala / To the embraces of this terror" (84:33–34/E352/359). The "terror" is Orc, and the Spectre is promising to carry out Enitharmon's request to "find a way to punish Vala . . . / To bring her down subjected to the rage of my fierce boy" (83:33–34/E352/359). Furthermore, Urthona's Spectre says, "I will destroy / That body I created then shall we unite again in bliss" (84:34–35/ E352/359). (Compare Urizen's earlier "I am God the terrible destroyer.") Enitharmon's response is a "fervent" embrace of "Her once lovd Lord." Then, almost immediately, the Spectre begins to keep his promise: Enitharmon gives birth to Vala (85/E353/360).

Enitharmon is Los's Shadow or separated self, much as Eve in book 8 of *Paradise Lost* is twice called Adam's "self." And the sighs and groans of Enitharmon's labor help Urthona's Spectre make his way into Los's bosom. "Enitharmon told the tale / Of Urthona" (85:28–29/E353/367), in something of the way that Eve unwittingly acts as Satan's agent in tempting Adam. But since for Blake the Shadow-Eve and the Spectre-Satan are both projected aspects of Los-Adam, Los must reclaim or "embrace" both. (This is Blake's major change in the temptation in *Paradise Lost*.) He embraces the Spectre "first as a brother / Then as another Self; astonishd humanizing & in tears / In Self abasement Giving up his Domineering lust" (85:29–31/E353/367). But the Spectre insists that Los cannot embrace Enitharmon until he is united with his Spectre. He sounds like the Milton of Blake's *Milton*: he asserts that the Satan-self can be overcome only by self-annihilation:

> Consummating by pains & labours
> That mortal body & by Self annihilation back returning
> To Life Eternal be assurd I am thy real Self
> Tho thus divided from thee & the Slave of Every passion
> Of thy fierce Soul Unbar the Gates of Memory look upon me

Not as another but as thy real Self. (85:33–38/E353/368)

But Urthona's Spectre is not to be wholly embraced because he is a medium not only between Los and Enitharmon, but also between Los and Urizen: the means by which Urizen tries to overcome Los. Though he urges self-annihilation, Urthona's Spectre is apparently carrying out a plan outlined earlier in Night VII by Urizen:

> To bring the shadow of Enitharmon beneath our wondrous tree
> That Los may Evaporate like smoke & be no more
> Draw down Enitharmon to the Spectre of Urthona
> And let him have dominion over Los the terrible shade.
>   (80:5–8/E348/355)

Thus the Spectre gives Los great tasks, "to destroy / That body he created"—apparently to work Los to death. (We remember once more that Urizen is "God the terrible destroyer.") Los proves to be a demon for work, however, and the first result is renewed work on Golgonooza, "the Center opend by Divine Mercy" (87:3/E354/368).

The Shadow of Enitharmon as the center Eno opened into infinitude now apparently opens to reveal "new heavens & a new Earth" (87:9/E354/368)—a Beulah paradise that has "a Limit Twofold named Satan & Adam" (87:12/E354/369). The Spectre of Urthona and Los now enact Satan and Adam as the limit of opacity and the limit of contraction created earlier (in Night IV) by the Elohim. As Los stands "on the Limit of Translucence" building Golgonooza, he is next to "Satan" (the Spectre of Urthona) as the limit of opacity. Enitharmon offers him the fruit, and he eats: "Then Los plucked the fruit & Eat & sat down in Despair / And must have given himself to death Eternal But" the Spectre comforts him, "Being a medium between him & Enitharmon" (87:23–26/E355/369). This is the nadir, and on this "But" the poem turns. Los and Enitharmon are Adam and Eve. One thousand of Enion's seven thousand years have passed, and human history (the myth of it) has begun.

A new version of Adam's temptation follows almost immediately; though vaguely put, it is to appease guilt and ward off punishment by sacrifice:

> Urthonas Spectre terrified beheld the Spectres of the Dead
> Each Male formd without a counterpart without a
>   concentering vision
> The Spectre of Urthona wept before Los Saying I am the
>   cause
> That this dire state commences I began the dreadful state
> Of Separation & on my dark head the curse & punishment
> Must fall unless a way be found to Ransom & Redeem.
>   (87:29–34/E355/369)

The "separation" is the separation of Luvah from the other Zoas and Vala, and the separation of Orc from Los and Enitharmon: ultimately the separation of Spectre from Shadow. Seeing—knowing in himself—that the Spectres "ravin" without counterparts, Urthona's Spectre proposes that they create counterparts for them, "For without a Created body the Spectre is Eternal Death" (87:38/E355/369).

The Spectre is the fear and guilt through which Urizen-Satan is artfully attempting to compel Los-Adam to die for him. But Los's response is enthusiastic and cheerful. He comforts the Spectre and encourages Enitharmon with a vision of Christ: "Turn inwardly thine Eyes & there behold the Lamb of God / Clothed in Luvahs robes of blood descending to redeem" (87:43–44/E355/369). Los moderates the Spectre's and Enitharmon's guilt, turning it toward forgiveness and acknowledgment of error. He tells Enitharmon that he (Los) appears before her "in forgiveness of ancient injuries": "let us converse together" (87:47, 50/E355/369). (Adam in book 9 of *Paradise Lost* twice refers to Eve's "sweet converse."("I also tremble at myself & at all my former life" (87:51/E355/369). "Conversation" would be the reintegration of man and Emanation. But Enitharmon—still influenced by the tree of mystery—fears that the Lamb of God will "give us to Eternal Death fit punishment" "to be a sign & terror to all who behold / Lest any should in futurity do as we have done in heaven" (87:54, 57–58/E355/370). (Again, Enitharmon sounds like a guilty Eve, and "heaven" seems to be Eden—a comparison Blake would have found in *Paradise Lost*.) Los, feeling that these "piteous victims of battle" "feed upon our life we are their victims" (90:7–8/E356/370), now proposes "To form a world of Sacrifice of brothers & sons & daughters / To comfort Orc in his dire sufferings" (90:12–13/E356/370), as if Orc were a Moloch-furnace.[9]

Los's proposal repeats and elaborates the Spectre's earlier one that they "find a way to Ransom & Redeem," and the Spectre speaks as Urizen. As guardian of Orc, the Spectre of Urthona has presumably been influenced by Urizen's readings to Orc from his iron and brass books and by the tree of mystery, which has grown up over Orc. The Spectre came to Los repeating Urizen's "The Spectre is the Man": he told Los that he was Los's "real self."[10] But if Urthona's Spectre is a tempter, Los does not recognize the temptation. He accepts the Spectre as in truth his self and enthusiastically accepts and responds to what he says. The pattern is again the Spectre vis-à-vis male and female: the Urizen-Luvah-Vala pattern of the Shadow of Enitharmon's tale (which is told in this night). It is also the usual two-males-and-one-female pattern of the short prophecies, such as *Visions of the Daughters* and *The Book of Urizen*. Like Urizen, the Spectre of Urthona claims to be the first born. Unlike Urizen, he is openly jealous of the male and desires the female, Enitharmon.

At best, the Spectre becomes a medium between Los and Enitharmon, with their guilt forming a link between them.

9. Most readers of *The Four Zoas* take the Spectre of Urthona in Night VII at face value and find nothing wrong with his emphasis on sacrifice or with Los's apparent agreement with it. Christine Gallant, for example, says of Los, "His desire to develop Golgonooza further is couched in words Christ might use:

stern desire
I feel to fabricate embodied semblances in which the dead
May live before us in our palaces & in our gardens of labour
. . . .
To form a world of Sacrifice. (7.90.8–12)

"Enitharmon acquiesces but encourages him to work on Golgonooza, but a Golgonooza with a religious as well as artistic purpose: to 'fabricate forms sublime . . . [that] They shall be ransoms for our Souls that we may live' (7.90.22–24). Christ has thus truly acted as an archetype of the Self for Los" (*Blake and the Assimilation of Chaos*, p. 76).

10. For a more favorable view of the Spectre of Urthona here, see Wilkie and Johnson, *Blake's Four Zoas*, p. 161: "The Spectre's claim that he is Los's self is a demand that Los acknowledge his errors; this claim on Los is entirely different from Urizen's . . . blasphemy in Night I, the insistence that 'The Spectre is the Man' (E303)." To me, the Spectre seems essentially to repeat Urizen's dictum, though in half-disguised form.

At worst, the Spectre's concern with ransom is a plan to bring into life—in order to sacrifice—the numberless dead (they are proleptically dead) who follow Vala. A messenger of Urizen-become-Satan, he speaks to a Los whose spirit and goodwill begin immediately to turn temptation to good, error to truth; but the conversion is so unconscious on Los's part that the outcome remains uncertain for a time. At first, Enitharmon seems to act as muse to Los as artist. She breathes forth piteous forms that would return to her bosom, but she proposes that Los "fabricate forms sublime" that they "may assimilate themselves into"; "They shall be ransoms for our Souls that we may live" (90:23–25/E356/370).

The temptation is almost buried by Los and Enitharmon's creative-procreative impulse. Los begins to "modulate his fires," which he draws from "the ranks of Urizens war & from the fiery lake / Of Orc," vanquishing them "with the strength of Art" (90:26–30/E356/370). Urthona was forging "spades & coulters" when the fall occurred. As Los, he now returns to productive labor, with the difference being that he now makes human forms, like the demiurge of Plato's *Timaeus* forming souls. Los's fires of art are modulated fires of war and hell. If war is energy enslaved, art is energy freed: art overcomes war and despair. If the Spectres, again, are obsessive fear of death—much as Milton's Adam and Eve fear death immediately and then foresee it for all their descendants—in Los and Enitharmon art overcomes this fear by converting despair into hope. Los draws

> a line upon the walls of shining heaven
> And Enitharmon tincturd it with beams of blushing love
> It remaind permanent a lovely form inspird divinely human.
>   (90:35–37/E356/370–71)

As if she were Enion, Enitharmon breathes forth the spectrous dead upon the wind: "Weeping the Spectres viewd the immortal works / Of Los Assimilating to those forms Embodied & Lovely" (90:41–42/E356/371). The soul as breath takes on form, the bound or outward circumference of energy. For Los—as for Pythagoras—it is limit that turns the unlimited into cosmos, soul into microcosm. But for Los, unlike Pythagoras, the soul as breath is not yet divine. In order to be "divinely human," at any rate, it requires form.

"First Rintrah & then Palamabron drawn from out the ranks of war / In infant innocence reposd on Enitharmons bosom" (90:44–45/E356/371).[11] Orc is comforted: "Orc became / As Los a father to his brethren" (90:47–48/E356/371). Like the speaker in "The Chimney Sweeper" of *Songs of Innocence,* Orc has learned the brotherhood that is fatherhood. And "Los loved them & refusd to Sacrifice their infant limbs" (90:50/E357/371). He and Enitharmon "rather chose to meet Eternal death than to destroy / The offspring of their Care & Pity" (90:52–53/E357/371). These "children" differ from Orc in that Los and Enitharmon have learned to be parents to them. Golgonooza is beginning to become a community of the redeemed and of prophets: Rintrah and Palamabron, drawn away from Urizen's war. If sacrificing children as ransom was Urizen's plan—spoken by the Spectre of Urthona—it has failed, for Los and Enitharmon cooperate in a mortal overcoming of death: making female counterparts for male Spectres begins the life of generation, or at least continues the start made in the birth of Orc. If Los and Enitharmon have expelled their Luvah-Vala selves by giving birth to them, when they choose death for themselves they prepare the way for Jesus. They have turned Satan, as the guilt and accusation that demand a death in payment for sin, into willing sacrifice or annihilation of self. In short, Los lives both Adam's and Christ's temptation by Satan. Blake assimilates

---

11. "Now the regenerated Los and Enitharmon reverse the process initiated by their spectrous mating in Night VII. They attract to Golgonooza the spectres who have entered Urizen's temple and are participants in the wars of Urizen and Tharmas." "The total form that Los and Enitharmon created for all the spectres combined is 'a Universal female form' Jerusalem (VIII E361)" (Wilkie and Johnson, *Blake's Four Zoas,* pp. 168, 171).

Milton Percival remarks, "Before Enitharmon can weave the new forms, Los has first to temper his wrath to the new ideal of mercy. He has then to draw 'the immortal lines upon the heavens,' [sic] in short, to restore the Divine Vision which has been lost.

"The 'Bodies' which Enitharmon weaves for the disembodied Spectres at this point are suggested by the Pauline division of mankind into Elect, Redeemed, and Reprobate. . . . This classification affords a vision of the whole regenerative process, for it is for these three classes that Creation, Redemption, and Judgment are devised." For Blake, "Man, who has been tortured by a conception of sin, is to be freed from his burden by the weaving of Enitharmon." In short, Percival reads Nights VII and VIII as an allegory of change in the Christian religion (*William Blake's Circle of Destiny,* pp. 229–30).

the two—immensely condenses time—so that the temptation is put aside almost as soon as it occurs. And Christ, as
Los, is given a feminine counterpart, Enitharmon.

We have reached the biblical, Christian, and Miltonic center of *The Four Zoas*. Nights VI, VII, VIII, and IX are the most
biblical nights, and Nights VI and VII are closest to *Paradise
Lost*. Urizen's journey to the cave of Orc in VI (to find the
source of the deep pulsation or heartbeat that he hears) suggests not only Satan's journey through chaos to earth, in
Paradise Lost, but also the Genesis tree of knowledge and the
Exodus wandering in the wilderness and the giving of the
Law: Urizen both plants the tree of mystery and composes
books of iron and brass.[12] The "wanderer" in the wilderness
in Night VI, then, is Urizen-Satan-Moses-Jehovah. (Later,
Los draws off from war the human part of Jehovah as the
prophet Rintrah, leaving the warlike "spectrous form"—
Satan—behind: separating prophet from warmaker, judge
from king, God from war-god.) Seen as Satan's journey, Urizen's journey in Night VI prepares for the temptation of Los-
Adam in VII, in which Satan and Eve are the Spectre of
Urthona and the Shadow of Enitharmon, both fresh from
conferring among the branches of the tree of mystery. Seen
as the Exodus wandering, Night VI prepares for Los's temptation as Jesus in Night VII by providing the equivalent of an
Old Testament type of Jesus's New Testament temptation in
the wilderness. Los's converting the temptation of Adam
into the temptation of Jesus converts loss into victory. And
Los and Enitharmon act not only as Adam and Eve, but also
as Jesus's human source and parents, Joseph and Mary. In
Night VII, four thousand years pass in a few moments. Having earlier enacted the pagan Eros vision of human love, Los
and Enitharmon now enact the biblical, and especially the
Christian, vision. All is presented as the history of a single
family, descended not from Abraham or Israel but from Los,
the power of vision and prophecy.

12. Percival observes that as Urizen explores, "he writes, endlessly record-
ing the terrors of the abyss. His records are today the Old Testament of
priestly literature. . . . As the eternal priest Urizen is also the eternal scribe"
(*William Blake's Circle of Destiny*, p. 192).

Blake's treatment of the Spectre of Urthona is complex and subtle. As a reminder of Los's former life as Urthona, the Spectre comes as renewal. Come from the tree of mystery, however, he is a fearful, confused, despairing tempter—not so much Satan as a messenger of Satan. At his best, he approaches the Michael of the late books of *Paradise Lost*. If Los is enacting Milton, then Urthona's Spectre is Milton's angel Michael as much as he is Milton's Satan. Both the Spectre and Michael act as medium between man and helpmeet, and both propound what is for Blake a mistaken idea of atonement. In Michael's account, Law was given mankind

> "to evince
> Their natural pravity, by stirring up
> Sin against Law to fight; that when they see
> Law can discover sin, but not remove,
> Save by those shadowy expiations weak,
> The blood of bulls and goats, they may conclude
> Some blood more precious must be paid for Man." (XII, 287–
> 93)

This is the idea whose seed the Spectre plants in Los and Enitharmon—to pay for their sins by blood: their children's blood.

The "Saviour," Michael continues,

> "shall recure
> Not by destroying Satan, but his works
> In thee and in thy Seed: nor can this be,
> But by fulfilling that which thou didst want,
> Obedience to the law of God, impos'd
> On penalty of death . . .
> . . . .
> So only can high Justice rest appaid.
> The Law of God exact he shall fulfill
> Both by obedience and by Love, though love
> Alone fulfill the Law; thy punishment
> He shall endure by coming in the Flesh
> To a reproachful life and cursed death." (XII, 393–406)

Like Michael's vision-lecture, the Spectre of Urthona's need to "find a way to Ransom and Redeem" is at best still contaminated by the Law and by punishment—by the notion of atonement as the paying of a debt. In Blake's view, Christ's dying "willingly" wipes out the Law and punishment. (The impulse to correct Milton seems to lead directly to Blake's *Milton*.) Blake's Christ comes not as both love and fulfillment of the Law, but as love alone: not in payment of a debt at all, but as peacemaker.

Much of *The Four Zoas* treats the payment as fear and guilt leading to human sacrifice in religious ritual and war. Luvah is the one who has been fulfilling the Law and paying the blood price, first in the furnaces of Urizen, then as Orc. The scapegoat—Luvah, Orc, Adam—keeps taking different forms, until Jesus dies "willingly." But it is for Satan, not for Adam—or for man, as Michael says—that Jesus dies. These payments are for, and sometimes as, Satan. They are demanded by Satan the accuser and paid by Satan the rebel outcast. (The first is, in the language of Blake's *Milton*, the elect; the second is the reprobate. Urizen in Night VI is Satan the elect accuser who finds Orc as reprobate Satan in hell.) Satan's "compelling" Adam by his "arts" to die for Satan reveals the complete double-form Satan: the tempter-accuser and the sinner whose transgression must be paid for. The first is always Urizen (or Vala); the second is always Luvah. They are the double-figure embodiments of a single error: the accusation of sin. Christ comes in Luvah's robes of blood to put an end to that error. Only in this sense does Christ die for man: not in payment of man's debt, but for the sake of man, for an end to the justice that is vengeance.

Urizen began by fearing the birth of "that Prophetic boy" and his own fall or servitude. By Night VII, he has achieved the binding of Orc and his transformation into a worm and sepent; and, through the tree of mystery and the Spectre of Urthona, he has attempted the sacrifice of all posterity, like Herod, in order to prevent the birth. In Night VIII, the "spectrous form of Urizen," which Los was unable to draw out of the ranks of war, makes machines of war. He communes with Orc

To undermine the World of Los & tear bright Enitharmon
To the four winds hopeless of future. All futurity

Seems teeming with Endless Destruction never to be repelld
Desperate remorse swallows the present in a quenchless rage.
  (VIII/100:34; 101:30–33/E359/374)

But in Night VIII (101/E358/373), Urizen sees a double-form
Luvah who balances Vala's double form as sin and death:
Orc, now a serpent, and Jesus in Luvah's robes of blood.
Urizen is "Perplexd & terrifid" (101:2/E358/373). Apparently
he has failed to identify the "Prophetic boy" he fears, and
soon he is "Terrified & astonishd" (101:33/E359/374) to see the
war take on the hermaphroditic form of Satan.

The series of metamorphoses, splittings, identifications,
and failures to identify others in *The Four Zoas* (the double-
form Vala, Tharmas's recognition of Urthona, Urizen's recognition of Orc-Luvah, Los's apparent failure to recognize
Orc as Luvah) come to a climax here. Los, having accepted
Urthona's Spectre in Night VII as his real self, in Night IX
recovers his suspended identity. In passing into new forms
in a new space, Los and Enitharmon have lost memory,
which resides in the Spectre of Urthona. With "I am that
shadowy Prophet who six thousand years ago / Fell from my
station in the Eternal bosom" (VIII/113:48–49/E365/380), Los-
Urthona remembers. The recall is like Oedipus's "How
strange, a shadowy memory crossed my mind" (Fitts-
Fitzgerald translation). Los and Urthona's Spectre are like an
Oedipus and Teiresias who were formerly one. Urthona's
Spectre, like Teiresias, is obsessed with memory and futurity
and seems helpless to change anything he foresees, though
he helps make it come to pass. That is, if one thinks of
Teiresias as the embodied and separated form of Oedipus's
memory of the past and fear of the future, one gets the Spectre of Urthona and Los. But with "I am that shadowy
Prophet," the previously self-divided Urthona becomes self-
conscious and one—identified. Then he names his descendants—ending with Paul, Constantine, Charlemagne,
Luther, Milton—and remembers his falling from his station
in the eternal bosom six thousand years ago. Cut off from the
Spectre of Urthona, he has been cut off from the knowledge
that is history, though he has been living and shaping it.
Summing it up now, Los-Urthona's account of the seven

guards of Satan—Seven Eyes of God—sums up seven thousand years of history in persons who symbolize eras.[13]

The most important development in Night VIII is that Los and Enitharmon's family become Jerusalem, with Jesus born in their midst. (Having closed Jerusalem out of her heart at the end of Night I, Enitharmon has now become Jerusalem.) Satan confronts Jesus; Jesus is crucified. As Satan and Jesus reflect one another in reverse, so Jesus and Los reflect one another really. What Jesus is, Los becomes. But he does so in such a way as to show Jesus working in time, to show his humanity not as assumed but as grown into through trial in what Keats calls "a world like this." Although by Night VIII Los has developed from a visionary of Jesus into living the humanity of Jesus, though he seems a foster father of the human Jesus, and though he has remembered that he is Urthona, he is like the disciples: he still does not understand. The crucifixion seems to him (and to Enitharmon) a final, permanent death. As Joseph of Arimathea, Los buries Jesus, and their family mourns him: "Jerusalem wept over the

13. It would be neat and simple if each Eye appeared, or "opened," in the order of his naming and occupied a single night. This is not quite the case. Very roughly speaking, however, Lucifer and Elohim appear in Night I ("Sudden down fell they all together into an unknown space" looks like Satan-Lucifer's being cut off from Golgonooza in Los-Urthona's account in Night VIII of the Seven Eyes [E366/381] and in the Bard's Song of *Milton*.) Night II is Molech; Night IV Shaddai; Night V Pachad; Night VI Jehovah; and Nights VII and VIII are Jesus (and Adam, perhaps dying the death of man). Satan appears first as Urizen-Lucifer, who falls, but escapes his bonds; then he appears as Orc-Luvah, bound. Together they form the double-form Satan who is both accuser and victim.

Compare Milton Percival's account: "The fact that Elohim comes with the Flood and shapes the world which rises after it makes the assignment of Molech and Lucifer certain. They divide the antediluvian world between them." Then come the triple Elohim, after the fall, and Shaddai. "He is the God (El Shaddai) who made the covenant with Abraham. . . . But in the course of time Shaddai grows angry. His people grow rebellious. . . . The moral law has to be created in order to restrain them. Orc is bound upon Mt. Sinai."

Pachad ("fear of the Lord") "comes in the nadir of the cycle. . . . Historically this period of fear has its climax in the Babylonian captivity. It is symbolized astrologically by the descent of the sun into the depths of winter." It is at the end of December, Percival maintains, when Urizen "takes his globe of fire . . . and explores the dark caves of his ruined world," preparing for deliverance (*William Blake's Circle of Destiny*, pp. 246–49).

Sepulcher two thousand Years" (VIII/110:33/E371/385).[14] The
failure to understand continues into Night IX. While Jesus
separates the spirit from the body, the spiritual body from the
corporeal body of death, Los weeps. "Terrified at Non Existence / For such they deemd the death of the body" (IX/117:5–
6/E371–72/386), Los tears down the time-space world of Urthona's Spectre and Enitharmon's Shadow as if it were the
scene or backdrop of a drama. What Los and Enitharmon fail
to understand is the Christian soul, or concept of the soul,
they have helped to form. Perhaps we should think of them
as the first Christians—or, since Joseph of Arimathea, in leg-
end, brought Christianity to England, as the first English
Christians. Perhaps their creation of souls is the conversion-
rebirth of Albion, Christianity recovered from its heathen
corruptions.

The spiritual body that Jesus separates from the mortal
body at the beginning of Night IX is a transformation of the
immortal, "divinely human" forms fabricated by Los and Enitharmon in VII. If their art was not salvation, it prepared for
salvation by giving the Spectres—naked need and fear of
death—"forms sublime," "divinely human." Without a
human or physical body, there can be no soul (as in the
Devil's account of soul and body in *The Marriage of Heaven
and Hell*). The Spectres are not only erotic need—males without female counterparts—but also phantoms: disembodied
thought and memory. They were born in the first steep fall,
breathed forth by females—males emanated from the female
in an Ulro asexual birth, as in Urthona's Spectre's birth from
Enion's nostrils. But this asexual birth may be followed by
generation, as Orc seems born of generation, though in him
generation is suspended. (Conceived in the loins, born in the
heart, Orc seems pure life opposed to the death of energy in
the Spectre.) Fully generational life begins only when the

14. Wilkie and Johnson also identify Los here as Joseph of Arimathea
(*Blake's Four Zoas*, p. 184) and the "two thousand years" as the "two millen-
nia of suffering . . . which correspond to the two days when the scriptural
Jesus lies dead and the disciples despair." This period "coincides with the
period of historical institutional Christianity when freedom succumbs to the
worship of death" (p. 190).

male Spectres embrace the female counterparts created for them. The offspring of these embraces are mortal. Their fathers, so to speak, are death—followers of the Emanation Vala, who denies the Man, or worshippers of Urizen, who has cast his Emanation out as weakness. (Vala and Urizen embody the two errors of Man-Emanation, or male-female, relations, both of which diminish man by separating him from his unique virtue and work.) When Los and Enitharmon embody in artful forms of "divine humanity" the Spectres of the dead, giving them "Female counterparts," they endow them—as if they were the Genius of Spenser's Garden of Adonis—with a renewed or second life. Los and Enitharmon become foster parents, and their children adopted, so that Orc has no siblings. Their foster care turns Generation into Beulah, repaying the Beulah care they received from Eno. If the Mental Fight of eternity has fallen into warfare in heaven, then Los and Enitharmon provide the Beulah care that allows its victims to be born into our world, on the verge of which their initial spectral state is fear of death. As in *The Book of Urizen*, life is a response to the image of eternal death. Los acts to answer Urizen.

*   *   *

Beulah is "Created by the Lamb of God," "around," "within," and "without" the "Universal Man" who is Eden (I/5:32–33/E299/303). Then, the Lamb of God enters Beulah— is born—and dies the death that is Ulro. His resurrection converts Ulro into Beulah again. The place of seed, Beulah is also the place of redemption, and redemption is in or of the body, is the divine mercy shown to the body through rebirth into the impermanent body for females, the permanent body for males. Beulah is feminine; and Eden—at least as seen from Beulah—is masculine. The man in Beulah is in a feminine state, resting or sleeping. A "feminine lovely" "mild & pleasant rest," Beulah is given to those who "sleep / Eternally" (I/5:31–32/E299/303). To sleep eternally is to sleep *from* eternity, and this is to be in the mortal flesh, male or female (as Eve sleeps in book 12 of *Paradise Lost* while Michael instructs Adam in what is to come). One may sleep or wake in Beulah, but the great awakening is into Eden. Los and Eni-

tharmon, then, fashion the mortal body that may be redeemed, awakened into the spiritual body of Eden, which is
neither male-female or mother-child, but Man-Emanation.
And the conversation of Man and Emanation is creation—
what Los and Enitharmon have begun to do. This is Blake's
great alteration of Milton's paradise.

Finally, Beulah is a kind of art, and the Daughters of Beulah
are Muses, carrying on a mental and creative life even in
sleep (as Eve dreams the future, her seed bruising the serpent's head, in book 12 of *Paradise Lost*): "The Daughters of
Beulah follow sleepers in all their Dreams / Creating Spaces
lest they fall into Eternal Death" (I/5:34–35/E299/303). As created by the Lamb of God, Beulah is mercy and salvation, the
redeemed, reborn body. As inspired by the Daughters of
Beulah, Beulah is dream or pagan art, or innocent pleasure:
art resting from the intellectual warfare of Eden. Most art,
then, is Beulah art—not the intellectual warfare that is Jesus
or Jehovah speaking, but Daughters of Beulah inspiring. The
Spectres are impulses or emotions not yet articulated into
words and built into lines. Without such embodiment they
would die, vanish into air as mere breath breathed out by
Daughters of Beulah. (For Milton Percival, "female" willingness to die is the willingness of form to be dissolved and re-
formed by the forming energy.)[15]

Blake-Los's illuminations rehabilitate sight from reading as
a power to decode abstract signs and make sight a sensuous
power—recover it from the remote, distancing, usurped
power of Urizen. In Night VII, Blake makes sight a power in
creating the poem by showing Los and Enitharmon beginning to illuminate the poem. When Los draws his line on the
shining walls of heaven in Night VII, Blake is reminding us
that the pure poetry of the Bible is or was illuminated, as in
the enormous visual power added to the Bible in painting
and sculpture and illuminated manuscript in the chapels and
churches and cathedrals of Europe. And Los's line on the
walls of heaven—both the artist's and the poet's "line"—
suggests the creation of a cosmos and of an ordered (*cosmios*)
soul. Line enclosing a space creates cosmos and organized or

15. *William Blake's Circle of Destiny,* p. 56.

ensouled body. Insofar as Los and Enitharmon participate in Jesus, the body they create is the myriad-bodied body of Albion, a Christian Albion and a nation of artists.

As souls, the Spectres are, so to speak, dead souls: the dead in Beulah who have perished in the obscure war between Tharmas and Urizen that is fought chiefly by the Zoas' sons, or the dead who have been drawn from the ranks of war by the intellectual force of prophetic art (as Rintrah is at the end of VII). They must pass through Urizen's Temple (built in VII): war as religion. They are dying to error; they are converts from the religion of war to the arts of peace and have undergone a Last Judgment. ("And the sea gave up the dead which were in it; and death and hell delivered up the dead which were in them; and they were judged every man according to their works" [Revelation 20:13].) If "the Man / Or Woman" who is not "A Poet a Painter a Musician an Architect . . . is not a Christian" ("The Laocoön"/E272/274), neither is the greatness of a nation in its generals, "heroic villains": it is in its artists. The Spectres are conceptions whose seed comes not from Blake but from elsewhere—from Chaucer, Shakespeare, Spenser, Milton, from Holbein and Hogarth, Wren and Inigo Jones, Byrd and Purcell. The seed would die if it were not kept alive by later artists and drawn out into a continuous line or tradition, such as the line that Los-Urthona names, ending in Paul, Constantine, Charlemagne, Luther, and Milton. Here the Christian generals are outnumbered by the Christian poet-prophets.

When Enitharmon tints the spaces outlined on the wall of heaven, Blake breaks through his own fiction. We see the family called Jerusalem as the characters created by Blake— those who will reappear in *Milton* and *Jerusalem* for example—and we see Los-Enitharmon as at that moment inventing the idea of illuminated printing and putting it into practice. (Male time and line suggest Blake as poet and engraver; female space suggests Catherine as colorist.) Perhaps Blake has taken us through Los's "child" Milton—through a complex corrective allusion to *Paradise Lost*—and has arrived at Los's "child" Blake, so that the poet-prophet has reached a time and place in history where he becomes a poet-prophet-artist. Creator of "divinely human" form, Los has also passed beyond the soul as breath or Spectre, beyond Hades and Sheol, to a fully Christian and fully human psychology: no soul without the human form divine.

The Urizen-Luvah-Vala pattern, which is repeated in relations among Urthona's Spectre and Los and Enitharmon in *The Four Zoas,* is—like that in the Tractates and many of the short prophecies—a version of the psychic triad of Plato's *Republic.* Urizen and Urthona's Spectre are reason; Luvah and Los are the spirited part; Vala and Enitharmon are not so much passions as forbidden objects of desire. This psychology, adopted by Christianity and by Milton in *Paradise Lost,* Blake opposed as the psychopolitics of tyranny, in which reason rules as internalized tyrant. Throughout *The Four Zoas,* as in the earlier prophecies, especially *Visions of the Daughters,* Blake treats this psychology as a pattern of sexual as well as political tyranny, with the female, as possession and forbidden object of desire, seen as the cause of male jealousy. In *Paradise Lost,* Adam as reason and Satan as desire fight over Eve as object of desire. In Night VII, Los frees himself from Milton's Platonic psychology, in which reason ought to rule over the passions with the help of the spirited part.

Los's action seems parallel to Blake's account in a letter to William Hayley of 23 October 1804:

For now! O Glory! and O Delight! I have entirely reduced that spectrous Fiend to his station, whose annoyance has been the ruin of my labours for the last passed twenty years of my life. He is the enemy of conjugal love and is the Jupiter of the Greeks, an iron-hearted tyrant, the ruiner of ancient Greece. I speak with perfect confidence and certainty of the fact which has passed upon me. Nebuchadnezzar had seven times passed over him; I have had twenty; thank God I was not altogether a beast as he was; but I was a slave bound in a mill among beasts and devils; these beasts and these devils are now, together with myself, become children of light and liberty, and my feet and my wife's feet are free from fetters. . . . Suddenly, on the day after visiting the Truchsessian Gallery of pictures, I was again enlightened with the light I enjoyed in my youth, and which has for exactly twenty years been closed from me as by a door and by window-shutters. . . . He is become my servant who domineered over me, he is even as a brother who was my enemy. Dear Sir, excuse

> my enthusiasm or rather madness, for I am really drunk with intellectual vision whenever I take a pencil or graver into my hand, even as I used to be in my youth, and as I have not been for twenty dark, but very profitable years. (E702–3/756–57)

Jupiter in Blake's letter parallels Urizen and his messenger, the Spectre of Urthona, in Night VII of *The Four Zoas*. Los too has "reduced that Spectrous Fiend"—the "ruin" of his "labours" and "the enemy of conjugal love"—"to his station." His response to Urthona's Spectre has converted Urizen-Jupiter from "domineer[ing] . . . enemy" to "servant" and "brother." In the letter, the result of Blake's "enlightenment" is a resurgence of "intellectual vision" and renewed energy and confidence in his drawing and engraving. Los, similarly, draws his line on the shining walls of heaven, and he and Enitharmon, like Blake and Catherine, convert "beasts and devils" to "children of light and liberty." Los has become an artist at the same time he has become a Christian and a peacemaker.

Furthermore, Los has been reintegrated with his Emanation in both a sexual reconciliation and a cooperative working whose "offspring" suggest what Blake elsewhere (and later) calls "Births of Intellect":

> Jesus is surrounded by Beams of Glory in which are seen all around him Infants emanating from him these represent the Eternal Births of Intellect from the divine Humanity A Rainbow surrounds the throne & the Glory in which youthful Nuptials recieve the Infants in their hands In Eternity Woman is the Emanation of Man she has No Will of her own There is no such thing in Eternity as a Female Will. ("A Vision of the Last Judgment," p. 85/E552/562)

Los-Enitharmon's creations in VII are at least halfway toward intellectual emanations, births of intellect from a divine man. The psychology here is that of the *Symposium*, in which intellectual births are superior to all sexuality; and conception, gestation, and birth are a complex metaphor for intellectual invention, work, and execution.

The man is clearly the moving force. The male or intellectual prolific in Blake's poetry competes with—is superior to—the female or bodily prolific, and Golgonooza as offspring is greater than Orc. Blake's Christianity is tinged by the "erotic" doctrine of the *Symposium*. For Blake, evidently, Los is still insufficiently free of the female, who gives birth to the corporeal body. Though Los is full of goodwill, though he begins apocalypse, and though, with Enitharmon, he is the artificer of the body, in Blake's view he is still ignorant; he does not understand the separation of the spiritual body of redemption and of art from the corporeal body. It appears that, having been born into Beulah, his life is Beulah; and even as Urthona, he has only glimpses of Eden.

The awakening in and from Beulah that occurs in Night IX is not so much from the sexes as it is from female will and from the claim to be God, which uses the doctrine of virginity and the refusals of the female will as its instruments. Though Blake sees sexuality as insufficiently creative and human, he sees its restraint by law as grievous error. His critical eye is on the gods, whose One Law is denial. In the resting Beulah visions of Night IX, the Zoas who have not yet been renewed or reborn—Luvah-Vala and Tharmas-Enion—are reborn, not as gods, but as humans. Luvah and Vala are "henceforth" to be "Servants" and to keep their "place [in] the place of seed not in the brain or heart" (IX/126:6–8/E380/395). (It is worth observing that keeping place and function is the "justice" of the *Republic*.) Tharmas and Enion—parent powers— are "renewd & brought into the gardens of Vala" as "little Boy" and "bright Girl" (IX/130:7–8/E383/398). These shadowy visions of renewal are Beulah visions: they entertain sleepers upon the couches of Beulah. Even after Urthona cries "Times are Ended" (IX/131:31/E385/400), *The Four Zoas* does not take us entirely into Jerusalem or Eden. Instead, though we end with the destruction of Ulro and Generation and One Law, we are left standing on the border between Beulah and Eden in a state that is still sexual.

The Final Harvest: Eden and Beulah, God and Man, Pagan Poetry and Christian Poetry

When the Eternal Man, Albion, says early in Night IX, "Immortal thou. Regenerate She, & all the lovely Sex / From her shall learn obedience & prepare for a wintry grave" to rise in "tenfold joy" in the spring (122:12–14/E376/391), it is clear that we have not left Beulah behind, that we have not progressed beyond the sexes or beyond female seasonal death. In the Beulah that surrounds Eden as its place of rest—"and our little life is rounded with a sleep"—females are consigned to winter death and spring rebirth as if they were vegetative life, while an Emanation is "a Self renewing Vision" (122:7/E376/391). *Female* and *Emanation* are analogous, but only analogous. Until the spiritual body of Eden that is Man-Emanation, not male-female, has appeared, and until the intellectual war that is the life of Eden has begun (the destruction of the old heaven and earth is not yet the warfare of Eden), Jesus as savior is still needed. And Jesus is different from the Eternals who look down into Beulah and are appalled by sexual generation and by the sight of females "Not born for the sport and amusement of Man but born to drink up all his powers" (IX/138:7/E386/401).

Jesus is mercy, and not only creates Beulah, which is feminine, but also enters it and takes on Ulro death as well as birth: he "die[s] the death of man." The opposed satanic and pagan principle is shown by Admetus, in *Alcestis*. Admetus is a king and Satan who gets another—his wife—to die for him. She is saved by Hercules, whom Blake would probably see as a type or "memory" of Jesus—both, like Los and Enitharmon, being immortals responding to the plight of mortals. If we take *man* in "die the death of man" to mean *male*, and if we take *female* to mean the mortal body (Vala as Luvah's "robes of blood"), then males living renewed by female deaths turns out, in Jesus, to mean that the spiritual body lives by the death of the corporeal body, and *female* remains stubbornly corporeal in Blake's lexicon.

But if we see Jesus, as most readers of Blake do (and as St. Paul did), as neither male nor female but *man*—the infant and the nurturer and the one who dies the death of man—then he has taken feminine virtue up in masculine form and has taken on and redeemed the whole human experience. And he has achieved the equality of god and man in death. But if *man*—Jesus—means "fully human," then in Blake's entirely human world, nature comes to be signified or enacted by female and by serpent, or perhaps by Eve and serpent. If *female* means nature, if Albion and the Eternals in speaking of female death mean that "greater" humans freely use and transcend the natural world and only rest in nature from their creative "war," then Eden remains masculine (like Milton's heaven) and Beulah feminine. That is to say, we never entirely leave Beulah in *The Four Zoas.* Man and Emanation remain in some way sexual, perhaps because Blake cannot concretely imagine a humanity that is not in some way sexual. When Jesus, having converted the family—which is Beulah—into the brotherhood of Eden, largely disappears from the poem, he leaves Albion and the four Zoas just entering into an Eden in which the sun is just rising, and in which a presumably asexual brotherhood is not very concretely developed.

Jesus's disappearance means also that Night IX seems less Christian than the two preceding ones, especially VII. It may be that Nights VII and VIII were composed later than IX, and that Christ's role and Los's Christianity came later than IX. If so, the night that was written earlier dominates: the apocalyptic energy of Night IX nearly obliterates the Christian conversion in VII, which is placed to precede and prepare for it. As we turn from Beulah toward an emerging fiery Eden, Christ's action gives way before that of the Zoas, humanity recedes before giant forms, and Blake's Christian poem, in spite of ending in apocalypse like the Christian Bible, tends to become pagan.[16] Since Los began, in *The Book of Urizen* and *The Book of Los,* as a kind of Hephaestus or demiurge and carries the role into *The Four Zoas,* which begins as a pagan poem, it is hardly surprising that the Christian myth in *The Four Zoas* is imperfectly fused with its pagan myth and often seems merely overlaid.

The last specifically Christian and merciful passage of any length in *The Four Zoas* alludes to the Lamb of God and to Jerusalem as Beulah—as bride, wife, and mother. In it Albion

16. In "A Vision of the Last Judgment," the very function of the Zoas seems to be the destruction of the old creation: "the Four Living Creatures mentioned in Revelations as Surrounding the Throne . . . I suppose to have the chief agency in removing the old Heavens & the old Earth to make way for the New Heaven & the New Earth" (pp. 83–84/E550/561).

describes an elevation of the sexes into Man-Emanation and a community of the redeemed through a "New Spiritual birth":

> Thus shall the male & female live the life of Eternity
> Because the Lamb of God Creates himself a bride & wife
> That we his Children evermore may live in Jerusalem
> Which now descendeth out of heaven a City yet a Woman
> Mother of myriads redeemd & born in her spiritual palaces
> By a New Spiritual birth Regenerated from Death. (IX/122:15–
> 20/E376/391)

By virtue of this "New Spiritual birth" enacted by Jesus, Jesus and the Eternals live in different worlds—Beulah and Eden, perhaps, but a very detached Eden. Since the Eternals are passive, choric, sometimes self-righteous spectators of a drama that to them is not fully real, Jesus and the Eternals sometimes seem to belong in different poems, one Christian and the other pagan. The same is even more true of Los and the Eternals, for Los, even more than Jesus, is in the thick of a struggle.

In *The Four Zoas,* as in the development of his poetry as a whole, Blake recapitulates the development-return of pagan poetry into Christian humanism. But the conversion is hard for him to make. Blake planned a triumph of the human over the pagan gods and Yahweh as punisher. Urizen, the Zoa who most needed to learn the principle, pronounces it in Night IX:

> If Gods combine against Man Setting their Dominion above
> The Human form Divine. Thrown down from their high
> Station
> In the Eternal heavens of Human Imagination: buried
> beneath
> In dark oblivion with incessant pangs ages on ages
> In Enmity & war first weakened then in stern repentance
> They must renew their brightness & their disorganizd
> functions
> Again reorganize till they resume the image of the human
> Cooperating in the bliss of Man obeying his Will
> Servants to the infinite & Eternal of the Human form. (126:9–
> 17/E380/395)

In the battle of giants, with each side claiming to be God, in which humanity finally prevails or is reasserted, Los and Enitharmon have developed a humanity recognizably our own. But in Night IX, the Eternals call humans "our shadows," and Los and Enitharmon become giant forms again, two among eight Zoas and Emanations in the Universal Man Albion, and in Jerusalem his Emanation. It is as if Los, like Christ, had taken on and put off flesh. Night VII ends "humanly," with generation an image of regeneration. Night IX ends at the edge of Eden, with the awakening and the violent putting off of the body of death, and with the "consummation" of the universe that corresponds to it. Los and Enitharmon as merely human—tender of the flesh—fail to understand the putting off of the flesh and are "consumed" to emerge as the giant forms Urthona and Enitharmon, who are immensely beyond what we know as human. If Blake planned a Christian epic on the humanity of Jesus, he folded so much pagan myth and metamorphosis into the poem that the development of a human Jesus—a human faith—is almost overwhelmed, and the poem ends as it began: as a heroic poem about giant forms whose actions constitute the world.

To put the fall-and-recovery in terms of speech, we begin with the nadir of self-obsession as a lower limit of speech, as in "every one wrapd up / In his own sorrow howld regardless of his words" (VI/70:42–43/E341/347), and we rise through speech as self-justification or the attempt to exert power, Urizen's "Am I not God . . . . Who is Equal to me" (III/42:19/ E322/328), to memory, as in Ahania's "Listen to her whose memory beholds your ancient days" (VIII/108:20/E369/383). Though Urizen complains, "My songs are turned to cries of Lamentation" (V/64:9/E337/343), songs of piercing beauty— often at the same time songs of piercing irony or love-and-hate—continue to be heard, as in Enitharmon's "The joy of woman is the Death of her most best belovd" (II/34:63/ E317/324). And we have the memory of man's talking with the rest of creation:

> in vain the voice
> Of Urizen in vain the Eloquent tongue. A Rock a Cloud a
>   Mountain

Were now not Vocal as in Climes of happy Eternity
Where the lamb replies to the infant voice & the lion to the
    man of years
Giving them sweet instructions Where the Cloud the River &
    the Field
Talk with the husbandman & shepherd. (VI/71:3–8/E341/348)

As *The Four Zoas* progresses, lament or speech or song
begins to evoke more response and moves toward dialogue
or responsive song—as Enion in Night VIII responds to Ahania's despairing cry "to the caverns of the Grave" by foresee-
ing the time when the "Eternal Man" will "reassume his
ancient bliss" (a response in which Enion also answers her
own lament in Night I). Finally, on the next-to-last page, we
have a "conversing":

                                  & one Sun
Each morning like a New born Man issues with songs & joy
Calling the Plowman to his Labour & the Shepherd to his rest
He walks upon the Eternal Mountains raising his heavenly
    voice
Conversing with the Animal forms of wisdom night & day
That risen from the Sea of fire renewd walk oer the Earth.
    (IX/138:27–32/E391/406)

But the imagery of sun as newborn man conversing with the
animal forms of wisdom is not yet the human conversation of
eternity. It is midway between that and the ancient poets
animating all sensible objects. Night IX presents the active
entering *into* Eden, but pastoral imagery remains dominant
until almost the end, and the poem ends more in final harvest than in conversation.

At the very end of *The Four Zoas,* however, Blake has ex-
ploited fully and has come to the end of the largely pastoral
imagery of the Bible and of pagan epic and myth.[17] The sci-

17. "This great metaphor of harvest and vintage is a rich elaboration and
synthesis of images appearing all through the Bible—especially in the toil of
Adam; the parables of the sower, the laborers in the vineyard, and the wheat
and tares; the joyful bringing in of the sheaves in Psalm 126; the beating of
swords into plowshares in Isaiah 2 and Micah 4; and the trampling of the
grapes in Isaiah 63 and Revelation 14. It is presented as a circumstantial
account of how bread and wine, the symbols of truly human communion,
are made. . . . Throughout, the seeds, grains, and grapes are human souls
and their cultivation is made possible only by the new cooperativeness

ences that dominate the end of *The Four Zoas* are architecture, for building the city and the poem, and knowledge, for intellectual warfare. Both look ahead, beyond the limits of the poem. If we have passed from innocence through experience to organized innocence, organized innocence is not much developed in the poem. Los-Urthona, who (though he mills grain and makes bread) is the only one of the Zoas who is not an entirely pastoral figure, with his hammer will build the city.[18] He became a builder of cities when he began work on Golgonooza at the birth of Orc. Now Golgonooza, which began as a defensive heart-labyrinth and became art as Mental Fight, has yielded to Jerusalem, but we have not yet entered into its life.

What is peculiar to the city of active brotherhood Los prepares to create is the transformed nature of the father. Here the father is a brother, and the Eternals no longer seem as cold or self-righteous as before. They have been enriched by the life-in-time of Jesus, so that they know

> That Man subsists by Brotherhood & Universal Love
> We fall on one anothers necks more closely we embrace
> Not for ourselves but for the Eternal family we live
> Man liveth not by Self alone but in his brothers face
> Each shall behold the Eternal Father & love & joy abound.
> (IX/133:22–26/E386–87/402)

---

among the Zoas and Emanations, with Albion as benevolent overseer and landlord" (Wilkie and Johnson, *Blake's Four Zoas*, p. 222).

Compare Christine Gallant: "At the end, what Albion sees is the 'eternal return,' the cycle of generation, death, and regeneration that the Zoas have just celebrated in their agricultural rituals. As Eliade predicts of the celebrant who experiences 'sacred' time, Albion sees the power behind the cosmos that manifests itself in the rhythms of that cosmos. . . . What Albion beholds is the play of polarities. His vision here is of a *perpetual process* rather than the final event of traditional eschatology, for as the Zoas' previous rituals have created Albion's 'mythic time,' so these rituals are here continually recurrent. They *maintain* the apocalypse" (*Blake and the Assimilation of Chaos*, p. 114).

18. "But in Eternity, when Urthona is restored to his ancient strength, his function is to make the weaponry for intellectual warfare, not to fight these wars himself (E392). He is closely identified with Hephaestus; he is not a splendid Apollo, Neptune, or Dionysus like his fellow Zoas." The stature of the artist is reduced at the end "in order to place all persons, humanity, mankind, at the acme of reality" (Wilkie and Johnson, *Blake's Four Zoas*, p. 237).

Since God the Father appears in *The Four Zoas* only as he is seen in one's brother, the relationship of the Eternals that is adumbrated in the poem is not hierarchical, like Milton's or Dante's heaven, but an equal and active brotherhood of free and unique persons: a community.

Los-Urthona dons his armor for intellectual war. The dark religions are gone, and sweet science reigns. It may be that the reign of sweet science is the beginning of a new poetry, going on from the Ulro, Generation, and Beulah of *The Four Zoas*. (Or it may be—though this is less likely—that sweet science supersedes poetry.) The new poetry could presumably be dialectic ending in conversation. The conversation is what Blake is not yet ready to do. When he does speak it, in the very different apocalypse that ends *Jerusalem*, it is poetry of an unprecedented sort in which poetry, painting, and music—man's surviving powers of conversing with paradise—have been freed and intensified into converse *in* paradise. And into *Jerusalem* the city of London comes much more: *Jerusalem* expands and develops the incipient awakening into human form that occurs in "London."

*   *   *

In *Milton*, which prefaces *Jerusalem*, Blake puts off apocalypse in order to prepare more carefully for the decisive role of the poet-prophet in its coming. *Milton* continues the account in *The Four Zoas* of the fall into the claim to be God and the rise into and recovery of the human. But the triumph of the human is greater and clearer now because *Milton* begins with a Los who retains the mature but beleaguered humanity he learned in *The Four Zoas*. Los now moves history by identifying himself with particular poets, with English prophets. The figure of the Bard singing of a human Los leads to the figure of Milton and then to Blake, and finally to the forming of one man from the Bard, Los, Milton, and Blake. The result is a human poet-prophet, the Awakener, who unites myth and history and who prepares for apocalypse in a much more deliberate and internal and psychologically subtle way than Blake had ever done before.

Los's relations with Urthona's Spectre in Night VII of *The Four Zoas* are resumed and transformed in the Bard's Song of

Milton in Los's (and Rintrah's and Palamabron's) relations with Satan. In *Milton,* Satan is Los's own son, his youngest. (A passage in Night VIII [E366/372], which identifies Satan as Los and Enitharmon's youngest son, may be a late addition to *The Four Zoas* from Blake's work on *Milton.*) In *Milton,* also, it is clearer that Satan is the second appearance of Urizen. Most important, Milton's wrestling with Urizen as Satan—as his own satanic Selfhood—immensely clarifies Los's conversion of the Spectre of Urthona's temptation in Night VII of *The Four Zoas.* Similarly, Milton's redemption of Ololon is a redemption of each by the other that clarifies and equalizes Los's relations with Enitharmon in Night VII. In all these ways the conversion action of Night VII seems the seed of Blake's *Milton.* In *Milton,* finally, Blake begins with his new insight into psychological classes. If in *The Four Zoas,* especially in Night VII, Blake converts the threefold psychology of the *Republic* and *Paradise Lost* into a Christian psychology, in *Milton* he Miltonically names the elements in the psyche "Elect," "Reprobate," and "Redeemed," locates each in one of Los's sons, and shows them to be not only psychic elements but also (as in the *Republic*) classes of men, classes in the city. The changes in *Milton,* as it turns out, bring Blake closer to what Shelley does later in *Prometheus Unbound.* Both identify active Poetic Genius in the single man—Milton or Los or Prometheus—with the community of men.

6

Milton

Milton is an inward and confessional poem, centering on Milton's conversion. Since Blake presents himself as a character in the poem and is throughout much of the poem united with Milton and Los, it centers also on Blake's conversion or illumination. *Milton* concerns the overcoming by unmasking of Satan, the anti-identity or Selfhood, in both Milton and Blake, and their assimilation to Los, the Spirit of Prophecy. In this way it prepares for—is really the prelude to—Blake's *Jerusalem*, his most ambitious completed work, and also for his more fully presenting the Divine Vision and the conversation in Eden in that poem.

Like *The Four Zoas* and *The Marriage of Heaven and Hell*, *Milton* is concerned with distinguishing between the reasoning-restraining-accusing Selfhood and the "true Poet," or Poetic and Prophetic Genius. In *The Four Zoas*, the true poet ceases to belong to the Devil's party. In *Milton*, he comes into full understanding. Milton becomes a true poet because he sees his error, which is his own distortions of vision and their effect on the religion that prevails in England. Inspired by a Bard's Song in which Los is divided in a family quarrel that issues in the warring nations of the fallen world, Milton descends from heaven to earth, annihilates his Selfhood by overcoming Urizen-Satan, and redeems his Emanation, Ololon.[1] (An Emanation is both a "bride" and a "form loved

1. Susan Fox has a better formulation: "Milton's descent is both simultaneous and identical with Ololon's descent; all the other actions of the poem, past and present, are merely component actions of the focal event" (*Poetic Form in Blake's "Milton,"* p. 17). At the end of the poem, it is clear that "she who descended to her husband has found him waiting for her; he has entered into the garden and found his bride waiting there. For they are and have been the same being. Ololon's bloody garments and Milton's Seven Angels are both manifestations of the Lamb of God" (p. 182). Fox's book is especially good on multiple perspectives and on simultaneous and mirroring action—"an elaborate system of parallels" (p. 24)—in *Milton*. As Fox says, "All the actions of the poem occur in . . . the last fragment of time itself, the instant before apocalypse puts an end to time" (p. 18).

because created.")[2] In *Milton,* then, a figure of identity is divided and falls as Los. As Milton, he is integrated with Blake, wrestles with his Spectre-Selfhood, and is reunited with his Emanation. Each of these events creates its appropriate human-centered world, fallen or redeemed.

Like *The Four Zoas* and *The Book of Urizen, Milton* concerns the divided self and the effort at reintegration. But in *Milton* the hero or champion is clearly the poet—Los in the Bard's Song; Milton, Blake, and Los in the remainder of the poem. Los, the source and father figure in the Bard's Song, is divided. He has first given off Enitharmon (as in *The Book of Urizen,* she is pity), and then further divided into Rintrah, Palamabron, and Satan, the major figures of the Bard's Song. As it concerns Milton, the implication of the Bard's Song is that in *Paradise Lost* the source and father figure is Milton, and that Milton, like Los, is divided.

*   *   *

Confusion begins in the Bard's Song when Satan, youngest of Enitharmon's sons, threatens to take over the powers and functions of his brother Palamabron. Palamabron is saved by the judgment falling on his brother Rintrah. The judgment leads to Satan's fall into hell, an internal hell, his "own place" (10:12/E103/104), but it is said by the Eternals to be the right judgment in that by the decision of the whole assembly the "Innocent" has been "condemn'd for the Guilty": "If the Guilty should be condemn'd, he must be an Eternal Death / And one must die for another throughout all Eternity" (11:17–18/E104/105). In the Eternals' view it is right that the judgment fall on Rintrah *because* Rintrah is innocent.

To understand this briefly stated action, we must look at it as a fall from identity, but a fall that offers the possibility of redemption. Los is what remains of identity. Satan is the anti-identity—the last born of Los's sons, thus the farthest removed from the source, inheritor of whatever tendencies to formlessness and evasion Los has. Refusing identifying form himself, he unconsciously seeks to destroy it in others. Having no identity himself, he tries to assume one by mas-

2. Northrop Frye, "Notes for a Commentary on *Milton,*" p. 128.

querading as one of Los's qualities or powers. The one most
available because Satan has the "Science" of it, and knows
how to use it, is pity. And the brother closest to Satan in that
he has powers of persuasion and political maneuver is Palamabron. Thus Satan tries to take over Palamabron's identity
and occupation by masquerading in Palamabron's own nature. He appeals to Los's pity by masking himself in Palamabron's mildness, which softens conflict. But since
Palamabron and Rintrah are brothers, mutually related Contraries, Satan cannot take over Palamabron's mildness without arousing its contrary, the wrath of Rintrah. The attempt
precipitates a conflict. Though the conflict seems to be between sons, the issue is really between son and father. Satan
is more or less consciously attempting to assume Los's
powers by dividing them further and taking them over one
by one. But he can assume them only by corrupting and
negating them. He is defeated both by Palamabron's political
cunning in calling a Solemn Assembly at just the right moment, when Satan's disguise of love is slipping, and by Rintrah's honest indignation and "firm perswasion," which
bring the conflict into the open. Since the Eternals refuse to
condemn mildness and pity, Satan playing Palamabron escapes condemnation. Thus Palamabron has to trap Satan into
showing rage. It is this rage—Satan as Rintrah—that the
Eternals condemn. Satan as Rintrah is exposed (but not
defeated) by Rintrah himself: frustrated rage is exposed by
justified wrath.

When expressed, Rintrah's honest wrath fuels Mental
Fight. Satan's denied and suppressed wrath bottles up a hell
inside, so that he is set apart, sacred, "in his own place."
Rintrah's wrath provokes wrath. Satan's pity (which he
never entirely loses the "science" of) evokes pity—as in Enitharmon's forming a protective womb or void into which
Satan escapes by falling, and which becomes the fallen world
of human experience. Dividing pity from wrath, the fall is a
misalignment of parties that obscures the issue of truth and
error: "All pitied the piteous & was wrath with the wrathful"
(5:4/E97/98).[3] Thus, Satan's effect on Los, the remnant of

3. Susan Fox observes, "Wrath was the constructive mode of Book I; it

identity, has been to exploit the division between pity and wrath in Los: to isolate them from each other, negating the progressive conflict of contraries, of truth and error. Separated from imagination, which is "the Human Existence itself" (32:32/E131/132), pity and wrath become rigid states. These states are a version of the absolute separation between good and evil in *The Marriage of Heaven and Hell,* a separation which leads to warfare. As in Night VIII of *The Four Zoas,* Satan is warfare, the negation of the Mental Fight which reveals identity.

As seen by the Eternals, however, the main effect of the three-way struggle among Satan and Rintrah and Palamabron is the delineation of three classes, an effect which prepares for the regaining of identity. To return to the lines I cited earlier, the question why "The Innocent should be condemn'd for the Guilty?" (11:16) is answered by an Eternal:

> If the Guilty should be condemn'd, he must be an Eternal
>   Death
> And one must die for another throughout all Eternity.
> Satan is fall'n from his station & never can be redeem'd
> But must be new Created continually moment by moment
> And therefore the Class of Satan shall be calld the Elect, &
>   those
> Of Rintrah, the Reprobate, & those of Palamabron the
>   Redeem'd
> For he is redeem'd from Satans Law, the wrath falling on
>   Rintrah (11:17–23/E104/105)

Without Rintrah's disinterested action, the conflict between Satan and Palamabron would be an eternal warfare. Though Satan in his fall has divided the nations and reduced Mental Fight to warfare, the fall allows for the separation of Satan, or Negation, from the contraries of reprobate and redeemed, so that the Mental Fight by which identity is regained may be carried on even after the fall.

Satan's being "new Created continually moment by moment" is a continual process of delineation and redefinition

---

burned away falsehood. Pity is the constructive mode of Book II; it re-creates truth." She further (and I think more accurately) insists that in Book II "Wrath is no longer left to wrath and pity to pity; the two are joined together" (*Poetic Form in Blake's "Milton,"* p. 163).

of classes, the gradual separation and isolation of error. Furthermore (though it has not yet become clear to the reader), the redeemed are to be saved from death not by atonement but by following the exemplary self-annihilation of the reprobate. Milton's self-annihilation is to be followed by Ololon's (and Ololon is multitudes of the formerly elect):

> And Ololon said, Let us descend also, and let us give
> Ourselves to death in Ulro among the Transgressors.
> Is Virtue a Punisher? O no! (21:45–47/E115/116)

Applied to others, the doctrine of atonement uttered by the Eternals is unspeakable. To "condemn the innocent" is to see atonement from the point of view of judge or prosecutor—Pilate or Caiaphas. It is the reverse of offering one's self as a willing sacrifice. Yet the latter way is the way Milton chooses after having heard the Bard's Song, and his sacrifice is redemptive. Though the Bard's Song is unfinished in that it contains no genuine self-sacrifice (Leutha's action is more self-accusation than self-sacrifice), the Song is cleansing in that it reveals the hidden Satan. It does so largely through Rintrah's wrath, which is condemned in both Rintrah and Satan. Although Satan's wrath, unlike Rintrah's, is concealed, it is nevertheless true. Since Satan lacks the "Science of Wrath" and is unable to make use of it to deceive, his wrath involuntarily betrays what is most genuine in him.[4] Ironically enough, *this* is what the Assembly condemns. Blake's understanding of this condemnation is complex. Satan has to show some flash of reality before he can be exposed, for he can only be "justly" condemned for what shows him as he is. But since that is what is least satanic in him—least evasive and lying, most direct and unknowing—the Satan who is condemned is always the reprobate, raging, sacrificial Luvah. This is to say that Satan cannot be justly condemned at all. In Blake's view, he is always elect, always the Accuser. Thus he cannot be eradicated in others, only annihilated in the self. This is also Milton's understanding of the Bard's Song. Milton's action in the remainder of the poem—annihilating Satan by offering himself as a willing

4. For pity and wrath as "sciences," see James Rieger, "The Hem of Their Garments," p. 268, n. 18.

sacrifice—completes the action of the Bard's Song, bringing truth out of error.

The major error corrected by Milton's act is derived from his own epic, *Paradise Lost*. In *Paradise Lost*, the judgment falls on a Satan who in Milton's view is guilty and must be punished, but who in Blake's view is guilty and therefore cannot stand punishment. To act wrongly is to suffer; in the wrong action itself is pain and suffering. This suffering is proper to the actor—or rather the hinderer—who commits a wrong. Now to suffer not only the original wrong but also its consequences, to be made responsible for the infinite ramifications of that wrong, is to suffer an infinitely multiplied loss. In Blake's eyes, then, the judgment in *Paradise Lost* is vengeance, and the vengeful justice Satan suffers makes him in turn an accuser and a seeker of vengeance. In the Bard's Song, Satan at first seems (and thinks himself) innocent while he accuses others, but ends by revealing himself and creating his own hell; whereas in *Paradise Lost* it is the vengeful justice Satan suffers that creates hell and makes him an Accuser. In the Bard's Song, Satan is a "false tongue"; in *Paradise Lost* he is made to seem (in spite of Milton's intention) a Rintrah or reprobate, one of "those form'd to destruction" (8:34), condemned in the eyes of the angelic host.

Since in Blake's view Christ is a reprobate, Milton's Satan is for Blake uncomfortably (because imperfectly, unconsciously on Milton's part) close to Christ. Milton's Messiah, on the other hand, is elect, far above all taint of sin. (This is almost equally true of *Paradise Regained*, which centers on Satan's temptation of Christ.)[5] Lacking a genuine reprobate

5. Florence Sandler has a different view, stressing what Blake owes to *Paradise Regained*: "In choosing the episode of Christ's Temptation in the Wilderness to bear most of the weight of the regaining of paradise and in reducing to a minimum any reference to the Cross, Milton appeared to suggest that the legal and sacrificial connotations of Atonement were beside the point; Redemption consisted rather in the Hero's rigorous self-examination and the re-integration of his personality. . . . When, after the rounds of temptation in which Jesus and Satan have probed the nature of Sonship and the basis of their antagonism, the Son stands finally in apotheosis on the pinnacle of the temple . . . while Satan falls, it is clear that Milton's short epic is the source from which Blake derived the pattern of self-annihilation and apotheosis for his own poem, and that he paid Milton no more than his due in making him the Agonistes of the latter-day epic" ("The Iconoclastic Enterprise," pp. 31–32). To me it seems that Blake's Milton, once he has removed the Robe of Promise, is a less elect figure than the Christ of *Paradise*

or outcast figure who combines justified wrath and identification with the sinner, *Paradise Lost* lacks the interaction of justice and mercy that Blake calls "Eternal Forgiveness" (*Jerusalem* 88:49–50). This is to say that it lacks Christ, who attacks not the sinner but the error, progressively recreating error and separating it into its own place. Insofar as it is dominated by a God the Father, a Messiah, and a Satan who are all Accusers and therefore all satanic, *Paradise Lost* in Blake's view centers not on redemption but on vengeance, and it does so because Milton, instead of finding Satan in himself, has projected him. The result is a thorough confusion of identity.

The Bard's Song enables Milton to recover those projections and to deprive Satan of his power by unmasking the real Satan—the elect accuser—in himself.[6] Satan's fall into fury in the Bard's Song exposes what he would conceal and shows Milton that the "pity" of the elect is hatred or desire for vengeance. When Satan says, "I am God," when he creates seven deadly sins and a scroll of moral laws and punishments, saying "transgressors I will rend off for ever," with his "bosom" growing "Opake against the Divine Vision" and the abyss of Ulro opening in it, and when he accuses "The Divine Mercy, for protecting Palamabron" (9:25, 28, 31, 42/ E102–3/103), he plays in exaggerated style the role of Milton's God the Father. Rintrah, on the other hand, plays the role of Milton's reprobate Satan. This suggests to Milton that the Satan of *Paradise Lost*, insofar as he is of the reprobate, is Christ. The shift from names to classes—elect, redeemed, reprobate—reveals the crucial spiritual choice that decides one's real allegiance and prepares for the final confrontation of truth and error.

Regained—one whose triumph is less certain and whose Satan is more threatening because more a part of himself.

6. With Blake's view of Milton, compare Jung's view of the Yahweh of Job: "Satan . . . owns Yahweh's ear and is able to influence him. He is the only one who can pull the wool over his eyes, beguile him, and put him up to a massive violation of his own penal code. A formidable opponent indeed, and, because of his close kinship, so compromising that he must be concealed with the utmost discretion—even to the point of God's hiding him from his own consciousness in his own bosom! . . . Truly, Yahweh can do all things and permits himself all things without batting an eyelid. With brazen countenance he can project his shadow side and remain unconscious at man's expense" (Carl Jung, *Answer to Job,* trans. R. F. C. Hull, pp. 47–48,49).

If Los in the Bard's Song vacillates between pity and wrath, and if Enitharmon's space that protects Satan spoils a potentially decisive confrontation between him and Rintrah, Milton in *Paradise Lost* is too quick to accuse and cast out. Those who cast others out are the elect. Ending with the birth and crucifixion of Christ, the Bard's Song shows Milton that in *Paradise Lost* he had put Christ (and himself) among the elect and that he should have put Christ (and himself) among the reprobate: "He died as a Reprobate. he was Punish'd as a Transgressor! / Glory! Glory! Glory! to the Holy Lamb of God" (13:27–28/E106/107). The Bard's Song not only shows Milton that hell is self-created, but also reminds him that Satan's innumerable disguises are self-deceptions. And it shows him how much the wrath that pursues Satan into hell in *Paradise Lost* is satanic—not the justified wrath of the reprobate but the fury of a self-righteous Accuser:

> The Elect shall meet the Redeem'd. on Albions rocks they
>   shall meet
> Astonish'd at the Transgressor, in him beholding the Saviour.
> And the Elect shall say to the Redeemd. We behold it is of
>   Divine
> Mercy alone! of Free Gift and Election that we live.
> Our Virtues & Cruel Goodnesses, have deserv'd Eternal
>   Death. (13:30–34/E106/107)

Later in the poem, Milton announces, "I have turned my back upon these Heavens builded on cruelty" (32:3/E130/131). Milton throws off his elect robe of promise and descends to earth because, acting the part of God, he has done man (himelf) wrong. He has identified himself with the Selfhood rather than with Christ and done violence to his own humanity.

*   *   *

Satan's relations with Leutha in the Bard's Song show much the same elect self-division and impulse to cast out, presented now as erotic division. Leutha is Satan's separated Emanation, and her story is the feminine mirroring of the earlier tale—its pity as distinct from its rage. It shows the fallen world as a feminine world of death clothed or softened by pity. (The birth of Jesus, which that pity unconsciously

prepared for, is of course outside the purview of Leutha's
story.) Leutha has aspects of both the Sin and Eve of *Paradise
Lost,* and Satan in her story often merges into Adam. Leutha's confession of sin is misplaced pity and delusive love:
half Satan's love for himself speaking through Leutha, half
Leutha's offering herself as a sacrifice in order to save Satan.
(This offer is purified of error in Milton's and Ololon's later
self-annihilation.) But according to Leutha in the Bard's
Song, Satan casts even that impulse out as Sin. Here Leutha's words have the ring of truth:

> in selfish holiness demanding purity
> Being most impure, self-condemn'd to eternal tears, he drove
> Me from his inmost Brain & the doors clos'd with thunders
> sound
>
> . . . .
>
> I humbly bow in all my Sin before the Throne Divine.
> Not so the Sick-one; Alas what shall be done him to restore?
> Who calls the Individual Law, Holy: and despises the Saviour.
> Glorying to involve Albions Body in fires of eternal War.
> (12:46–48;13:3–6/E105/106)

The Eve and Adam of *Paradise Lost* 9 and 10 are here
merged with Sin and Satan, giving us an inclusive "State"
Satan, which embodies Milton's effect on English culture.
Puritan England calls the Emanation "Sin," thus denying
sexuality, the arts, and the powers and fruits of the individual
imagination and fostering warfare. Milton is an unwitting
cause of this denial; according to Rintrah and Palamabron,
the daughters of Los "weave a new Religion from new Jealousy of Theotormon! / Miltons Religion is the cause: there is
no end to destruction!" (22:38–39/E116/117). Milton accepts
the imputation of error or responsibility in the Bard's Song
and responds immediately to the threat to his eternal
salvation:

> I will go down to self annihilation and eternal death,
> Lest the Last Judgment come & find me unannihilate
> And I be siez'd & giv'n into the hands of my own Selfhood.
> (14:22–24/E107/108)

The implication of the Bard's Song is that Milton has saved
only "himself"—the elect or self-righteous Milton. Others

remain in jeopardy, and Milton's work remains unfinished: "What do I here before the Judgment? without my Emanation?" (14:28/E107/108), with the daughters of memory (memory is of the self) and not with the daughters of inspiration. Instead of being true to his own intention of writing a *Christian* epic, Milton has followed the classical Muses who inspired an epic about Priam's war; he has ended by glorifying war.

As often in Blake's poetry, imagination miscarries because of an internal division between reason and imagination that leaves a Spectre pursuing a separated Emanation. Milton has "turn'd [his] back upon these Heavens builded on cruelty," but

> My Spectre still wandering thro' them follows my Emanation
> He hunts her footsteps thro' the snow & the wintry hail
>   & rain
> The idiot Reasoner laughs at the Man of Imagination
> And from laughter proceeds to murder by undervaluing
>   calumny. (32:4–7/E130/131)

The Spectre here is the "idiot Reasoner," tracking down and murdering the Emanation that is the creation of the "Man of Imagination." And both Spectre and Emanation are Milton's, so that the conflict between "idiot Reasoner" and "Man of Imagination" is a conflict within the poet himself. If the "new Religion" woven by the daughters of Los is perverse, Milton comes to see that the cause is his own self-division, by which Man and Emanation have become Spectre and Shadow, the one erotically pursuing the other.

All of this is highly instructive to Milton because figures in the Bard's Song are treated symbolically, as psychological forces in the poet (Los) himself: the major figures are Los's offspring and their Emanations. Milton sees that he had put himself into *Paradise Lost* unconsciously and that he should have put himself into it consciously—as Blake, following his own implied advice, puts himself into his poem *Milton* as visionary witness. He sees that the effect of Satan's doings in the Bard's Song is to divide wrath from pity and set them at odds, in Rintrah and Palamabron, while Satan himself seems to be outside or above the struggle. He sees that this is what he himself did in *Paradise Lost*: *that* Milton, then, is Satan, and Milton sets out to overcome the Satan in himself.[7] "I in my Selfhood am that Satan: I am that Evil One!" (14:30/ E107/108).

Milton's struggle with the Spectre, Urizen or Satan, is accompanied by his redemption of his Emanation, Ololon. As W. J. T. Mitchell points out, Ololon is the host of the elect who had thrust Milton's "real and immortal Self" out of heaven like the Satan of *Paradise Lost*.[8] Converted to the redeemed, they have followed Milton from heaven to earth. Compared to Milton's struggle with Urizen, then, his redemption of Ololon is no struggle at all. Ololon is searching for Milton, as he for her, and her tracking Milton's course through chaos (pl. 34) reverses Milton's Spectre's pursuit of his separated Emanation through the snow (pl. 32). Thus, Milton's reintegration with Ololon perfects the relation between Satan and Leutha in the Bard's Song, where the Emanation is rejected as sin, and completes the Eros plot in *Milton*. It also reverses Milton's understanding of Sin in *Paradise Lost*.[9] Ololon's confession of sin late in *Milton* is the coun-

7. For a similar view, see Edward J. Rose: "Milton passed through the state of the youthful republican rebel (Orc) into the state of the Cromwellian censor (Urizen), so that when writing *Paradise Lost* he draws Lucifer in the image of Orc as he does Jehovah in the image of Urizen. Milton must return and become one again with Los in order to cast his selfhood into the lake. In order to do that he appears as Urizen in Los's world, that is, Rintrah or prophetic wrath. . . . The Jehovah of *Paradise Lost* is God from a Urizenic point of view. . . . Because Milton enters the State of Satan, a new state called 'Eternal Annihilation' (M 32:21–22) must be created and it is *Milton*, a new category of metaphor in which Milton becomes one with the inspired Bard, Los and Blake" ("Blake's Metaphorical States," p. 30).

8. "Blake's Radical Comedy," p. 285.

9. Compare the parallel or analogous event in Jung's *Answer to Job*: Yahweh "has remembered a feminine being who is no less agreeable to him than to man, a friend and playmate from the beginning of the world, the first-born of all God's creatures, a stainless reflection of his glory and a master workman, nearer and dearer to his heart than the late descendants of the protoplast, the original man, who was but a secondary product stamped in his image. There must be some dire necessity responsible for this anamnesis of Sophia: things simply could not go on as before, the 'Just' God could not go on committing injustices and the 'Omniscient' could not behave any longer as a . . . thoughtless human being. Self-reflection becomes an imperative necessity, and for this Wisdom is needed" (p. 63). Blake's "Emanation" is Jung's "self-reflection," and Ololon—and Jerusalem—is very close to Sophia, or Wisdom.

terpart of Leutha's, but clearer, no longer deluded, because she realizes that she is Milton's "Feminine portion." The confession, that is, is Milton's own, and it is a confession not of sin but of error. Milton sees that he has furthered religious error rather than eradicated it:

> Are those who contemn Religion & seek to annihilate it
> Become in their Feminine portions the causes & promoters
> Of these Religions . . . ? (40:9 –11/E140/141)

Since Milton's returning to earthly life or the "sepulcher" is an entering into his own Shadow (the fallen aspect of his Emanation), he is surrounded (or at least his "Mortal" and "redeem'd" parts are surrounded) by a separated and fallen "imaginative world" of his own making, by a "Female Space." ("Imaginative world" is one of Frye's definitions of Emanation.) Milton's wrestling with his Selfhood, the satanic "Reasoning Power" that inhabits his Shadow, has the effect of recalling his Emanation, Ololon. In Book II, Ololon is redeemed, re-enters Milton, and is contained in him as the regenerate community of which he is the seed. The poet lives again in his work, and the prophet is reunited with an awakened people. From this point of view, the action of *Milton* is the final separation of Shadow from Emanation, or error from truth, in Milton's work. Taken again into the man after the annihilation of his Selfhood, his Emanation becomes an expression of his vision and his love purified of his need or jealousy or fear, so that Milton stands identified.

Throughout *Milton*, Ololon has symbolized Milton's created world insofar as it is good. At the end of the poem the remaining sexual or jealous element is removed from that love. With the sexual separated from the human, Ololon becomes the divine community—she becomes a figure like Sophia or Wisdom or Jerusalem—and the confrontation that leads to apocalypse has been prepared. Like all the crucial acts of *Milton*, the marriage of Milton and Ololon is essentially a recognition and a division of truth from error. It occurs in the same time or pulsation of an artery as Milton's final breaking of the chain of vengeance and corporeal warfare by refusing to annihilate Satan. The two acts together are the triumph of identity over the satanic Selfhood.

The Mental Fight in *Milton* is Milton's struggle with the Spectre and the separated Emanation, both of whom, like Satan and Eve, are fallen aspects of himself. These three figures may be assimilated to the three classes of elect, redeemed, and reprobate. The separated Emanation may ally herself with the Spectre, the elect who casts the reprobate (the man) out of paradise. Or she may return to the man, becoming redeemed. (The Eve of *Paradise Lost* allies herself first with Satan, then with Adam.) The Milton and Ololon who are in heaven at the beginning of *Milton* have, so to speak, cast the Satan of *Paradise Lost* into hell. They are elect, Satan reprobate, and the division between them is the apparently absolute division between heaven and hell. But Milton mistakes himself as elect. He is reprobate like the Milton of *The Marriage of Heaven and Hell*, who is of the Devil's party without knowing it. Awakened by the Bard's Song, he throws off the Robe of Promise, becomes redeemed, and as reprobate annihilates his satanic Selfhood and redeems his Emanation—who, as the elect, having first driven him from heaven, later follows his example.

The three classes of reprobate, elect, and redeemed are—like Man, Spectre, and Emanation—related dynamically as elements of identity, and their relations dominate *Milton* from the very beginning.[10] As Rintrah, Palamabron, and Satan are elements of Los, so, evidently, every man has these possible elements or characters in him. One character or the other predominates, so that the man is in the class of reprobate, redeemed, or elect. But since class is not identity, it may be changed, as Milton himself is converted from elect to redeemed and finally to reprobate by the Bard's Song and by his own struggle with Urizen-Satan. Especially during Milton's wrestling with Urizen, Blake insists that Milton contains within himself all three possibilities:

> Silent Milton stood before
> The darkend Urizen; as the sculptor silent stands before

10. "The major principle of unity in *Milton*, and a major element in the neo-Christian provision Blake worked out for man's salvation, is the conversion of sets of twos (apparent opposites) into threes (genuine contraries separated from an unreal negation). . . . All forms of duality have to be meticulously subdivided into Three Classes, two contraries and an excluded negation" (Mary Lynn Johnson, "'Separating What Has Been Mixed,'" p. 11).

His forming image; he walks round it patient labouring.
Thus Milton stood forming bright Urizen, while his
    Mortal part
Sat frozen in the rock of Horeb: and his Redeemed portion,
Thus form'd the Clay of Urizen; but within that portion
His real Human walkd above in power and majesty
Tho darkened; and the Seven Angels of the Presence attended
    him. (20:7–14/E113/114)

The Urizen that Milton the sculptor works on is Milton's own "Mortal part," frozen into the rock Horeb, the elect Milton, the God of *Paradise Lost*. "Forming bright Urizen" is a restoring of the accusing figure of *Paradise Lost* into a redemptive figure. The Milton who acts as sculptor (as Los), forming red clay on Urizen's bones, giving Urizen life while Urizen gives him death, is the redeemed Milton. "Within" the redeemed Milton, his "real Human" walks above. That the "real Human" is both within and above may suggest not only a third, reprobate Milton, but also the figure that contains the others in the fourfold vision of Christ. As the redeemed Milton is between the elect "Mortal part" outside and the "real Human" within and above, so Los, as long as he is between Satan and Rintrah, unable to choose, confused and tormented by Satan, is also in the class of the redeemed. Los ceases to be Palamabron, the redeemed, and becomes Rintrah when Milton faces Satan and refuses to annihilate him only to become "a greater in [his] place," to be a "covering" for Satan to do his will. But unlike the Milton of *Paradise Lost*, Blake's Milton is a genuine Rintrah, facing an unmasked Satan.

*   *   *

The poem *Milton* is from one point of view a watching of Milton's progress through Ulro and Urizen's chaos to Los's universe, built in the center. Through a change of perspective, we see Milton's journey focus on the increasingly minute and local, and on what is closer and closer to the self. The climax of this development is Milton's unmasking of Satan in his last and most deceptive disguise—the very Selfhood that would "smite" Satan and, in doing so, become his new abode. In this change, Milton ceases to be elect and regains his authentic status as reprobate. Milton's progress is observed by Blake, and the action comes increasingly close to the inner Blake as it does to Milton. As Milton regains the identity that had been overwhelmed by the Selfhood, Blake as man is identified as the poet-prophet. But he retains his local and particular identity as Blake.

When Milton enters Blake's foot just before the midpoint of the poem, Blake sees into the "nether regions of the Imagination, / In Ulro beneath Beulah" (21:6–7/E114/115). But he does not see into Los's universe. He sees Urizen opposing Milton's journey toward the world of Los and Enitharmon and Milton silently striving with Urizen in the chaotic world of Urizen near the borders of the Mundane Shell. (In Blake's diagram of Milton's track, Milton enters where the worlds of Luvah and Urizen overlap, passes close by Satan, the limit of opacity, in Urizen's world, and ends at Adam, the limit of contraction, in Urthona's world. Satan and Adam are shown as opposed poles or foci within the Mundane Egg. Milton's ending at Adam suggests his ending in regenerated man, as a regenerate Urizen, and at the same time ending in Blake's garden as a figure of "normal" size, since he has reached the limit of contraction.) Milton's struggle with Urizen has the effect of regenerating Blake and assimilating Blake (and Milton) to Los, so that Blake can then see into Los's universe. Thus, the end of Book I—the center of the poem—is a visionary account of Los's universe, built in the center, and this is the universe of the remainder of the poem. Urizen's universe is that of the prophet whose message has been abstracted into rigid law. Los's universe is that of the prophet of mercy and of Poetic Genius, showing the present action of creative vision, a new seeing. Milton's second meeting with Satan (the meetings are actually simultaneous) takes place in Los's universe, and Milton's words to Satan express this new seeing and the identity that has been regained.

Throughout, Milton confronts Milton. In Book I, Milton divides into the sculptor Milton and the stony Milton, who is both the skeletal Urizen and Milton's "mortal part" as a rock in Horeb. In Book II, Milton's "Human Shadow" divides into human (reprobate) and Shadow (Milton's elect portion,

Satan). When Milton in Book I meets Urizen-Satan, a fallen dying part of the human form, he restores him to human form, identifies him. Driven out of Urizen, the Spectre of Satan—which cannot be humanized—is forced in Book II to take on a clearer and more furiously threatening form and insists that he is God. But Satan's fury masks the fact that he is tempting Milton's Selfhood to annihilate him, and thus to become his "covering." Again, Milton confronts Milton in a distorting mirror, a Satan whose every act responds to and mimics Milton's, confusing identity. Milton in black, severe and silent, evokes the Spectre of Satan, a twenty-seven-fold mighty demon. Milton speaking evokes Satan as the God of Apocalypse, "Coming in a cloud, with trumpets & flaming fire / Saying I am God the judge of all . . . / Fall therefore down & worship me" (38:50–52/E138/139). Satan's reference to the seven angels ("Seven Angels bear my Name & in those Seven I appear" [38:55/E140/140]) evokes the "Starry Seven" around Milton. They speak, and their illumination of Milton's path causes Milton's "Human" self to be no longer "darkend." Since the Milton who finally speaks ("I know my power thee to annihilate") is the Milton who has merged with Blake and Los and thus gained strength, what he tells Satan terrifies him and makes him muster all his terrors to masquerade as the God of Apocalypse and to consolidate: "Till All Things become One Great Satan" (39:1/E139/140). The final identifying struggle has been prepared.

In the first meeting between Satan and Milton, we follow Milton into a landscape essentially biblical. The struggle is on earth, earthly. The opponent, Milton's "mortal part," is stony skeleton and rock, and the struggle takes place in time frozen into the past: the world of Milton's poetry insofar as it repeats the Old Testament Law, especially the Ten Commandments. In the second meeting, we follow the cloud redounding from Blake's foot over Europe. The struggle is in air, and Satan appears as Prince of Air. Here the opponent is Milton's elect portion, his external shadow, inhabited by Satan. This is the world that Blake's contemporaries would call the present—Blake's Felpham garden, the English coast, and Europe—and the shadow is the fallen aspect of Milton's contemporary influence. In this contemporary perspective,

Milton's historical aspect—the severe and silent Puritan, dressed in black—comes into prominence. In Books I and II, Milton is traveling through the Seven Eyes of God or the twenty-seven churches of Beulah toward contemporary history, toward the time and place in which Blake is writing, and Blake's garden is the center and present he arrives at in Book II. Here Milton and Blake are identified as Los, as the community of man acting through the poet-prophet.

In the first confrontation, Milton meets the satanic in his own works, especially as they impose a frozen and tyrannical law. The struggle with Urizen is an attempt to remake Milton's poetry and to change Moses, the prophet as law-giver, into Christ—to change Old Testament Law into New Testament mercy. The struggle is to make the intellect anew or to humanize it. Since the hills and mountains of the biblical landscape of Book I are made up of Milton's own body (Sinai) and those of his sixfold Emanation, it is his own body as well as the body of his work that Milton strives to make human. It is also Blake's body; and the Urizen Milton struggles with is Blake's as well as his own. In the midst of the wrestling Blake breaks in in his own voice:

> O how can I with my gross tongue that cleaveth to the dust,
> Tell of the Four-fold Man, in starry numbers fitly orderd
> Or how can I with my cold hand of clay! But thou O Lord
> Do with me as thou wilt! for I am nothing, and vanity.
> If thou chuse to elect a worm, it shall remove the mountains.
>   (20:15–19/E113/114)

Blake's "gross tongue" reflects the silence of the Urizen-Milton struggle, and his "cold hand of clay" gives him characteristics of both Milton and Urizen, so that he seems a Urizen halfway brought to life or redeemed, thus halfway between Urizen and the sculptor Milton. Milton as regenerator or awakener is forming the body of a new prophet, Blake, and the work is completed when Los and Blake and Milton are identified.

Simultaneously, as we see in Book II, Milton is trying to awaken Albion. It becomes increasingly clear that the figures in *Milton* are both particular and universal. In Book II, Milton is both a black cloud "redounding over" Europe and the figures (Milton and Satan) struggling over the sleeping Albion. Albion himself is a landscape-body in which Milton and Blake participate so deeply that they are almost identical with it. Earlier, when Milton descends, "Feeling the electric flame of Miltons awful precipitate descent," "Albions sleeping Humanity" begins to stir (20:25–26/E113/114). What Milton does, all men do in him. Similarly, what Blake sees in the nether regions of imagination, in Ulro, all men see. Both Milton and Blake are both human figures and worlds. When Albion tries to awaken (pl. 39), it is the sleeping humanity of every man that tries to awaken, and when Albion stirs, Blake and Milton and Los are the stirring force awakening in him. Insofar as Blake and Milton are asleep, or mortal, they are Albion. Insofar as they are awakened conscience and will, they are Los—man identified. Identity is the community of men acting through the individual man to create a human world.

The effect of *Milton* is to confirm Blake and Milton as prophets, Blake in the line of Milton, both contained in Los. Since the Bard takes refuge in Milton's bosom after he has finished his song, and since Milton descends to and enters Blake, the implication is that the prophetic poet is one figure made of many, and that Milton needs Blake's help if he is to be heard. At the same time, *Milton* is Blake's own calling as poet-prophet and Blake's own wrestling with Satan, presented through Milton. When the virgin Ololon appears to Blake as an angel of God might appear, Blake—the poet as imperfect and suffering man—asks

> What am I now to do
> Is it again to plunge into deeper affliction? behold me
> Ready to obey, but pity thou My Shadow of Delight.
>   (36:29–31/E136/137)

Ololon seeks Milton, but since Milton has entered Blake's left foot, when Ololon says,

> Are those who contemn Religion & seek to annihilate it
> Become in their Feminine portions the causes & promoters
> Of these Religions (40:9–11/E140/141),

the warning is directed at Blake as much as at Milton.

The combined sublimity and lyricism of *Milton* is largely in its making man infinitely greater without ceasing to see him as a "Minute Particular," and at the same time centering all of time and history in a single act, so that time and space no longer contain but are contained. Milton is both a twenty-seven-fold shadow reaching from earth to heaven and the human and unenlarged form that descends into Blake's garden. And when Blake and Milton are assimilated to Los, and Blake binds on this vegetable world as a sandal to walk forward through eternity, we see that "more extensive / Than any other earthly things, are Mans earthly lineaments" (21:11/ E114/115). But if the action of *Milton* is to make Blake, Milton, and Los one figure, at the end it returns Blake to his mortal body, so that we finally see the poem as an instantaneous act of vision.

When Blake midway in the poem becomes "One Man with [Los] arising in my strength" (22:12/E116/117), he is given both an immense power of vision and an immense burden of responsibility. In Los, Blake sees that every moment of time is eternally present and that every act is eternally significant: "for not one Moment / Of Time is lost, nor one Event of Space unpermanent" (22:18–19/E116/117), though on earth "all things vanish & are seen no more / They vanish not from me & mine, we guard them first & last" (22:22–23/E116/117). Having begun by speaking of "my Brain, where . . . / The Eternal Great Humanity Divine. planted his Paradise" (2:7–8/ E95/96), Blake is left at the end of the poem, like Coleridge's Ancient Mariner, struck by a terrible beauty. When the four Zoas sound their trumpets,

> Terror struck in the Vale I stood at that immortal sound
> My bones trembled. I fell outstretchd upon the path
> A moment, & my Soul returnd into its mortal state
> To Resurrection & Judgment in the Vegetable Body
> And my sweet Shadow of Delight stood trembling by my
>   side. (42:24–28/E142/143)

This return from the greater man, from Los as "combinations of individuals" to the single man, the historical Blake and his wife, is the final crucial event in *Milton*.[11] It unob-

---

11. Compare Susan Fox: "As Ololon came into the garden to join Milton,

trusively relates poem to poet and attaches timeless vision to the concrete particulars of his historical time and place. The effect is not only to put off the vision of apocalypse but to redeem time, to show eternity *in* time by showing us that "Eternity is in love with the productions of time," as Blake puts it in the "Proverbs of Hell."

*   *   *

As the fall in the Bard's Song is Los's fall in that it is a division of his family, so the recovery in the remainder of the poem is Los's recovery. That recovery is reflected in the world built in the center of the fallen creation. Los's universe is a turning back to the primitive world in which "the ancient Poets animated all sensible objects," the world of Poetic Genius, full of responsiveness to human desire. Like Wordsworth's natural world, it is potentially a human community. Seen from this point of view, the action of the poem, beginning with Milton's wrestling Urizen on the banks of the Arnon, is making the desert flower. Los's world has its own kind of Natural Religion—not religion naturalized, but nature made visionary—the speaking creation that utters the glory of God in the Psalms and Proverbs and Sirach. Los's world in *Milton* is moral, sensuous, visionary, and "common" all at the same time, expressing the whole self, and Los as the awakening human identity comes more and more to contain both the world and the actors in it. What is peculiarly Romantic is not so much the correspondence of man and world as the richness and inexhaustible potentiality of their relationship. Since Los's world is one in which all human forms are on the verge of being identified, Blake's account of that world is an account of emerging identity—identity concealed, yet revealed to the awakened eye and ear. The beauty

Catherine has come to join Blake: they are the embodiments in Generation of the union that is the action of *Milton.* Book I presents us with the cosmic, mythic dimensions of that union; for its purpose, Blake was himself a mythic figure who strode toward eternity with all Generation on his foot; he was the herald of inspiration taking part in the drama of apocalypse. Book II presents us with the individual, human dimensions of the union; for its purpose, Blake is a single human being with a sick wife and a modest garden" (*Poetic Form in "Milton,"* pp. 188–89).

of Los's world comes from its concealment-revelation of human energy and desire.

Against the merely "Natural power" that "continually . . . tends to Destruction," *Milton* is especially an effort to humanize nature. Against Satan and "Natures cruel holiness," Blake pits Los and Los's universe. Since Los knows that he is fallen and imperfect, he does not assert holiness. Instead, he labors ceaselessly toward human form, his workmen "All the Gods of the Kingdoms of Earth . . . / Every one a fallen Son of the Spirit of Prophecy" (24:74–75/E120/121). The work of Los and his sons is a "putting off the Indefinite" by setting "bounds" to the "Infinite" (28:4/E124/125), a focusing of what is scattered and separating of what is mixed, drawing every "scattered Atom / Of Human Intellect . . . from Animal & Vegetable & Mineral" (25:18–19, 21/E120/121), identifying the world as human. The Sons of Los give form to spectrous souls that are mere "Passions & Desires / With neither lineament nor form" (26:26–27) and reveal the paradisal "inward form" that Satan has blocked out from men's senses:

> And every Generated Body in its inward form,
> Is a garden of delight & a building of magnificence,
> Built by the Sons of Los. (26:31–33/E122/123)

Reversing the Newtonian cosmic perspective that dwarfs man, Blake shows Los's world as a single family or household. The "unwearied Sun" is created by Los "To measure Time and Space to mortal Men. every morning" (29:23–24/E126/127), and Blake insists on the human dimensions of the universe:

> The Sky is an immortal Tent built by the Sons of Los
> And every Space that a Man views around his dwelling-place:
> Standing on his own roof, or in his garden . . .
> . . . such space is his Universe (29:4–7/E126/127),

so that when a man moves, "all his neighbourhood bewail his loss" (29:13/E126/127).

From the perspective of Beulah, eternity is concealed in the infinitely small:

> Every Time less than a pulsation of the artery
> Is equal in its period & value to Six Thousand Years.

> For in this Period the Poets Work is Done: and all the Great
> Events of Time start forth & are concievd in such a Period
> Within a Moment: a Pulsation of the Artery. (28:62–63;29:1–
> 3/E126/127)

Communication between time and eternity, earth and Eden, takes place only in a chosen moment: "There is a Moment in each Day that Satan cannot find" (35:42/E135/136). In this moment Ololon descends to Los and Enitharmon, arriving in Blake's garden. And in this moment that Satan cannot find, a fountain gives rise to two streams:

> Just in this Moment when the morning odours rise abroad
> And first from the Wild Thyme, stands a Fountain in a rock
> Of crystal flowing into two Streams. (35:48–50/E135/136)

One stream is time as recurrent cycle; the other is time opening into eternity. The fountain in Golgonooza is time as a perpetual beginning, and Golgonooza in Beulah faces one way on eternity or Eden, the other way on time, which may be Beulah or Ulro. The moment is made equal to eternity on the one hand, and to the cycles of time on the other. And it can "face" either way—either to Eden, or through the twenty-seven churches of time, the "aerial void," back to Golgonooza.

In Los's world, the poet-prophet's world, every space larger than a globule of blood is "visionary"—part of Los's creation, created by Los's hammer, embodying Los's vision of eternity. "Every Space smaller than a Globule of Mans blood. opens / Into Eternity" (29:21–22/E126/127), as does the odor of the center of a flower: "within that Center Eternity expands / Its ever during doors, that Og & Anak fiercely guard" (31:48–49/E130/131). Here *Milton* comes close to "Auguries of Innocence," but the universe of "Auguries" is moral-intellectual rather than lyrical or "Beulah," and its innocence is radically joined to wrath. In *Milton* Blake identifies God in the world of the transformed and minutely focused senses as much as in moral intellect or vision: "Seek not thy heavenly father then beyond the skies: / There Chaos dwells & ancient Night & Og & Anak old" (20:32–33/E113/114). The way to eternity seems barred by Og and Anak in both the flower and the remote heavens. But the flower is a visible

symbol of eternity on a human scale, while heaven beyond
the sky is a remote outer void or chaos. In the center of a
flower there is a window on eternity, a vortex of vision in a
"Minute Particular," which identifies the world as human in
scale and beauty by condensing time-space into a single
"Particular." "Minute" refers to time as much as to space.[12]

In *Milton* as in *Jerusalem* or "Auguries of Innocence," one
feels the gap between image and what it represents in intellect or spirit. One feels it especially in Blake's spatial images—Golgonooza, Los's eastern wall, western wall, the
gates of the body, and so on—and in the images that dissolve
time into space and space into time. Such images are often
very concrete but not visualizable or "sensable" as a *whole*.
One strains to visualize them nevertheless. The effect is of
fallen sense experience being intensified to a point at which
it is about to overcome its limits and to reveal the world as
human. One of the secrets of Blake's energy is the pulsation
of his vision between the minutely particular or the personal
and the universal, treating time and space as illusory, re-
imagining the structure of the universe by seeing it again as
human life.

Thus it is not until very late in the poem that Albion, who
has been sleeping in "the Night of Beulah," stirs but is unable
to rise:

> Then Albion rose up in the Night of Beulah on his Couch
> Of dread repose seen by the visionary eye; his face is toward
> The east, toward Jerusalems Gates: groaning he sat above
> His rocks. London & Bath & Legions & Edinburgh
> Are the four pillars of his Throne; his left foot near London
> Covers the shades of Tyburn: his instep from Windsor
> To Primrose Hill stretching to Highgate & Holloway
> London is between his knees. (39:32–39/E139/140–41)

We are reminded that Albion contains the action of the poem,
and Albion's creature sleep of history begins to give way
before a myth of reawakened powers. The vision by which
Blake, more radically than any other Romantic poet, assimilates landscape and city to the human body begins to fall into
place, but the identity of man and world is never quite real-

---

12. As Edward J. Rose says, the word *minute* contains "a . . . subtle en-
tendre: mi-*nute* is also *mi*-nute" ("Los, Pilgrim of Eternity," p. 96).

ized in *Milton*. Though Albion strives "to rise to walk into the Deep" (39:50/E140/141), his strength fails, and he sinks down "upon his Couch / In moony Beulah," while "Los his strong guard walks round beneath the Moon" (29:51–52/E140/141).

Blake's vision ends in the marriage of Milton and Ololon and in the conversion of "the Starry Eight," the eight eyes of history, into "One Man Jesus the Saviour," who comes clothed in the "clouds of Ololon," a garment woven in letters that are "the Divine Revelation in the Litteral expression." It is a "Garment of War . . . the Woof of Six Thousand Years" (42:14–15/E142/143). What remains to be done is to put off the garment of six-thousand-years' history. Jesus comes to put an end to fallen rage or warfare, but Blake reserves that act for *Jerusalem*. *Milton* ends in suspended time. With Los listening "to the Cry of the Poor Man: his Cloud / Over London in volume terrific, low bended in anger" (42:34–35/E142/144), *Milton* ends in expectation of "the Great Harvest & Vintage of the Nations" (43:1, the last line of the poem [E143/144]), and points toward Blake's more thorough engagement of the world's error in *Jerusalem*. [13]

In *Jerusalem* the struggle of self-annihilation—the struggle with both Spectre and Shadow—proves to be enormously more complicated, confused, and difficult than it is in *Milton*. This is to say that *Jerusalem* is a poem of extremes, of Ulro and Eden, and that *Milton* is a poem of Beulah. *Jerusalem* is apocalyptic, *Milton* redemptive. In *Milton*, Blake at his Felpham cottage in Beulah has glimpses of Eden:

> As the breath of the Almighty. such are the words of man to man
> In the great Wars of Eternity, in fury of Poetic Inspiration,
> To build the Universe stupendous: Mental forms Creating.
> (30:18–20/E128/129)

But *Milton* confirms Blake's determination not to "cease from Mental Fight" until he has built Jerusalem in England. Thus, although Blake at the end of *Milton* has fallen outstretched upon the path and returned to his mortal state, his "real Human" nevertheless seems still to be walking forward through eternity. In *Milton*, Blake is identified.

13. Since "the Great Harvest & Vintage" takes place in the Night IX of *The Four Zoas*, it is tempting to read the Night IX after *Milton*, but *Milton* has of course progressed beyond *The Four Zoas*.

7

Jerusalem

As in *The Four Zoas* and *Milton,* Los in *Jerusalem* is the remnant of identity, the active agent, and the champion of mankind.[1] Unlike *The Four Zoas,* however, where Blake's vision grows and changes as he writes the poem, *Jerusalem* implies the whole of his vision from the start, but presents it in fragments or flashes. *Jerusalem* is organized like a more fragmented *Milton*—not by time but in a timeless pattern and contest of extremes. Albion and Los, Satan and the Divine Vision, Vala and Jerusalem, are present from the beginning, as the extremes of sleep and wakefulness, anti-identity and identity, whose contest moves the action of the poem. Identity is defined in large part by its opposite, the height of human possibility by its nadir, with the whole struggle contained in the figure of Albion and its progress revealed in his Emanation Jerusalem, the dispersed or outcast community of mankind.

"Jerusalem in every man" is the "peculiar light" by which the "particular Form," the Divine Vision, is identified (*Jerusalem* 54:1–3/E201/203). Jerusalem is one seen as many, the family of which Jesus is the universal form. But most of *Jerusalem* is about the divisions and disguises of human identity in time—"Reason Dividing Families in Cruelty & Pride!" (57:11/ E205/207). In time, the person no longer is his world; the community of man is divided; and the open bosom of eter-

1. I must express at the outset a general debt not only to Northrop Frye and David V. Erdman, to whom all present-day writers on Blake are indebted, but to Harold Bloom, both in *Blake's Apocalypse* and in his commentary to Erdman's edition of Blake. Martha England's conversation about *Jerusalem* has been an informing delight.

For other accounts of *Jerusalem,* see Karl Kiralis, "The Theme and Structure of William Blake's *Jerusalem*"; Edward J. Rose, "The Structure of Blake's *Jerusalem*"; Stuart Curran, "The Structures of *Jerusalem*"; Anne Kostelanetz Mellor, *Blake's Human Form Divine,* chap. 8; Christine Gallant, *Blake and the Assimilation of Chaos;* and W. J. T. Mitchell, *Blake's Composite Art.*

nity is closed off. Jerusalem is separated from Albion and becomes a nebulous form, seen at an immense distance, cast out among "Starry Wheels." For fallen man, absorbed in his nightmare of division and death, community no longer exists. Disorganized and separated from her prophets, Jerusalem is tempted to turn her back on the Divine Vision, as Albion does. But when Albion rejects error and brings time to an end by turning again to the Divine Vision, Jerusalem comes into organized existence, and the poem ends. Identity for Blake, then, is a dynamic plot rather than a static theme because of the fall. It can be adequately treated only in its full range: the extremes of Christ and Satan, Jerusalem and Babylon, Eden and Ulro. *Jerusalem* is the only poem of Blake's which presents these extremes fully.

Albion looms larger and is more continuously present in *Jerusalem* than he is in *Milton,* as befits the greater completeness of *Jerusalem's* plot. Once the "Angel of the Presence" (43:7) and the "Image of God surrounded by the Four Zoas" (42:23/E187/189), Albion is described in "A Vision of the Last Judgment" as "our Ancestor patriarch of the Atlantic Continent whose History Preceded that of the Hebrews & in whose Sleep or Chaos Creation began" (p. 80/E548/558). The classical paganism of *The Four Zoas* is largely absent from *Jerusalem,* largely because "your Greek Philosophy . . . is a remnant of Druidism" (52/E198/200), and Blake wants to go to the root of the error in his own nation. He wants to focus on Albion as the local place and personal source of error, as "the Parent of the Druids" (27/E170/171) who fell into error. Satan appears often as "the Druid Spectre of Albion," and in *Jerusalem* "the Tree of Good & Evil [springs] from the Rocky Circle and Snake / Of the Druid" (92:25–26/E250/253). (The "snake" is less prominent in *Jerusalem* than in *The Four Zoas,* sometimes replaced by "Mortal Worm" as what Satan has shrunk the human form into.) Furthermore, Blake wants to derive Abraham and Israel from Albion's fall, and the religion of the Jews from Jesus. He wants to stand accepted history on its head and affirm not only that "Ye are united O ye Inhabitants of Earth in One Religion. The Religion of Jesus," but also that it is "the most Ancient, the Eternal: & the Everlasting Gospel" (27/E169/171).

Since Albion contains not only the English but also the Jews and *all* nations, it is in Albion that Israel—and the Deists and Christians—may "Return" and "Take up the Cross . . . & follow Jesus" (27/E172/174). *Jerusalem* is the vision of a single man's conversion: it is the struggle for Albion's soul, and it is in him that all men undergo a Last Judgment.[2] If Satan's "first victory" "in Offerings of Human Life" (27:28, 32/E170/172) was won on Tyburn's brook and Tyburn's tree, it is in Albion and in London—and in Blake—that Mental Fight and Mental Sacrifice and the forgiveness of sin must contend against their opposites, and the "bright Preacher of Life" must overcome the "dark Preacher of Death" (77:19, 22/ E230/232). Summing up all human experience (in the two poles of England and Israel), yet capable of being imaged or represented in any of the figures he contains, Albion is the giant form in whom mankind and each man pass from "death" to "awaking": "Of the Sleep of Ulro! and of the passage through / Eternal Death! and of the awaking to Eternal Life" (4:1–2/E145/146). The sleep of Ulro is disbelief. From this point of view, the plot of *Jerusalem* is a descent into disbelief followed by a turn to belief: the passage through "Eternal Death" to "Eternal Life." As in *Milton*, the death that leads to life is the willing sacrifice of one's self for another. But until almost the end of the poem, Albion's passage through death is involuntary rather than voluntary, a sleep rather than a waking.

Albion's fall consists of a division and "diaspora" in which his Emanation and his children and the sun and stars are cast out or flee from him: "'But now the Starry Heavens are fled from [Albion's] limbs'" (27/E170/171). As it centers on Albion, *Jerusalem* is about the distribution of the human into the animals and birds and vegetables and the very rocks and grains of sand of this world, and about this world's reintegration and reawakening into the human. *The Four Zoas* offers the

2. The "longest and probably the oldest extant Moral, *The Castle of Perseverance*, ca. 1450 . . . [had] beneath the castle a bed under which lay, till his cue came, the actor who played Humanum Genus, i.e. Mankind" (Thomas Marc Parrott and Robert Hamilton Ball, eds., *A Short View of Elizabethan Drama* [New York, 1958], p. 17). "Humanum Genus," waiting for his cue while others contest for his soul, sounds like Blake's Albion.

most condensed image of Albion's "distribution" into the
natural world and his loss of human identity:

> He touches the remotest pole & in the Center weeps
> That Man should Labour & sorrow & learn & forget & return
> To the dark valley whence he came to begin his labours anew
> In pain he sighs in pain he labours in his universe
> Screaming in birds over the deep & howling in the Wolf
> Over the slain. (VIII/110:18–23/E370/385)

But the poetry of lamentation is equally powerful in *Jerusalem*, and human conflict more bitter:

> His Children exil'd from his breast pass to and fro before him
> His birds are silent on his hills, flocks die beneath his
>   branches
> His tents are fall'n! his trumpets, and the sweet sound of his
>   harp
> Are silent on his clouded hills, that belch forth storms & fire.
> . . . .
> And self-exiled from the face of light & shine of morning,
> In the dark world a narrow house! he wanders up and down,
> . . . .
> All his Affections now appear withoutside: all his Sons
> . . . .
> Raging against their Human natures. (19:1–4, 13–14, 17, 23/
>   E162/164–65)

What is true of Albion is almost equally true of his Emanation. Once a "World / Of Love & Harmony in Man" (39:41–42/
E185/187)—the community and mutual harmony in which
the nations lived—Jerusalem has been debased and exiled
"distant far from Albion":

> Naked Jerusalem lay before the Gates upon Mount Zion
> The Hill of Giants, all her foundations levelld with the dust!
> Her Twelve Gates thrown down: her children carried into
>   captivity
> Herself in chains. (78:21–24/E231–32/234)

At her lowest point, when she is imprisoned in the dungeons
of Babylon, driven mad by the despair and unbelief that are
the fruits of reason, Jerusalem might say with Albion, "Hope
is banish'd from me" (47:18/E194/196). Without having wholly
ceased to exist, she seems somehow to have been replaced by

or transformed into her Shadow or fallen image, Vala. Unity has become division, and the inner world an outer one. The separation of Jerusalem from Albion, and the drawing of Jerusalem's emanative life into the Shadow Vala, results in the thorough confusion of Jerusalem and Vala, so that Jerusalem throughout most of the poem is in the "State" Vala, who uses Jerusalem as her "cover": "Vala is but thy Shadow, O thou loveliest among women! / A Shadow animated by thy tears O mournful Jerusalem!" (11:24–25/E153/154). Jerusalem is innocence driven out; Vala, even at her best, is experience turned to despair. At her worst, she is the focus and cause— as in *The Four Zoas*, but more violently—of destructive sexual warfare. In *Jerusalem* identity is divided by the fall into a murderous "Sexual Religion."[3] It is regained, in Los, through brotherhood.

From Sexual Religion to Brotherhood

In eternity, embraces are "Cominglings: from the Head even to the Feet," not a "pompous High Priest entering by a Secret Place" (69:43–44/E221/223), brotherhood conversing through Emanations, not sexual congress. In eternity the sexual center—a form of mistaken emphasis on and idolatry of a part and of the self—gives way to the outline and to the holiness of all the "Minute Particulars." The formula is organic and stresses the interdependence of parts and whole

3. Milton Percival writes, "Blake adopts St. Augustine's triple division of spiritual history and gives to it a sexual interpretation. . . . He designates these three divisions as 'churches.' The first is hermaphroditic, the other two are double-sexed. In the hermaphroditic church, which extends from the Creation to the flood, we have duality resolved by man's complete absorption in the feminine self. Nature and Natural Religion are the result. In the double-sexed churches, which complete the temporal cycle, we have an open dichotomy, the energetic male in revolt against feminine dominion. Here we no longer have good alone, but good and evil. We no longer have pity alone, but pity and wrath. We no longer have nature alone, but nature and man. . . . Because Albion's preoccupation with Vala ends in repression and vengeance, the fall into sex is present, with Blake's characteristic irony, not as a fall into license, but as a descent into chastity. . . . With the double-sexed churches, which arise after the hermaphroditic church has been destroyed in the flood of time and space, the mortal and Generative world begins" (*William Blake's Circle of Destiny*, pp. 115–17).

in the universal body of man, of which we are all members. In *The Marriage of Heaven and Hell* and *Visions of the Daughters*, where his emphasis was on the prolific and on energy, Blake was willing to use the bodily prolific as symbol of the imaginatively prolific. Throughout most of *Jerusalem*, he treats sexuality as divisive and associates it with the binding down of the body and senses, as in the threefold closing off of brain from heart and from loins in Vala and in other expressions of the female will. Sexual division is thus symbolic of the Selfhood; in creating the sexual body the loins are given "bends of self interest" that are opposed to the open bosom of eternity, which contains one's world and at the same time reveals it to others—identifies the man. Sexuality is clothing, not identity—"Male & Female clothings" and "sexual garments"—and in the Resurrection men change their sexual garments at will. But sexuality is easily confused with identity, and the confusion leads to sexual conflict. In the process of the fall, imagination is limited and thought engrossed by sexual need; intellect gives way to sexual torment:

> Once Man was occupied in intellectual pleasures & energies
> But now my soul is harrowd with grief & fear & love & desire
> And now I hate & now I love & Intellect is no more:
> There is no time for any thing but the torments of love &
>   desire. (68:65–68/E220/222)

When the need is denied, as by the torturing female will, the result is the exacerbated erotic desire that becomes hatred and warfare. Blake sees the fall as a continuing process of dividing and closing in, a limiting of both imagination and identity, until the individual has become entirely closed off from others. Without their Emanations, "Which stand both Male & Female at the Gates of each Humanity," "Man cannot unite with Man" (88:10–11/E244/246), cannot be identified in community. But in the fall, these original elements of man fall asunder: "The Feminine separates from the Masculine & both from Man, / Ceasing to be His Emanations, Life to Themselves assuming!" (90:1–2/E247/249). They become male and female, Spectre and Shadow: "Man divided from his Emanation is a dark Spectre / His Emanation is an ever-

weeping melancholy Shadow" (53:25–26/E201/203). The male
Spectre becomes an unsatisfiable lust or desire, the female
Shadow an apparently external object world. At its worst,
the division into Spectre and Shadow results in the "adjoin-
ing" by hatred and mutual destruction—conflicting self-
hoods moved by a devouring destructive lust. The
condensed form of this relationship is in "The Mental Traveller." Its elaboration in *Jerusalem* emphasizes its horror and
shows its institutionalized form in idolatry, human sacrifice,
and bloody warfare:

> Look: the beautiful Daughter of Albion sits naked upon the
> Stone
> Her panting Victim beside her: her heart is drunk with blood
> . . . .
> In pride of beauty: in cruelty of holiness: in the brightness
> Of her tabernacle, & her ark & secret place, the beautiful
> Daughter
> of Albion, delights the eyes of the Kings. their hearts & the
> Hearts of their Warriors glow hot before Thor & Friga.
> (68:11–17/E219/221)

Vala, Blake's symbolic form for this female aspect of the
fall, tells Jerusalem that her children are "Children of
whoredoms: born for Sacrifice . . . to sustain the glorious
combat & the battle & war / That Man may be purified by the
death of thy delusions" (45:64–66/E193/195). As in *The Four
Zoas*, in Vala community changes into containing place; she
is "Mother of the Body of death" (62:13/E211/213), nature as
womb and grave. She is "that Veil which Satan puts between
Eve & Adam" (55:11/E202/204)—the veil of separation between Albion and Jerusalem, sexual division as quarrel and
jealousy and assertion of female pride, with the female warring against and torturing the male. The result of Vala's false
love for Albion—"a pretence of love to destroy love" (17:26/
E160/161)—is man as worm or phallus and love as submission
to the mortal body:

> They know not why they love nor wherefore they sicken &
> die
> Calling that Holy Love: which is Envy Revenge & Cruelty
> Which separated the stars from the mountains: the mountains
> from Man

And left Man, a little grovelling Root, outside of Himself.
(17:29–32/E160/162)

Vala is the degeneration of brotherhood into sexual strife, the
perversion of community into organized worship of nature.
In that worship, life feeds upon death, and community,
which is the life of identity, becomes a machine for warfare
and human sacrifice.

Albion's fall is a version of the Fall in Genesis, but one in
which man is born of woman as mother—Adam becoming
the child of Eve, losing human identity to the dominance of a
female nature. The myth is enacted by the male and female
figures in "The Crystal Cabinet" and "The Mental Traveller,"
and by Luvah and Vala, Los and Enitharmon, in *The Four
Zoas* and *Jerusalem.* In the account of Albion's "internal" fall
brought back by Enitharmon and Urthona, Luvah and Vala
enact the myth. They

> Went down the Human Heart where Paradise & its joys
> abounded,
> In jealous fears & fury & rage, & flames roll round their fervid
> feet:
> And the vast form of Nature like a serpent playd before
> them. (43:74–76/E190/192)

As in *The Four Zoas,* where this passage also appears, the
expulsion from Eden and the accompanying dominance of
female will or selfhood is the creation of a fallen nature that
overcomes identity: "And from her bosom Luvah fell far as
the east and west. / And the vast form of Nature like a serpent rolld between" (43:79–80/E191/193). In Luvah's falling
from Vala's bosom, it is as if he were being reborn, no longer
one of the immortals but subject now to Mother Nature.
(This account fits Luvah's association with Christ, if one
thinks of it as an account of Christ's taking on the mortal
body.) The being cast out of paradise is the being born of a
mother, with the womb being not paradise but Generation.

In another version, Vala tells Albion that she is not an
Emanation of man, but mother of mankind:

> Know me now Albion: look upon me I alone am Beauty
> The Imaginative Human Form is but a breathing of Vala

> I breathe him forth into the Heaven from my secret Cave
> Born of the Woman to obey the Woman O Albion the mighty
> For the Divine appearance is Brotherhood, but I am Love
>
> Elevate into the Region of Brotherhood with my red fires.
>   (29:48–52; 30:1/E174/176)

By using love as sexuality, Vala obscures the Divine Vision that is brotherhood, and Albion comes to worship her as "Nature Mother of all!" Love with its red fires elevated into the region of brotherhood is Mars ascendant and sex raised from the loins to the breast, thrusting out love and brotherhood. *Philia* or agape becomes eros; sexuality becomes the selfish center and masquerades as man's very identity, crushing the minute particulars.

Los laments that "Albion is the Tabernacle of Vala & her Temple":

> O Albion why wilt thou Create a Female Will?
> To hide the most evident God in a hidden covert, even
> In the shadows of a Woman & a secluded Holy Place
> That we may pry after him as after a stolen treasure
> Hidden among the Dead & mured up from the paths of life.
>   (30:29–35/E175/176–77)

"To hide the most evident God . . . even / In the shadows of a Woman & a secluded Holy Place" is to put God into the "tabernacle" of the womb and to make him exclusive to a chosen people.[4] Thus the Jews, and thus England. In both cases, it is for Blake a religion of moral righteousness and of sexual denial. The tabernacle and hidden God exclusive to a chosen people have their origin or revealed form in sexual

4. Florence Sandler elaborates on the biblical sources of Blake's symbolism; speaking of God's "marriage with the 'Virgin' Israel," she points out that "the marriage contract or covenant . . . had been negotiated on Mount Sinai, and thereafter the sign of God's dwelling with Israel was his tent or tabernacle that accompanied her through the wilderness. The temple on Mount Zion was still called God's 'tent' . . . preserving, it was thought, the original prescriptions laid down in Leviticus. . . . In the complex of symbols within the Holy of Holies (the ark behind the curtains, the Tables of the Law, the Covering Cherub) Blake sees the conjunction of legalism and mystery (Satan and the Whore) that he calls the 'Sexual Religion' and, even, the 'Abomination of Desolation.' The original use of that phrase in the Book of Daniel had been to designate a defilement of the Holy of Holies; Blake uses it to designate the Holy of Holies itself" ("The Iconoclastic Enterprise," p. 39).

division and concealment and denial, and in female will. The typical forms of the worship of the projected Selfhood that Blake calls the "Sexual Religion" are the holy tabernacle, the closed chapel, the selfish center, the secret places of a woman. All are of course opposed to the openness of identity, and all are much more elaborated in *Jerusalem* than in Blake's earlier prophecies.

Albion's sexual repose in Beulah has cost him dearly. Like Adam or Samson, he has lost his powers to the woman. "Eternity" has been overcome by "Marriage"; identity has become erotic division. The fall is in submission to female beauty—in allowing it to eclipse the Divine Vision. In relations between Albion and his Emanation—sometimes Jerusalem, sometimes Vala—one sees dimly adumbrated a reading of Genesis in which Albion-Adam hides his Emanation, Jerusalem-Eve, "in Jealousy." Sometimes it seems that Eve's separation from Adam has left him a Spectre, which, projected externally, adopts Eve as his cover. Sometimes it seems that the Emanation that has been thrust out becomes a Shadow that appears to the man as a Spectre, a delusive "God" whom he falls down before and worships: Satan or the serpent.

> Albions Emanation which he had hidden in Jealousy
> Appeard now in the frowning Chaos prolific upon the Chaos
> Reflecting back to Albion in Sexual Reasoning
>   Hermaphroditic. (29:26–28/E173/175)

It is as if Eve, separated from Adam, had become a Shadow that appeared to Adam as Satan-in-the-form-of-Eve and tempted him to eat the fruit.

The separated Emanation becomes the apparent outside world, the satanic quality of nature. As in *Milton,* Satan as the Spectre or Selfhood is hidden in this Shadow and is always in some way an anti-identity—the female covering the male Spectre, instead of the man's containing the female Emanation that identifies him. The Spectre is a separated reason taking exclusive refuge in the female tabernacle and speaking through the cover of the female. In sum, Satan, who has no identity, is always concealed or disguised. Identity, in contrast, is always revealed openly—in creative act, in brotherhood or community, and ultimately in Christ or the Divine Vision.

*   *   *

What accounts for Albion's awakening from his fall into the sexual religion and the death that is despair and unbelief is the power of vision to rouse energy to act. Inspired by the Divine Vision, Los shows Albion how to regain the identity he barely remembers. In the last chapter of *Jerusalem*, the history of Vala and the female will is enacted by Los and Enitharmon and Los's Spectre. It is the familiar triad that goes back through *The Four Zoas* to *Visions of the Daughters of Albion* and can be derived from the Tractates. As in the story of Vala, the Spectre works through the cover of the separated female will. But finally, as in the vision of the birth of Jesus presented to Jerusalem in the center of the poem, Generation gives birth to Regeneration and the Religion of Brotherhood.

Opposing Los's struggle to save Albion, Enitharmon separates from Los, leaving him "Lured by her beauty outside of himself in shadowy grief," his identity divided: "Two Wills they had; Two Intellects: & not as in times of old. / Silent they wanderd hand in hand like two Infants wandring" (86:60–62/ E243/245–46). As Enitharmon says, "In Eden our loves were the same here they are opposite" (87:17/E244/246). In Enitharmon's opposition to Los, sexual generation and jealousy arise together: she threatens to "Create / A round Womb beneath [her] bosom" and asserts, "I never will be thy slave" (87:14–15/E244/246). Los's Spectre (like Milton's Satan), "Gratified / At their contentions," "Knowing himself the author of their divisions & shrinkings," exults: "The Man who respects Woman shall be despisd by Woman / And deadly cunning & mean abjectness only, shall enjoy them" (88:37–38/E245/247). Spirit, as always in Blake, expresses itself in bodily form or process. "Despair" takes on a physical embodiment, making their "places of joy & love, excrementitious" (88:39/E245/247).

Satan shows himself in his fruits, but Satan begins to yield to Christ, the anti-identity to identity. Though Enitharmon's defiance scatters Los's "love on the wind / Eastward into Eden," it nevertheless prepares for the birth of the Savior, "creating the Female Womb / In mild Jerusalem around the Lamb of God" (88:51–53/E245/247). At the same time, out of Enitharmon's assertion of Selfhood the "Covering Cherub" suddenly appears, "majestic image / Of Selfhood," in its brain a "reflection / Of Eden all perverted" (89:9–10, 14, 15/ E245/248). Enitharmon has been his cover, as Eve is the serpent's cover in the temptation of Adam. As at the end of *Milton*, "A Double Female now appeard within the Tabernacle, / Religion hid in War, a Dragon red & hidden Harlot" (89:52–53/E246/249). But Jerusalem is hidden within the Covering Cherub. The "Religion of Generation which was meant for the destruction / Of Jerusalem" has "become her covering till the time of the End" (7:63–64/E149/150). Eve-Vala has involuntarily protected Jerusalem and prepared for the coming of Regeneration:

> when Man sleeps in Beulah, the Saviour in mercy takes
> Contractions Limit [Adam], and of the Limit he forms Woman: That
> Himself may in process of time be born Man to redeem.
> (42:32–34/E187/189)

Vala, though Jerusalem's shadow, is also her image, and the delusive image may evoke or awaken the reality: love, "mutual forgiveness," may issue from the sexual love whose source is spiritual hatred, and Generation may become the image of Regeneration, "point of mutual forgiveness between Enemies! / Birthplace of the Lamb of God incomprehensible!" (7:65–67/E149/150). In "The Dead awake to Generation! Arise, O Lord, & rend the Veil!" (44:40/E192/194), the "evident" God who has been hidden in the shadows of a woman becomes "evident" again by rending the veil, by being born. And by dying and living again, he not only rends the veil of the mortal body, the veil between eternity and time, but also rends the veil of the tabernacle by opening up the tabernacle and making an exclusive religion universal, thus regaining the identity in community which had been lost.

Los has prepared for this conclusion by putting squarely the issue of open brotherhood against exclusive sexuality, Jerusalem against Vala. The question is whether humanity is sexuality or brotherhood, sexual congress or conversation:

> When in Eternity Man converses with Man they enter
> Into each others Bosom (which are Universes of delight)
> In mutual interchange. and first their Emanations meet
> Surrounded by their Children. If they embrace & comingle
> The Human Four-fold Forms mingle also in thunders of
>   Intellect
> But if the Emanations mingle not; with storms & agitations
> Of earthquakes & consuming fires they roll apart in fear
> For Man cannot unite with Man but by their Emanations
> Which stand both Male & Female at the Gates of each
>   Humanity
> How then can I ever again be united as Man with Man
> While thou my Emanation refusest my Fibres of dominion
> When Souls mingle & join thro all the Fibres of Brotherhood
> Can there be any secret joy on Earth greater than this?
>   (88:3–15/E244/246)

Jerusalem begins (roughly speaking) with the words of the Savior as brother:

> I am not a God afar off, I am a brother and friend;
> Within your bosoms I reside, and you reside in me:
> Lo! we are One; forgiving all Evil. (4:18–20/E145/146)

Christ and man are "One"—identified—but the "Perturbed Man," Albion, turns away, and in him the Divine Vision splits into a multitude of "weak visions of time and space." Having turned away, Albion falls into the sleep of unbelief, and only at the end of the poem does he see Jesus as a brother for whom he can sacrifice himself. The time between the turning away and the return belongs to Los, "the friend of Albion who most loved him," and who sacrifices everything for that friendship, entering "the Door of Death for Albions sake inspired" (1:9/E143/144).

When Albion hardens himself "lest any should enter his bosom & embrace / His hidden heart" (34:2–3/E177/179), closing off the identity that can only be revealed openly, Los tries to break up Albion's "rocky" Selfhood, his rigid moral attitudes and accusations of sin. But Albion remains "obdurate! . . . counting [his friends] enemies in his sorrow" (40:35–36/ E186/188). What is worse, Albion has put on death—despair—as a dress or garment: "on my feet / Bound these black shoes of death, & on my hands, deaths iron gloves: / God hath forsaken me, & my friends are become a burden" (35:21–22/E179/181). The danger is not from despair so much as from the effects of despair—"Law" and "vengeance." The danger is that Albion's fall into despair and disbelief may free his Spectre to live in a hell of self-created torment. If Albion falls, "Man himself" may "become a Fiend, wrap'd in an endless curse, / Consuming and consum'd for-ever in flames of Moral Justice" with "his mighty arms brandish'd against the heavens" (36:29–30, 37/E180/182). Forgiveness may be lost in the "Moral Justice" of the false self, human identity lost in Satan.

As in *Milton*, only Los keeps his former active energy and identity, though it turns increasingly to rage: "Then Los grew furious raging: Why stand we here trembling round / Calling on God for help; and not ourselves in whom God dwells" (38:12–13/E182/184). When Albion in his nightmare delusions of "Moral Virtue" curses his offspring (like Urizen in *The Book of Urizen*), Los acts as providential watchman and teacher: "I have innocence to defend and ignorance to instruct" (42:26/E187/189). Seeing that the "Opressors of Albion in every City & Village / . . . . mock at the Labourers limbs! they mock at his starvd Children!" (44:27–28/E191/198), Los "In all the terrors of friendship" descends into the rocky bosom of Albion in search of the cause of Albion's suffering. It is a harrowing of hell as mere barren nature, ending in London as Babylon or the Egyptian captivity. Coming "from Highgate thro Hackney" to "Stepney & the Isle / Of Leuthas Dogs," Los

> saw every minute particular, the jewels of Albion, running down
> The kennels of the streets & lanes as if they were abhorrd.
> Every Universal Form, was become barren mountains of Moral
> Virtue: and every Minute Particular hardend into grains of sand. (45:14–20/E192/194)

The "Minute Particulars" who were men have become stones and rocks and grains of sand: "enquiring in vain / Of stones and rocks he took his way, for human form was none" (45:26–27/E192/194). Human identity seems entirely lost in barren nature, and Los at this point is helpless to act. He can only await Albion's conversion, his turning toward the truth:

If I should dare to lay my finger on a grain of sand
In way of vengeance; I punish the already punishd: O whom
Should I pity if I pity not the sinner who is gone astray!
(45:33–35/E192/194)

Los's devotion to "Minute Particulars" is a devotion to the
individual existence and character that is the life of identity
and without which community cannot exist. His perceptions
are not rational but symbolic and evaluative. They identify
the unique individual with the universal form rather than
burying the individual in the general: they see the universal
identity in or through the unique particular. In this seeing,
Los follows the words of Jesus, who says that the "Eternal
Vision," the "Divine Similitude," must be seen in individuals, in "loves and tears of brothers, sisters, sons, fathers,
and friends." Otherwise, man "ceases to exist" (34:11–13/
E178/180). Los is following Christ, then, when he says

He who would see the Divinity must see him in his Children
One first, in friendship & love; then a Divine Family, & in the
   midst
Jesus will appear; so he who wishes to see a Vision; a perfect
   Whole
Must see it in its Minute Particulars; Organizd . . .
. . . .
But General Forms have their vitality in Particulars; & every
Particular is a Man; a Divine Member of the Divine Jesus.
   (91:18–21, 29–30/E249/251)

In Blake's radically human vision, the universal form that is
the whole body or community of man is to be seen and loved
in the minute particular that is the unique person. The relation—the equation or metaphor—is identity. When Jesus appears to Albion "at the end of time," Albion knows that it is
"the Lord the Universal Humanity." But Albion "saw his
Form / A Man and they conversed as Man with Man, in Ages
of Eternity" (96:5–6/E253/255). The man Albion sees and converses with in the "Divine Appearance" is Los.

Whether we follow the changes of Albion or Los or Enitharmon, then, we arrive at the same place—Christ, the Divine Vision, realized in experience, eternity breaking into
time and space and bringing time to an end. The center of

Jerusalem, the point around which all its events arrange themselves, is the recovery of identity by seeing the divine in the minute particular of the human form.

The Labourer of Ages

Albion is saved not only by Los's love, but also by his creative energy. Los is the energetic center and organizing force in the poem. As in *Milton,* he is visionary and prophet and creative laborer, creating through mercy the visible world that appears in the void and carrying out the work of Providence. If the name *Los* suggests *Logos,* the prophetic and creative word, then Los is both Old Testament prophecy and the Gospel, and in him the word as creative principle is "adapted to the weaknesses of men." Standing midway between the Universal Form, Jesus, and the chaos of the indefinite, Los assumes the whole burden of the fallen world, saving the vision of identity.

In *Jerusalem* as in *Milton,* Los sets limits to and makes permanent the division of mankind into sexes, nations, and families, and presides over the whole creation that appears in the void. By dividing the sexes into masculine and feminine, he produces the sexual Contraries without which there is no progress in the fallen world and thereby fosters life. He works "To create a World of Generation from the World of Death: / Dividing the Masculine & Feminine" (58:18–19/ E205/207). From Los as the Poetic Genius in a fallen world "the body or outward form of Man is derived" (E2/1). He forges the threefold fallen body, brain, heart, and loins divided and closed off from one another, and thus from the fourfold total vision of eternity. But he must construct limits and divisions without ceasing to see in them the infinite. As in *Milton,* Los creates the perceptions of time and space and protects moments and joys and visions—"Gates" or windows into eternity—from Satan's watch-fiends. ("I am the door: by me if any man enter in, he shall be saved" [John 10:9].) He is the central ear and eye of the poem, and what he sees and hears *is* the poem as much as his furious labors.

But because imagination or creative power is fallen in Los, his labors are overwhelmingly laborious and materialize the vision. Los calls himself "the labourer of ages in the Valleys of Despair!" (83:53/E240/242). Since he is himself fallen and works with a fallen material, his creation is only a shadow of the clarity and permanence and freedom of eternity. But he watches and protects, exhorts and encourages, and labors mightily to unite in the Divine Vision. Los divides and binds only because of a horror of the void (as in *The Book of Urizen*), and it is a merciful binding, to put a limit to the fall. The last survivor of the four Zoas, mediator between time and eternity, Los might be called "the mercy of Eternity." He binds form to time and space and matter only because form cannot otherwise be revealed in a fallen world, and he does it for the sake of the liberation to come. The enemies Los battles are the indefinite and the void, and the rigid or petrified—both forms of death. He labors to give definite form to the indefinite: in definite form and minute particulars identity resides.[5]

In eternity, vision and creation are one, yielding the identity of unfallen man. In time, the creative power reveals itself only imperfectly: "Creation is, God descending according to the weakness of man" (Annotations to Lavater, *Aphorisms on Man*, E589/599). As the creation is imperfect and annihilable, so the identity achieved through creative work is imperfect. Perfect mercy, forgiveness, and brotherhood appear only in the Divine Vision, the exemplar of Los's work. Nevertheless, since in this world "God only Acts & Is, in existing beings or men" (*Marriage of Heaven and Hell*, pl. 16), through Poetic Genius the Divine Image is kept alive in the world. Los is the power of organization in the fallen world—humanity di-

5. For Los as both unique and universal, see Edward J. Rose, "Los, Pilgrim of Eternity." The perception that is "capable of seeing . . . the 'One Central Form' and all forms . . . is called Los. Los's descent into Albion in *Jerusalem* is a process of self-exploration. It is a pilgrimage through history, but it is experienced as Kairos rather than as Chronos. It is the search for identity through a vision of the particular man in his infinite variety. The labor of Los is the imagination's view of itself" (p. 85). "Blake stresses the wholeness and oneness of the creative process, which is forever organic, while emphasizing the liberating character of particularity; that is what he means by identity" (p. 86).

vided, yet struggling to keep the Divine Vision of unity. Los destroys and he "circumcizes." He divides individuals from "States." Breaking up rigid forms and ideas, or "rocky forms of Death," with his hammer, he destroys, re-forms, and transforms in a continual process of destruction and rebuilding that prevents the solidifying of the world into unalterable form, and in that way allows change and redemption: "a World of Generation continually Creating; out of / The Hermaphroditic Satanic World of rocky destiny" (58:50–51/ E206/208). When the Spectres of Albion's twelve sons threaten "to devour / The sleeping Humanity" (Albion in his tomb), Los with his iron mace breaks up "the rocky Spectres, as the Potter breaks the potsherds: / Dashing in pieces Self-righteousnesses," dividing them into "Male & Female forms in his Furnaces / . . . lest they destroy the Feminine Affections" (78:2–8/E231/233).

In these divisions and re-formings, Los carries on the essential imaginative activity of dissolving in order to recreate. His "Furnaces" are the crucibles of imagination; his "Hammer" creates justice and mercy: "The blow of his Hammer is Justice, the swing of his Hammer: Mercy / The force of Los's Hammer is Eternal Forgiveness" (88:49–50/E245/247). Los both gives definite form to and watches over individuals or minute particulars, and strives to unite these particulars into universal form. "As all men are alike in outward form. So (and with the same infinite variety) all are alike in the Poetic Genius" ("All Religions Are One," E2/1). In Los, identity divides into multitude and strives to regain its identity as the Divine Vision.

As imagination in the fallen world holds in balance one's actual or apparent state of alienation and the vision of one's identity, so Los is the fallen form that in the end takes on its real form: the particular form in which the universal form is visible. The difficulty is to see the universal in the particular. Seeing only the universal, one destroys or negates individual identity (minute particulars). Seeing only the particular, one fails to see it as divine, as the human *identity*. To see the particular forms as human is to see them in their source and to see the source as the end to which they return: "God is a man not because he is so percievd by man but because he is the creator of man" (Annotations to Swedenborg, *Divine Love and Divine Wisdom*, E592/603).

Los creates the language and the arts and tools of man and plants "The seeds of Cities & of Villages in the Human Bosom" (83:55/E240/242). As artisan and builder, Los's great work is the creation and salvation of human value. He is a Promethean source of culture. Once, "In the exchanges of London every Nation walked / And London walkd in every Nation mutual in love & harmony" (24:42–43/E168/170). But London has become or is becoming Babylon, built by the children of Albion: "Albion is cast forth to the Potter his Children to the Builders / To build Babylon because they have forsaken Jerusalem" (24:29–30/E168/169). The materials are misery, destruction, and death. Against the building of Babylon, Vala's city and the city of death, Los (as in *The Four Zoas* and *Milton*) builds Golgonooza. In it, the destruction and death of Babylon are answered by brotherhood and forgiveness: "The stones are pity, and the bricks, well wrought affections . . . The mortar and cement of the work, tears of honesty" (12:30, 33/E154/155). Golgonooza aspires to be the "fourfold spiritual London," but throughout most of the poem it is so only in hope and expectation, for "Jerusalem wanders far away / Without the gate of Los: among the dark Satanic wheels" in Ulro (12:43–44/E154/156). As in *Milton*, again, though Golgonooza is built and destroyed and rebuilt in time, in it "all that has existed in the space of six thousand years" remains "Permanent, & not lost not lost nor vanishd, & every little act, / Word, work, & wish, that has existed, all remaining still" (13:59–61/E156/157–58). Blake himself claims to "walk up and down in Six Thousand Years: their Events are present before me" (74:18–19/E227/229).

Golgonooza is not only a city but a poem, and Los as poet labors with imperfect powers—the "soft affections" condensing into "forms of cruelty . . . beneath [his] hammer" (9:26–27/E151/152). Still Los labors "in hope," forging the poetry of spiritual warfare to combat Albion's increasing inhumanity—his denial of genius and inspiration. He takes "the sighs & tears, & bitter groans" and in his furnaces forms of them "the spiritual sword. / That lays open the hidden heart" (9:16–19/

E151/152) and reveals identity. The poem Los is creating appears later:

> For a Tear is an Intellectual thing;
> And a Sigh is the Sword of an Angel King
> And the bitter groan of a Martyrs woe
> Is an Arrow from the Almighties Bow! (52:25–28/E200/202)

In its expression and overcoming of states of grief and despair, Los's poetry seems primarily emotional in its motive force, with its most immediate effect psychological and expressive. But this expression serves the needs of Mental Fight by melting apparent surfaces away and by releasing and giving shape to suppressed forces. What is forged under Los's hammer is understanding and intellect. The great need is that men should

> understand . . . the distress & the labour & sorrow
> That in the Interior Worlds is carried on in fear & trembling
> Weaving the shuddring fears & loves of Albions Families.
> (59:50–52/E207/209)

Finally, in chapter 4, Los is ready to say,

> I care not whether a Man is Good or Evil; all that I care
> Is whether he is a Wise Man or a Fool. Go! put off Holiness
> And put on Intellect. (91:54–56/E249/252)

Los is a furnace of furiously burning emotional energy coming into form and intellect in Blake's mind. As in *Milton,* when Blake sees himself in his function and in the tradition he is working in, he sees himself as Los. But Los is of course not Blake. He is a depersonalization of the individual poet, of the poet as man, who by means of his "Furnaces of Affliction" forges tears, groans, and sighs into the arrows and swords and spears of Mental Fight. Los is the prophet as he has existed for thousands of years. Blake is the unique form or individual "weakness" to which the prophetic genius adapts itself, as Blake says in "All Religions are One."

Since Albion sees the Divine Vision in the image of Los at the end of the poem, and since Blake's battle is against the inhuman image of God, it is necessary that Blake see Los as human. We have seen that the essential human qualities of moral commitment, brotherhood, and fidelity of vision developed late, that in Blake's early vision of Los, desperate and instinctive energy predominate, and that the crucial change toward loyalty, brotherhood, Jesus, and constructive prov- idential labor—the great conversion—occurs in Night VII of *The Four Zoas*. There Los becomes less the fallen Eternal in desperate conflict with the other Zoas and more a figure of salvation, the friend and brother of Albion, and from that point on he becomes Blake's symbolic figure of humanity making a world. Los is in the thick of a battle. His engage- ment in the world reveals the force of his concern. His instru- ments are neither pastoral appurtenances nor weapons of war, but the tools of the builder. He is no gentleman but an artisan and a demon for work. Through Los, Blake might have worked a revolution in the image of the artist in English poetry, but Los has few notable descendants.

Los's humanity is in his relative weakness and his enormous goodwill: his struggle against temptation, doubt, despair— and against a resistant Spectre and Emanation. Though Los is a giant form, he is neither all-powerful nor full of divine certi- tude. Blake does not create in Los a figure to make up for his solitude or his apparent failure. Instead, he gives Los the power of brotherhood and goodwill and makes Los's "System" or creation less important than the faith and loyalty of the builder. These qualities can be given reality only by the system Los creates, but the system is less than the imagination and human- ity of the creator. Though Los is a depersonalization or mask— the poet as prophet—when one thinks of Blake, one thinks of him in the image or similitude of Los.

*   *   *

But Blake is of course Urizen as well as Los.[6] The system-

6. John Sutherland notes, "Some sort of *reason*, of course, was necessary to Blake in his system-building. In *Jerusalem*, Plates 10 and 11, Blake/Los drives his Spectre, the 'Holy Reasoning Power' which is also the 'Abstract Object- ing power,' to great and painful labors, as he attempts to 'Create a System.' There seems little doubt that Blake's primary ability was his creative, vision- ary imagination—as symbolized by Urthona/Los. However, the clear, hard lines with which he insisted on delineating his visions, and the precision with which he worked out complex relationships in his writings, point to reason—symbolized by Urizen—as a strongly developed secondary ability" ("Blake and Urizen," p. 245).

atic part of Los's creation comes from the Urizen—the Spectre—in him. Urizen too is a creator, and at the same time the false identity that Blake struggles to throw off or convert. He is the part of Blake that demands a solid and permanent accomplishment—a "solid without fluctuation," an embalment of the artist—and the part that asks Blake what he has to show for twenty years' work. He is the reason that ought to be the polar contrary to the fiery energy of imagination, but he has asserted himself in separation, as a restrainer: "O Urizen! Creator of men! mistaken Demon of heaven: / Thy joys are tears! thy labour vain, to form men to thine image" (*Visions of the Daughters of Albion*, 5:3–4/E47/48).

The Urizenic or spectrous element in Los-Blake's work helps to account for the systematic element in it. As organization, system is rational, dividing, and abstract; it is to be distinguished from Universal Form—the human form divine that comes into existence only at the end of the poem. Morally, system is to be distinguished from the spirit of brotherhood and the forgiveness of sins: "Brotherhood is Religion / O Demonstrations of Reason Dividing Families in Cruelty & Pride!" (57:10–11/E205/207). Here I want to concentrate on Los's moral system. He labors to create separable states and to divide individuals from states, on the one hand, and on the other to consolidate states into a system that must be thrown off because it obscures identity: his function is to "Divide us from these terrors & give us power them to subdue" (84:26/E241/243).[7]

7. Perhaps the best account of Blake's "States" is Edward J. Rose, "Blake's Metaphorical States." States, Rose insists, are metaphors, and states given the same name are often different: "'Beulah in Ulro,' for instance, is not Beulah, the first of the 'Four States of Humanity in its Repose,' or the three-fold Beulah of the four states of existence. Blake's symbolism always energizes. Symbols change other symbols when one symbol moves into a context ordered or influenced by another symbol. Blake uses the word 'state' as an alternative for 'world' (J 49:196–97), for the contrary states of the soul, for the state of innocence, experience, happiness, or wisdom, for Eden, Beulah, Generation, and Ulro, for three states within Ulro ('Creation, Redemption & Judgment'), for some of the sons of Los, including Milton. . . . He uses the word for . . . countless Biblical persons, for the state 'Called Eternal Annihilation' and for 'Memory' and for 'Reason' and for 'Churches.' . . . As a metaphor, a state is many things . . . a metaphorical or symbolic context and a process. . . . A state is essentially an artifice of the imagination" (p. 11).

States may be real or illusory—"Supreme" or "States of Sleep":

> I do not consider either the Just or the Wicked to be in a Supreme State but to be every one of them States of the Sleep which the Soul may fall into in its Deadly Dreams of Good & Evil when it leaves Paradise following the Serpent. ("A Vision of the Last Judgment," p. 91/E553/563)

An illusory or "sleep" state is a permanent but separable psychic set or vision—often the apparent reality formed by the fragmentary self, or Selfhood, and its world. A system is a series of connected and mutually interdependent states forming a cooperative enterprise or a shared vision of reality. States are a result of division and fragmentation. Systems are forms of interconnection or consolidation that fall short of Universal Form, and that, if they impose, become a kind of law or outward fate. States are psychological; systems are intellectual and social. Deism, Epicureanism, state religion, and warfare are systems—for Blake, erroneous systems. Reason, the Selfhood, and the accusation of sin are states, but systematically related states in that they are mutually supporting and increasing. All fall short of the "Supreme State" of Eden.

States appear to be external and are associated with the "Selfish Center," which is "Without." To turn one's gaze outward and to be fascinated by what seems outside is to fall into the Selfhood; states (even the state of self-annihilation) concern the Selfhood. Every delusory state has its apparent outside world—the external projection or the fallen appearance of a paradisal and fully human world within. This external world is what Blake calls the "Shadow." But the real world of imagination that constitutes the identity of every person is inward: brotherhood is an inner and translucent circumference (opposed to the "Selfish Center") that "still expands going forward to Eternity" (71:6–9/E222–23/225). In *Jerusalem* as a contest of visions, the two forces or directions of vision are outward toward the abyss, seeing that as source and end of life, or inward toward the imaginative world of human identity and value—the paradise of delight and harmony within:

For all are Men in Eternity.
Rivers Mountains Cities Villages,
All are Human & when you enter into their Bosoms you walk
In Heavens & Earths; as in your own Bosom you bear your
   Heaven
And Earth, & all you behold, tho it appears Without it is
   Within
In your Imagination of which this World of Mortality is but a
   Shadow. (71:15 –19/E223/225)

Since perception and identity are interdependent, states or shadow worlds mask and confuse identity. But in a fallen world the creation of states is an act of mercy—Christ working through Los—a bulwark against "Eternal Death." Los's works are gates or windows into eternity, but also systems that may impose the kind of unquestioning belief that Blake, in *The Marriage of Heaven and Hell,* calls "subjection." The creations of Los always have this double aspect, and throughout most of *Jerusalem* the systematic aspect appears to dominate. From the "Limit of Opakeness Satan & the Limit of Contraction / Adam" (73:27 –28/E226/228), for example, Los creates the succession of religious "churches" or systems in time: "Satan & Adam are States Created into Twenty-seven Churches" (*Milton,* 32:25/E131/132). Created by Los through the "Spectres" that are mortal men, such systems are "Shadowy," yet "to those who enter into them they seem the only substances" (13:64 –65/E156/158).

In "A Vision of the Last Judgment," Blake writes, "There is not an Error but it has a Man for its Agent. . . . There is not a Truth but it has also a Man" (p. 86/E553/563). All of *Jerusalem* embodies truths and errors in persons and gives them form. Each state or church is named after the person or figure in which it has its source, but "Multitudes of Men" may inhabit the same "State":

> It ought to be understood that the Persons Moses & Abraham are not here meant but the States Signified by those Names the Individuals being representatives or Visions of those States as they were reveald to Mortal Man . . . in the Bible these various States . . . when distant . . . appear as One Man but as you approach they appear Multitudes of Nations. ("A Vision of the Last Judgment," p. 76/E546/556)

Most of the biblical persons or names in *Jerusalem*—Adam, Satan, Reuben, Abraham, Moses, and so on—are representative of states. So are such other figures of Blake's own invention as Vala, Hand, Hyle, Gwendolen, and Cambel. But Albion, Urizen, Luvah, and Los are not. Thus "Satan is the State of Death, & not the Human existence: / But Luvah is named Satan, because he has enterd that State" (49:67–68/ E197/199).

The state Satan is "A World where Man is by Nature the enemy of Man." Since it has been created "that Men / May be deliverd time after time evermore," we must

> Learn . . . to distinguish the Eternal Human
> That walks about among the stones of fire in bliss & woe
> Alternate! from those States or Worlds in which the Spirit
>   travels. (49:72–74/E197/199)

Like man, "The Spiritual States of the Soul are all Eternal" (pl. 52). But they are not the man, and though Blake reads the Bible as representing states through persons and adopts the same practice himself, it is essential to "Distinguish between the Man, & his present State" (pl.52). States are opposed to individuality in being "general," a product of reason and thus a matter of appearance: "Death / And Hell & the Grave" are "States that are not, but ah! Seem to be" (*Milton*, 32:28–29/E131/132). Thus they change, but identity does not: "States Change: but Individual Identities never change nor cease: / You cannot go to Eternal Death in that which can never Die" (*Milton*, 32:23–24/E131/132). States change, but are eternal. In Blake's view, men change states by passing from one to another, as travelers pass through various countries, so that both states and individuals seem to change. But states only appear to change; the apparent change in the states themselves is the passing from one state to another. "As the Pilgrim passes while the Country permanent remains / So Men pass On: but States remain permanent for ever" (73:44–45/E227/229).

The permanence of states serves their function of delivering or freeing individuals. States are made permanent so that they may be forever separable from individuals and may forever be thrown off. Thus death, as a state, is eternal. It is the state, not the individual, that is "for ever accursed." When "Albion goes to Eternal Death," the Voice from the Furnaces says that he has

> enterd the State Satan! Be permanent O State!
> And be thou for ever accursed! that Albion may arise again:
> And be thou created into a State! I go forth to Create
> States: to deliver Individuals evermore! Amen. (31:13–16/
> E176/177–78)

Not only is "Righteousness" a state, but sexual identity as male or female is not identity but a state, and the Shadow and Spectre are states. The flower, rock, tree, and metal that Los creates (on pl. 73, for example) are states, and at the end of the poem they are among the objects that are identified as human. Heaven and hell are states of the soul, as are the "Three States of Ulro; Creation; Redemption. & Judgment" (32:42/E177/179).

Los's system of states, since it is created as a limit to the fall, is definitely organized and is a kind of life. Thus it is a great deal better than the rock or void. But it is life in division and violent conflict, a way-station between immortality and death—the belief in death that accompanies loss of the Divine Vision. What is in comparison to the void a system of life is in comparison to eternity a body of death, so that Los's system is profoundly ambiguous. Like the whole of creation, it mediates between extremes, so that any element in it may be turned two ways—toward conflict or unity, death or life, hell or heaven, Satan or the Divine Vision. Los's desperation comes both from the inhumanity of his creation—what he creates is a degeneration of the human—and from the turning further toward death of what he creates. He labors unceasingly to turn it around, but his creative labors seem partly involuntary, and his power is limited. The deluded figures of the poem take the forms Los creates as fates—as upper rather than lower limits—so that everything he does is perverted in delusional falls to lower forms. His creation of the vegetated body of Reuben, for example, may be a warning that miscarries when those who see Reuben "become what they behold," fall into the power of the state they behold, and become vegetated themselves.

Finally, Los of course has to struggle against division and delusion in himself and against a tendency to construct systems that do not free but bind. Insofar as system is imaginative, it helps to reveal or assert identity: "I must Create a System, or be enslav'd by another Mans" (10:20/E151/153). Insofar as it is of the Selfhood, it distorts identity. But the systematizing of error helps to define identity negatively—as what is *not* this system of error—and gives error an organization and body that can be thrown off. The systematizing and clarifying of error prepare for the "Destruction of Error" and for "Circumcision," and it is thus a means of freeing from error: "Striving with Systems to deliver Individuals from those Systems" (11:5/E153/154). Los's system counteracts system, fighting fire with fire. If he were to take the system as a final reality, it would change from Shadow to "rocks in Horeb" and become an apparently permanent and inescapable hell, as it does for Albion. Los's effort to divide individuals from states, to show that states are not identity, is an effort to get intellectual and voluntary control of what would otherwise be invisible or confused, bringing it to clear consciousness and organized form, so that what is seen becomes separable from one's identity. Thus (as in *The Four Zoas*) Los builds "the stubborn basement" of the language lest Albion be a "dumb Despair." By articulating the despair and making it conscious, the language gives it a separable form of its own, and in this way rescues us from being enslaved by it. Once seen as a state, it loses its obsessive power and its apparent inevitability. Thus individuals can be delivered from states, as Albion is delivered at the end of *Jerusalem* when he recognizes Satan as his Selfhood.

In seeing a state, the possibility of other states is revealed, and it becomes clear that the state is not necessary or integral to the seer: "We are led to Believe a Lie / When we see not *Thro* the Eye" ("Auguries of Innocence," E484/492; my italics). The power of seeing through or around states is the power of changing state, the reverse of becoming what one beholds. This is the expressive, visionary, and redemptive power of the poet in which humanity finds its voice and its freedom:

> The Imagination is not a State: it is the Human Existence
>   itself
> Affection or Love becomes a State, when divided from
>   Imagination
> The Memory is a State always, & the Reason is a State
> Created to be Annihilated & a new Ratio Created
> Whatever can be Created can be Annihilated Forms cannot.
>   (*Milton,* 32:32–36/E131/132)

Whatever is not humanity—what has separated itself from the root or source and become the Selfhood—is a state, even if it call itself "Love," "Memory," or "Reason." Los tells the "Fiends of Righteousness" who pretend "Holiness" to "obey their Humanities":

> Go, tell them that the Worship of God, is honouring his gifts
> In other men: & loving the greatest men best, each according
> To his Genius: which is the Holy Ghost in Man; there is no
>   other
> God, than that God who is the intellectual fountain of
>   Humanity. (91:7–10/E248/251)

Blake's God—like Shelley's Prometheus—is "the intellectual fountain of Humanity," the human identity fully revealed.

The Form of Mental Fight

The way to truth in a fallen world is through error. This is the version in *Jerusalem* of Blake's doctrine of experience and of excess: "Enough, or too much"; "The road of excess leads to the palace of wisdom." The alternative or opposite to this is "Chastity"—holding oneself apart from and superior to experience, or fleeing terrified from it (as in *The Book of Thel*). The central part of each chapter in *Jerusalem*, then, is a descent into error or illusion in an attempt to redeem it. At the nadir of each chapter, Blake-Los reaches the limits of the intelligible, where experience or history or the mind's internal turmoil ceases to be understandable and "human." Through Los, Blake seeks to destroy error by seeking its psychological and internal roots in his own mind. The process is

one of self-annihilation. In order to deliver individuals from
states he must enter these states. Although they are a history
of the states of the human mind, in order to express them
adequately he must find them within himself. A Montaigne
or a Thoreau might descend into himself with a sense of
detachment; Blake does so without reserve. To enter into the
delusional states Blake presents in *Jerusalem* is to enter hell,
to accept the hell as one's own, to accept one's self, or Selfhood, as Satan, and to open the labyrinth of error to the light
in a "laying open the hidden heart." *Jerusalem* is a descent
into and taking on of error, delusion, loss, inhumanity, fear,
and cruelty. The delusion and crime of six thousand years
have to be recognized, accepted as implicit somewhere in
one's self, and confessed before they can be thrown off. The
alternatives would be indifference or the accusation of sin.
The first is humanly unthinkable, though it is a commonplace
reaction of fallen man. The second would be, or would lead
to, vengeance, a continuation of cruelty and violence.

The fires of Los's furnaces are hellish fires—the furious
form that hope threatened by despair takes in him. In this
phase, Los is like Luvah. Acting in wrath, hammering the
soft affections into forms of cruelty, forging justice under the
blows of his hammer, Los creates hell perforce for salvation.
Jerusalem depicts a descent into Ulro—"Meer Nature, or
Hell"—and a consolidation and revelation of the figure of
Satan; at the same time, it opens hell to heaven:

> Even from the depths of Hell his voice I hear,
> Within the unfathomd caverns of my Ear.
> Therefore I print; nor vain my types shall be:
> Heaven, Earth & Hell, henceforth shall live in harmony.
> (3:7–10/E144/145)

In *Jerusalem* as in *The Marriage of Heaven and Hell*, the two
extremes of imagination prove to be Contraries—partial and
complementary visions of a single order, eternity. Opening
hell to heaven does not destroy hell but illuminates it
through a change of perspective that makes it part of eternity. When Albion awakens from his involuntary delusion to
the fact that his nightmare world is his Selfhood, which
threatens the Divine Vision, he attempts to save his brother

by sacrificing himself. But when the fires of hell into which he throws himself reveal themselves as rivers of life, Albion rises in fourfold glory. Whatever appears on the void has come from within himself. The vision of the world as human (or, in its fallen state, as Selfhood) could scarcely be more clear. What follows on the vision of the world as human is total responsibility. And Albion, in the act that brings time to an end, accepts responsibility for the world. That done, the divisions that have plagued him end, and the battle for his soul is won. He has regained identity.

Jerusalem is designed to show the multiplicity, yet recurrence and essential sameness, of the forms and disguises of error, to show not just the "*two* contrary states of the human soul," though that is finally at issue, but to suggest the variety of the states of the human soul between the two extremes of Satan, or the Selfhood, and self-annihilation, or the forgiveness of sins. Blake wants, furthermore, to show the states from within, in their own vision, and to express each in its own voice. Hence the enormous variety and conflict of visions and voices and points of view in the poem, almost all gradually revealed as forms of the reasoning Selfhood. (Blake's structure of voices, which is particularly pronounced in *The Four Zoas,* might owe something to *The Divine Comedy,* particularly *The Inferno,* and even more to *The Canterbury Tales,* which in Blake's view sums up the characters of men.) Like *The Four Zoas, Jerusalem* is a system of vision, a series of visions and voices, often laments, sometimes one inside another, arranged so as to carry on and portray a Mental Fight—the struggle to reconstruct human identity out of the contesting variety of individual visions.[8]

8. "Blake's technique of the dramatic voice reaches its most sophisticated development in the epics, and perhaps especially in *The Four Zoas.* In this poem, we are given no consistent authorial voice to serve as a norm by which to gauge the dramatic speakers. We are thrown in among a series of speeches by characters, each trying to persuade us that only he or she is correct in his interpretations, assumptions, and programs" (Thomas R. Frosch, *The Awakening of Albion,* p. 115). Frosch's book is an especially good account of the last plates of *Jerusalem,* and while its subject is "The Renovation of the Body" in Blake's poetry, it is also very suggestive on the subjects of conversation and touch. See especially pp. 49, 106–7, and 131. For hearing and speech in Blake's poetry, the sections "Hearing and Speaking" (pp. 103–10) and "An Auditory Style" (pp. 110–23) are both excellent.

In "Man is born a Spectre or Satan & is altogether an Evil, & requires a new Selfhood continually & must continually be changd into his direct Contrary" (52/E198/200), it is Blake speaking, as it is earlier, where we see him carrying out his own hard saying and showing the way for Albion's reclaiming of his Spectre at the end of the poem:

> Spectre of Albion! warlike Fiend!
> In clouds of blood & ruin roll'd:
> I here reclaim thee as my own
> My Selfhood! Satan! armd in gold. (27:73–76/E171/173)

On plate 34 it is the "Saviour":

> Saying. Albion! Our wars are wars of life, & wounds of Love,
> With intellectual spears, & long winged arrows of thought:
> Mutual in one anothers love and wrath all renewing
> We live as One Man; for contracting our infinite senses
> We behold multitude; or expanding: we behold as one.
>   (34:14–18/E178/180)

Without such preparatory visions of the incessant interchange of Mental Fight, we would not be ready to see and hear and touch the conversation with which *Jerusalem* ends.

In the immense range and variety of speech in *Jerusalem*, Blake's voice breaks into widely different and opposed voices, as if it were the medium through which all the persons of a dispersed and isolated and groaning creation spoke. Soliloquy ("So Los in secret with himself commund" [17:48/E161/162]), lament, accusation, imposition, Mental Sacrifice, prayer, lecture, sermon, dialectic or Mental Fight, and responsive song make up an immense chorus from which sections and solo voices detach themselves. In the kaleidoscope of points of view and the cacophony or discord of voices coming into order and harmony in the great choral vision of the poem, the modulation between Blake's voice and Los's, and Los's voice and the Divine Voice, is necessary so that the vision of the whole may be repeatedly present in its parts. Blake claims both that he is a "true Orator" and that he "see[s] and converse[s] with daily, as man with man . . . the Friend of Sinners" (3/E144/145). The "Saviour" is seen "Dictating the words of this mild song" (4:5/E145/146), and

Blake or the Divine Voice or Vision repeatedly breaks into the poem, reaffirming the terms of a ceaseless battle. The issue of belief or disbelief is joined again and again; all events are variations on the crucial issue. To show the multiplicity of error, Blake shows division and proliferation fragmenting the original unity. At the same time, he reveals emerging unity or identity—renewed brotherhood.

The "change" or plot of *Jerusalem* is constituted by the unchanged human form and power of forming and the metamorphoses of state that it nevertheless undergoes—the incrustation of outline by false growth and the "Circumcision" of it; the descent into division and the re-ascent to unity. At the end of the poem Albion finally sees "The Visions of my deadly Sleep of Six Thousand Years" as a "Serpent," and that serpent as "my Self" (96:11–13/E253/255). Like *The Four Zoas,* *Jerusalem* separates human form from serpent form. Blake's whole concern in *Jerusalem* with identity and its disguises has in fact been condensed into the dissolving perspectives and shifting speakers of "For the Sexes: The Gates of Paradise."[9] Both poems are about the "Deadly Dreams of Good & Evil" that "the Soul may fall into . . . when it leaves Paradise following the Serpent" ("A Vision of the Last Judgment," p. 91/ E553/563).

The issue in "For the Sexes" is "Mutual Forgiveness" versus the accusation of sin, an issue which takes dramatic and identical shape as Christ versus Satan. In the prologue, Jehovah, having written the law of Sinai in response to the Accuser's "chief desire," relents and weeps and buries the law as a "dead Corpse" beneath his "Mercy Seat." The epilogue addresses that corpse, the accusing law embalmed as the crucified Christ and worshipped by Christians: Christ

9. From its beginning as "For the Children: The Gates of Paradise" in 1793 to its revision as "For the Sexes: The Gates of Paradise" (with the addition of the "Keys to the Gates") in 1818, "The Gates of Paradise" spans the most productive years of Blake's career. For the seventeen emblems of "The Gates of Paradise," and for the large and complicated and shifting "matrix" of fifty or sixty emblems out of which they came, see *The Notebook of William Blake,* ed. David V. Erdman and Donald K. Moore. Chapter 2, "Emblems of Fear and Hope," and tables IV and V of chapter 2, contain very full commentary on and analysis of the emblems. "For the Sexes" has been applied to the structure of *Jerusalem,* in a very different way from my own application, by Edward J. Rose, in "The Structure of Blake's *Jerusalem,*" p. 44.

become Satan. After the prologue, the framing action of the poem and epilogue is the fall and return of light. The poem begins with "My Eternal Man set in Repose," passes through his lending his light to the female moon and his descent into the darkness of the "cave," and ends with Lucifer, "Son of Morn," and the expected awakening from a dream. The root or identity figure at the beginning is "My Eternal Man"— Albion or Blake. He returns later (is "descried") as "The Immortal Man that cannot Die." "My Eternal Man" is premortal, so to speak, while "The Immortal Man that cannot Die" has conquered death. In the body of the poem, the speaker, being fallen, is Adam—"only the Natural Man & not the Soul or Imagination," as he is identified in "Laocoön" (E271/273). The poem is about the fall of Eternal Man to the limit of contraction, Adam, and the limit of opacity, Satan, and it looks forward to Eternal Man's resurrection as the second Adam, Christ.

When the female moon leaves the Eternal Man and hides within her veil the mandrake that she finds beneath a tree, the Eternal Man has fallen, to be reborn in a vegetated, virginal birth as the unfathered child of mother Eve, like Luvah in *Jerusalem* or the male babe in "The Mental Traveller." As usual in Blake's poetry, the figure covered by the veil or womb is Satan. At the depth of his fall, Adam knows himself as Satan; he keeps changing identity, taking successive forms as "Mandrake," "Serpent Reasonings," "Two Horn'd Reasoning Cloven Fiction," and finally as a "dark Hermaphrodite." The "dark Hermaphrodite" is Satan as the reasoning sexual strife between Adam and Eve, man and wife. In "I rent the Veil where the Dead dwell," Satan is violently born of the female, rapes her, and fathers on her incestuous, mortal offspring, or Death itself (as in the incestuous relation between Satan and his daughter-wife Sin in *Paradise Lost*). But rending the veil also implies Christ, as in the rending of the veil of the temple at Christ's crucifixion (Matthew 27:51), and in Blake's repeated allusions to rending the veil in *Jerusalem*. Satan begins to yield to Christ. In fact, the "Saviour" is mentioned almost immediately, presiding over the death-birth of "weary Man," whose "Cave" is womb or tomb:

When weary Man enters his Cave

> He meets his Saviour in the Grave
> Some find a Female Garment there
> And some a Male, woven with care
> Lest the Sexual Garments sweet
> Should grow a devouring Winding sheet (21–26/E266/268),

and identity be lost in sexuality and the death that is generation. In the Resurrection man changes his sexual garments at will.[10]

Having discerned the "Immortal Man that cannot Die," fallen man learns to see death as a state and enters the "Door of Death" as a freeing from mortal life, and thus from death. He now sees the "Serpent Reasonings" as only "the Worm Weaving in the Ground"; he sees Satan not as his own identity but as the servant of life, doing the work of the Savior by weaving the sexual garment or mortal body that is to be put off. "My Mother *from* the Womb" and "Wife, Sister, Daughter *to* the Tomb" (my italics) accurately reflect the history the speaker has told and imply the sexual images that dominate the history of Vala and Luvah, Vala and Albion, in *Jerusalem* (and the male and female in "The Mental Traveller"). "Weaving to Dreams the Sexual strife" suggests that the "reasonable" state of Ulro, death, and Generation has been a dream, and that Satan is the Eternal Man's dream self.

In the epilogue, Adam, thrust out of paradise, lost traveler through various satanic states as mandrake, dark hermaphrodite, and worm, has awakened from his serpent dream of good and evil. He addresses Satan as the Selfhood that, still sleeping, takes its dream for reality:

> To The Accuser who is
> The God of This World
> Truly My Satan thou art but a Dunce
> And dost not know the Garment from the Man
> Every Harlot was a Virgin once
> Nor canst thou ever change Kate into Nan

10. About the lines "their Emanations / Which stand both Male & Female at the Gates of each Humanity" (IV/88:10–11/E244/246), Frosch says that apparently "each Edenic Humanity emanates what we would consider to be two sexual persons, a male and a female at its points of communication with other human forms, as if each Edenic being, then, appeared to others as a deeply and radically unified couple" (*The Awakening of Albion*, p. 174).

> Tho thou art Worshipd by the Names Divine
> Of Jesus & Jehovah: thou art still
> The Son of Morn in weary Nights decline
> The lost Travellers Dream under the Hill. (E266/269)

Satan is a dunce in failing to recognize that neither harlotry nor virginity is a "Supreme State." More fundamentally, he is a dunce in being unable to identify man: to separate man from "Garment" or state, and thus to realize that identity—including his own—does not change.

The structure of "To the Accuser" is a series of identifications of Satan that strip him of his assumed identity as Jesus and Jehovah. He is furthest from Jesus and Jehovah in his masquerade, when he is worshipped by the Divine Names. He is closest in his identity as "Son of Morn." The Prince of Lies has deceived not only man but also himself—himself most of all—and has to be told that he is the "Son of Morn," about to awaken from the deluded dream of the Selfhood, the body of death that is put off by all men at the resurrection. The Satan who is the state death or the state negation will be negated. In one sense, "Son of Morn" is a diminishing image like "lost Travellers Dream." The light of the morning star—Lucifer—serves only to announce a greater light that follows and extinguishes it. But "morning star" is a traditional image of Christ. In Revelation 22:16 Christ says, "I am . . . the bright and morning star." This suggests that his coming promises a second and greater coming, but one that does not obliterate him. Similarly, beneath Satan as illusion, in Satan as herald of the coming light, there is a core of real identity. Beneath the change of state he is still the morning star—much as, in Night IX of *The Four Zoas*, the serpent Urizen reassumes his human form as Prince of Light.[11] For Blake, Urizen or Lucifer is a human power that, when fallen, de-

---

11. Written above the picture in *Job,* plate 11, is "Satan himself is transformed into an Angel of Light" (2 Corinthians 11:14). Leopold Damrosch, Jr., who points this out, goes on to say, "This Satan, the consolidation of error, is the agent by whom Job is awakened to illumination, and the true Lucifer or 'morning star' will later be revealed as Jesus, as anticipated by the quotation of Job 19:25, 'For I know that my Redeemer liveth'" (*Symbol and Truth in Blake's Myth,* p. 279).

For "To the Accuser," see Isaiah 14:12–15, which Blake's vision of unchanged identity in "To the Accuser" incorporates and transforms.

mands worship, and often *is* "Worshipd by the Names Divine / Of Jesus & Jehovah" (E266/269). But Blake identifies all human powers and risen humanity with the Christ who is the "Human Form Divine," and who appears not as a God demanding worship, but as a brother. The risen Lucifer, the morning star, is Christ. Awakened, Adam and Lucifer, and all men, are Christ.

For Blake, man identifies himself with one of two polar figures, Satan or Christ. Satan is confusion of identity; Christ is identity. The speaker in "For the Sexes" first misidentifies himself as mandrake, hermaphrodite, and worm, but later identifies himself with "the Immortal Man that cannot Die" by detaching Satan from himself as a state. (Like most of Blake's figures, the "I," though fallen or misidentified, is nevertheless a vital force, a kind of identity beneath identity that prophesies success.) Blake's speaker in "For the Sexes" is Adam, Blake, Albion—all men—undergoing a Last Judgment by rejecting error and embracing truth, by dying as Satan to be resurrected as Christ.

It is as true of *Jerusalem* as of "For the Sexes" that "the Imaginative Image" is permanent and eternal and "returns by the seed of Contemplative Thought" ("A Vision of the Last Judgment," p. 69/E545/555). But in *Jerusalem* the one dreaming, metamorphosing figure of "For the Sexes" becomes multitude, so that the single "Imaginative Image," and the pattern of return, are harder to see. Blake means to show in *Jerusalem,* through the condensed pressure of vision, "Every Affinity of Parents Marriages & Friendships" and "All that can happen to Man in his pilgrimage of seventy years" (16:65–67/E159/161): "All things acted on Earth are seen in the bright Sculptures of / Los's Halls & every Age renews its powers from these Works" (16:61–62/E159/161).

"Speaking . . . in Human Forms"

From one point of view, *Jerusalem* presents a falling into the silence and immovability of writing and the awakening into acting speech.[12] When all Los's "Friends & Brothers," as he complains, "stand silent" (38:77/E184/186), and the Divine Family delegates Los to "Watch over them / Till Jesus shall appear . . . / Naming him the Spirit of Prophecy" (39:29–31/ E185/187), and when Albion himself falls silent after his "last words. Hope is banish'd from me," the sixteen-pillared "Couch of Repose" on which he is placed by the "merciful Saviour" has "Spiritual Verse" written on it:

> The Five books of the Decalogue, the books of Joshua
> & Judges,
> Samuel, a double book & Kings, a double book, the Psalms
> & Prophets
> The Four-fold Gospel, and the Revelations everlasting.
> (48:9–11/E194/196)

Albion's sleep is watched over and his silence filled by the Bible, itself filled by the "Spirit of Prophecy," Los. But in the later solo chorus and response between Los and the Daughters of Albion—"This World is all a Cradle for the erred wandering Phantom: / Rock'd by Year, Month, Day & Hour" (56:8–9/E204/206)—Los's song is "utterd with Hammer & Anvil." This is to say not only that Los works to turn Generation into Regeneration in the birth of the infant Jesus, but also that in his hammer speech is already becoming act. In the "stubborn structure of the Language" Los is building, English is the "rough basement" of the act-speech Albion is to utter in eternity. As usual in Blake's poetry, the man and the city he is building—Los and Golgonooza—are identified as metaphor. But in *Jerusalem*, both are embodied speech— the man-city *is* his power of speech—and Los is preparing to disappear in the completed work, the risen, speaking Albion.

At the end of *Jerusalem*, the "wond'rous art of writing" given to man in "Sinais awful cave" (3:3–4/E144/145) comes to life. The risen Albion appears as Jehovah and speaks as "salvific" and loving intention: "And I heard Jehovah speak /

12. "Urizen's creation of 'order' out of what he saw as chaos by the mediation of language is a parody of the traditional creation of the cosmos by 'the Word': in this sense the origin of language is the origin of the fallen world" (Ault, *Visionary Physics*, p. 167). I would add that Urizen is associated with written language engraved on stone tablets.

Terrific from his Holy Place & saw the Words of the Mutual
Covenant Divine / . . . Humanize / In the Forgiveness of Sins
according to the Covenant of Jehovah" (98:40–45/E255/258).
Throughout the poem, Jehovah has descended through the
Divine Vision—the Word—to Los. Los has realized that intention by giving it temporal and changing form. Seen only
from within itself, the creation seems earthly and corporeal
and is unintelligible. Seen from eternity, it is intellectual or
visionary, revealing spirit. The creation, then, is truly seen
when it is seen to be mental, not corporeal—a body, with all
its minute particulars and definite outline, but a spiritual
body, begotten through the Spirit rather than the flesh. Creation when burned up leaves all human, liberated from the
inhuman; and the created object disappears before creative
energy, the fire that delights in ever-changing form, from
which Urizen fell at the beginning of *The Book of Urizen,* and
in which Angels find torment in *The Marriage of Heaven and
Hell.*

In the last half-dozen plates of *Jerusalem,* words take on
life. When Albion rises, his "clay cold ear" "pierc'd" by Brit-
annia's voice,

> into the Heavens he walked clothed in flames
> Loud thundring, with broad flashes of flaming lightning
>   & pillars
> Of fire, speaking the Words of Eternity in Human Forms.
>   (95:7–9/E252/255)

Albion speaks as Jehovah spoke earlier, in "Thunder of
Thought, & flames of fierce desire" (3:6/E144/145). Words become acts and speak "in direful / Revolutions of Action &
Passion" (95:9–10/E252/254). Words "speaking . . . in Human
Forms" (95:9/E252/255) are now not personified ideas or ab-
stractions, but words "regenerated," their "excrementitious /
Husk & Covering" (98:18–19/E255/257) cast off. These forms
become one form, and that "Word of Eternity in Human
Form" is Jehovah speaking. Discourse becomes dramatic act,
and the poem comes to life and clear outline in "Visionary
forms dramatic," in speaking visions that are both "bright"
and "thunderous," "Creating Space, Creating Time" (98:28–

31/E255/258). Presumably, "Childhood, Manhood, & Old Age" (98:33/E255/258)—any one of the "Three Regions"—may now be chosen at will. At the same time, all forms come to life and become one form, and all poems part of one poem: "& they walked / To & Fro in Eternity as One Man reflecting each in each & clearly seen / And Seeing" (98:38–40/E255/258). The poem is the risen form of Albion. As one it is the Word: Jesus, or the Universal Form. As many it is Jerusalem: "And I heard the Name of their Emanations they are named Jerusalem" (99:5/E256/259). As the identity of one and many, the divine and the human, it is the human identity.

The "end" of a poem, as of human life, is Eden. In Eden, creation is direct, unmediated by material husk or by the senses in abstraction, since in paradise words dance in harmony, "rejoicing in Unity / In the Four Senses" (98:21–22/E255/257). In Eden, "Organs of Perception," varying, create a moving and changing time and space, and all "nervous fibre" is "translucent" and responsive: the whole body hears, sees, smells, touches, speaks—"converses," as Blake says, "according to the Expansion or Contraction, the Translucence or / Opakeness of Nervous fibres" (98:36–38/E255/258). And "every Word & every Character / [is] Human" (98:35–36/E255/258). Jerusalem as "Liberty" is the condition of liberation from the weakness of the flesh, of creation unlimited by time or space or matter. The generating idea of Blake's poetry is "the liberty both of body & mind to exercise the Divine Arts of Imagination" (77/E229/231).

But the poem *Jerusalem* is itself a system in part, and what is a systematizing of error in it is designed to fall away, to move back so that it no longer looms in the foreground and overwhelms the mind, and can thus be seen in the perspective that reveals error. What remains when Satan is annihilated is simply the risen Albion, the great body of universal humanity, the family of men living in universal brotherhood. As identity in the fallen world cannot be revealed directly and intuitively through the Emanation but only indirectly through system, so the city that Los works day and night to construct is not Jerusalem but Golgonooza. Although it is the saving artifact and the community through creative work of fallen man, Golgonooza is nevertheless a system, with fallen elements, and not an Emanation. When Albion rises at the end of the poem and sees Los as Jesus, the part of Los's system that came from the Selfhood is presumably left behind as a cast-off garment and remains as a warning in the "Outward Spheres of Visionary Space and Time," so that "we may Foresee & Avoid / The terrors of Creation & Redemption & Judgment" (92:17, 19–20/E250/252).[13]

And if Blake sees himself in writing *Jerusalem* as participating in Los's work in the world and in his powers of prophetic vision, if Los's labors at Golgonooza include Blake's labors on the poem *Jerusalem*, then Blake would expect his poem, having taken its place among the structures of Los's halls along with the prophecies of Ezekiel and Isaiah and the Gospels, to undergo the same test and "Circumcision" as the rest of Los's creation. What is of the Spectre or Selfhood or Satan would be cast off. What is of the imagination and eternal would become Emanation and take its place in Jerusalem, part of the form that is a city, yet a woman:

> All Human Forms identified even Tree Metal Earth & Stone.
>   all
> Human Forms identified, living going forth & returning
>   wearied
> Into the Planetary lives of Years Months Days & Hours
>   reposing
> And then Awaking into his Bosom in the Life of Immortality.
>   (99:1–5/E256/258)

13. As Milton Percival notes, "Creation, Redemption, and Judgment are continuous, and it would seem also, simultaneous, processes. In them we have . . . the 'creation' or error, the release of man from error's power, and the destruction of error in mental fires"; "In the main, Creation is for the Spectre, who can never be regenerated, but must be 'created continually . . . in the cruelties of the moral law.'" For Percival, "the generative body which Los creates is the Christian Church. Since it too rests upon the hypotheses of good and evil, it too is a body of error, but it differs from the hermaphroditic form which preceded it in its forgiving spirit. This appearance of the spirit of selflessness within a Satanic system is the equivalent of Christ's assumption of the body of death" (*William Blake's Circle of Destiny*, pp. 223, 226).

Eternity appears at the end of *Jerusalem* not simply as a poem brought to life, but as all creation identified—brought to life in the divine community that is one man made of many.[14]

*   *   *

In *Jerusalem*, time and eternity, "this world" and Eden, remain distinct realms until eternity—in the Divine Vision— breaks into time and transforms it. Though its garments change, identity for Blake is eternal. Nevertheless, the implication of Los's faith and labors and of Albion's responding sacrifice at the end of *Jerusalem* is that they have developed in time, through experience, into unique persons with a history. They retain the virtues called forth by their life in time, and these virtues are the seed of the poem's final community—its Eden. From the perspective of *Jerusalem*, then, Blake's aphorism in the Tractates—"God becomes as we are, that we may be as he is" ("There Is No Natural Religion"/E2/3)—describes the creation of a community of souls each of whom is unique, yet forming one body. And "God becomes as we are" suggests that God is changed by the descent as well as we, though all become "as he is." The Eden into which Albion leaps at the end of *Jerusalem* follows on and cannot obliterate the six thousand years whose images and events have been the major substance of the poem. Although eternity has prevailed, time remains; it has become permanent—though transformed—in eternity.

Although *Jerusalem* focuses on the Apocalypse more than on Genesis, so that paradise comes into concrete existence

---

14. Leopold Damrosch, Jr., maintains that *Jerusalem* ends in "a perpetual return to the world as we know it, where we are sustained by the Beulah-comforts of Albion's Emanation Jerusalem until we can break through into Eden" (*Symbol and Truth in Blake's Myth*, p. 348). It is true that *Jerusalem* ends with

> living going forth & returning wearied
> Into the planetary lives of Years Months Days & Hours reposing
> And then Awaking into his Bosom in the life of Immortality
> And I heard the Name of their Emanations they are named Jerusalem.

But this is not "the world as we know it." It is Eden-Beulah, not Beulah-Generation-Ulro. The repose of Beulah does not necessarily lead to the fall into warfare and "Deadly Dreams of Good & Evil," though Blake seems to leave open the possibility that it will do so again.

only at the end of a task and trial, paradise comes (as in *Prometheus Unbound*) as the regained and unfolded origin, the original good.[15] This is to say that imagination works with a given world, however much it changes it; and plot demands that the beginning be shown as pregnant with the end. But plot—a structure of change—demands also that the end be different from the beginning. And what comes between beginning and end cannot simply be canceled. Briefly and theologically, we may describe the shape of time as circular, as Blake seems to do in "God becomes as we are, that we may be as he is." But in poetry—in a long poem—time can be no more than spiral. Whether or not the middle transmits a causal force to the end, it serves, and remains, as a way to the end. (This is true even if the middle is the state of time as delusion, as it is for Albion in *Jerusalem*, and it is doubly true if the middle is the struggle *against* delusion, as it is for Los in *Jerusalem*.) The form of time in *Jerusalem* is spiral: revolutionary, and, if only by implication, evolutionary as well. That form is implicit in Blake's Tractates; and in the poetry that follows, the sentence "God becomes as we are, that we may be as he is" is seen to describe not quite a circle but a spiral. In the next chapter, however, I will argue that the form of Blake's prophecies is not Aristotelian, because the change that takes place in them is largely restorative.

15. For the observation that the return of the Golden Age as conscious knowledge or science in *Prometheus Unbound* makes the shape of time in it "spiral," see Milton Wilson, *Shelley's Later Poetry.*

8

Blake's Los

What first occupies Blake's attention in Los is his fall into Urizen and Orc, king and priest battling revolutionary. But Blake gradually turns from the extraverted rebel in fire who fights kings and priests to the increasingly conscious radical reformer who opposes kings and priests and the Satan who is his Selfhood: as Blake's myth develops, Orc is superseded as active savior by his source and father, Los. Furthermore, Blake's personal link with Los is slow to emerge. Los only gradually appears as an angel or mighty demon who visits Blake in epiphanies, whom Blake wrestles with in the letter poems to Butts like Jacob with the angel, and whom Blake later becomes one with. But gradually Los becomes the "artist as hero" of the whole body of Blake's long prophecies, and he becomes (in *Milton*) an English dissenting prophet—a Milton who is a painter and engraver as well as an "Awakener," and a Milton who revises Milton (and Genesis).

The repeated implication of Blake's poetry from "All Religions Are One" of 1788 through *The Marriage of Heaven and Hell* and *The Book of Urizen* to *Milton* and *Jerusalem* is that Los is our progenitor: that Poetic Genius is the source and creator of our humanity, the seed that makes us both Homo sapiens and unique human persons, and at the same time the cultural ground that fosters this development. Los subsumes both the classical and the Judeo-Christian traditions, so that in him we see Hephaestus and the Platonic demiurge—creator of the cosmos and of human embodied souls—turn into the visionary of Jesus who finally images Christ as Creator and Redeemer. Los is Blake's great mediator between man and the divine, the disciple as artisan, in whom history becomes religous history and religious history becomes the history of the artist. In fact, Los is a second mediator—between man/Blake and Christ and between the authors of the Gospels and Jesus.

If the interplay between eternity and time, the divine humanity and fallen generation, is the great structural polarity or "X" of Blake's poetry, when Los in *The Book of Urizen* is assigned by the Eternals to "confine the obscure separation alone," and he starts into distinct existence as the link between Blake's two worlds, everything depends on him. Eternity shows that time is fallen, but eternity is nevertheless "in love with the productions of Time," and they are, for the most part, Los's productions. It is in Los that creation—and error—becomes possible within time. Los is "the faculty which experiences" of the Tractates, the Zoa who is able to learn and change, and finally to identify and correct error. (That Los is capable of changing is seen best in his relations with both his Spectre and his Emanation, Enitharmon, in Night VII of *The Four Zoas*.) The Los who begins in *The Book of Urizen* as desperate and apparently mindless action and who at the end of *Europe* and even of *The Four Zoas* still bursts out in violent act (apparently without insight into the present or foresight of consequences) is physical act, process, change through violence: "the wine-press of Los." This is the Los who is close to Orc and Luvah. The Los who tells Albion that he has innocence to protect and ignorance to instruct, who enters the door of death for his friend's sake, and who teaches him by his example to annihilate self, is the same Los—but matured—who begins the Apocalypse in Night IX of *The Four Zoas* out of terror.

We see, then, that it is in Los particularly that the "road of excess leads to the palace of wisdom," and that as the father of Orc comes to preach the forgiveness of sins, act becomes knowledge, the father becomes a brother, and the Eternals themselves learn and are changed. If the Eternals are enriched by the life in time of Jesus, Los is that life embodied in the work of the artist and builder and prophet.

As time, Los is the mercy of eternity. The cosmos he creates is centered in the local landscape that we know as the here-and-now given by the awakened senses—for example, the Felpham garden, which is the goal of Milton's cosmic journey into time and space in *Milton*, and the lark and thyme, which are messengers. With these Adam-atoms Blake counters the Natural Philosophy of Democritus and Lucretius (which sees the source as atoms in motion in a void) in its most powerful reviser, Newton. After Los's initial cosmic creation of an erroneous Urizen, his religion, and his world (in *The Book of Urizen*), Los's own world becomes a sustained and continual human creation in which men themselves, as minute particulars, stand as synecdoches for the whole. If, in Los, work dominates, with his conversion it becomes the work of faith and redemption, so that the world-artificer becomes also the world-savior. It is Los who proves the claims of *The Marriage of Heaven and Hell*—that Poetic Genius and "firm perswasion" remove mountains, that in large part we create ourselves, and that "God only acts & is, in existing beings or men." And it is Los who shows us the poet's/ artist's/savior's faith: "There is a Moment in each Day [and a Grain of Sand in Lambeth] that Satan cannot find" (*Milton* 35:42/E135/136; *Jerusalem* 37:15/E181/183).

But from the start, Los's creation is both error and the attempt to correct error. Like Blake's prophecies, it is always in change and revision, and Los increasingly learns to separate error from truth. Because "Truth has bounds, Error none," error appears everywhere. Gradually it becomes clear that it has one source—the claim to be God and to make universal laws from one's own identity—but it still needs to be identified in all its ramifications. Blake's Mental Fight to identify and cast out error or Satan on all fronts—art, poetry, psychology, history, politics, economics, natural science, and religion—makes his poetry both philosophic and epic, or all-inclusive.

As demiurge, Los can recreate his creation and correct even deep-rooted historical errors, such as those deriving from the Bible and from pagan poets, or from misreadings of both. Los knows all (Western) history because he began it all, and finally, in the great anamnesis of "I am that shadowy Prophet who six thousand years ago / Fell from my station in the Eternal bosom" (*Four Zoas* VIII/113:48–49/E365/380), re-members it and sees that all time is present. For Los and Blake, if all time is eternally present, all time is redeemable. Los's recall of history enables Blake to write it from a new point of view—that of the Divine Vision created and given by Poetic Genius: to show it as beginning in the fall from the

Everlasting Gospel of Jesus and ending in that Gospel regained in Los.

In recreating the world in human form Los embodies souls by building on atoms of "feeling"—often "mere passion and appetite." Blake imagines the mortal body as a work of art, a garden or building or city, made by the sons and daughters of Los: "And every Generated Body in its inward form, / Is a garden of delight & a building of magnificence" (*Milton* 26:31–32/E122/123). Los's cosmos and ordered souls reflect the "Wars of Eternity," which build the universe through visible, acting speech:

> As the breath of the Almighty, such are the words of man
>   to man
> In the great Wars of Eternity, in fury of Poetic Inspiration
> To build the Universe stupendous: Mental Forms creating.
>   (*Milton* 30:18–20/E128/129)

Los's making the world shows the poet-prophet remaking the world. But Blake's metaphor is bold: he simply shows Los making the world (where he is a giant form and an immense hyperbole) and cherishing the minute particulars (where he is a "small Sir" or modest understatement). Los builds with the smallest units of creative perception: the pulsation of an artery, a globule of man's blood, the center of a flower. In them, he is able to "shew [us] all alive / The world, when every particle of dust breathes forth its joy" (*Europe* iii:17–18/E59/60).

In "General Forms have their vitality in Particulars; & every / Particular is a Man; a Divine Member of the Divine Jesus" (*Jerusalem* 91:29–30/E249/251), Blake shows the work of art as a divine community of men. Los's work identifies the minute particulars that are elements of his world with the universal human form as seen in a work of art and in Jesus. For Blake "Art is the Tree of Life God is Jesus" ("The Laocoön" E271/274), and Los is the dynamic image of his remaking everything from that point of view. In Los, art is faith and salvation as labor: the sons of Los "With bounds to the Infinite put off the Indefinite / Into most holy forms of Thought . . . / They labour incessant" (*Milton* 28:4–6/E124/125). Blake's epistemology and psychology, his cosmology and theology, is an aesthetic of faith derived from his experience as a working artist and poet.

As Los changes from pagan hero (demiurge in the books of *Urizen* and *Los*, Mars in *Europe*) to Christian hero (in *The Four Zoas*), he develops form and consciousness; and he begins to forge words, building the stubborn basement of the language "lest Albion be a dumb despair." In Los—and under Los's hammer—act becomes speech; and the spiral is completed when speech, finally, transforms itself into act at the end of *Jerusalem.* If Los's development is a return to and recovery of the origin, the recovered origin is speech. We move with Los from the solitary struggle and lament of *The Book of Urizen* and *The Book of Los* and *The Song of Los* through Mental Fight to the conversation of eternity. As Los turns back from pagan demiurge to visionary of Jesus, we turn back through the creation to its source and end in the Word as eternal life. When the human poem, in the person of Albion centered in Los, arises as Jehovah-Jesus, and the "art of writing" given in thunder and fire at Sinai becomes the thunderous "conversation" of equal exchange in the many-in-one of Albion as Jehovah, questions are no more answered than they are in Jehovah's "response" in the book of Job. But we have reached the end of a great action in the form of a comedy, and Los's work for the time being is done.

Blake cuts short the conversation in Eden by presenting it only at the end, and it remains mysterious. What he describes as the coming of figures and mental forms into perfect clarity is for us a vanishing point in which we know what we know through having watched its coming into existence in the whole body of the poems and prophecies. Like Coleridge in "Kubla Khan," Blake in *Jerusalem* causes the poem to turn back on itself and to show its building as language, and language as a risen body. Los's building the language with which he builds a world can be taken as summing up the whole of his work as demiurge, awakener, and savior. As creator of the word, Los becomes Logos and disappears into the poem as Word, along with the other Zoas as Gospel writers. When Los disappears into his achieved work, he images any poet or artist or worker, but language has been his last great work, and in it Blake has been his prime agent.

When Los "builds" or alters language, he comes closest to literally imaging what Blake has been doing from the start. He is the Universal Form of Blake's action in the poem.

* * *

More than most poets, Blake prevents us from seeing his figures or images or lines as finished and stilled. In reading him we move with the unfolding life of imagination and are carried by the action of imaginative production and transformation. For Blake, the fact that our initial or founding works of criticism are the *Republic* and the *Phaedrus* and the *Poetics* must have seemed unfortunate. Plato suggests that poets do not know what they are saying. Aristotle thinks they do; but he treats poetry in such a powerfully analytical way that the terms of the analysis have proved determining and overriding. Blake's first act in his defense of poets in the Tractates and again in *The Marriage of Heaven and Hell* is to change the terms by turning back to the source, which is generative and productive. The source and new initial term is "Poetic Genius." Everything is to be seen in terms of the imagination and through the work—through the mind and hands—of the producing poet-artist.

Without mentioning Aristotle's *Poetics*, Blake sees that the usual terms of criticism do little justice to the impulse, generation, production, or movement of poetry; they are not genetic, not productive, not dynamic.[1] In Los, Blake's image of poetry is his image of the poet, and it is profoundly genetic. Los is in almost constant action, so that the excitement of Blake's poetry is in its growth and building through Los's work as demiurge. In Los, furthermore, Blake's poetry becomes an imagined or mythical history of poetry in which the genesis of poetry is the genesis of culture (which often falls into "religion"), and human history is the history of the artist and a history in which Blake is a latecomer who turns back to the beginning in order to regain the source and to correct the errors of the past.

1. For a view which recognizes the importance of genesis and fosters the production of writing, see Marie Ponsot and Rosemary Deen, *Beat Not the Poor Desk*.

To say that the figure of Los dominates Blake's poetry, and to say further that Los is an image of the poet and of the making of poetry, sounds depressingly modernist and self-conscious and all too familiar. But Blake's search for or turning back to the primitive, to the ancient poets who animated all sensible objects with gods and geniuses, has an amazing, labyrinthine force. It cannot be called self-conscious because Blake's exploration as it unfolds is in part blind, feeling its way into the primitive that is still present within the human psyche, underground, in caves and caverns. Blake expands and proliferates within his primordial image, causing the inside of his cave to be infinite. This is one pole of Blake's practice. At the same time, he *does* know what he is saying. His knowledge takes the form of vision on the one hand and the form of the knowledge that emerges through realization on the other. He has the whole abstract form of it in his mind. Blake's seed statement in "There Is No Natural Religion" is the statement both of an action and of a change or coming-to-be, which has a chiastic back and forth pattern of *God, we, we, he,* and four verbs of becoming-being: "Therefore God becomes as we are, / that we may be as he is." The end turns back on itself, and we work back and forth chiastically between beginning and end. The form is that of a circle with diameters crossing in an X, or the sign for infinity:

> God becomes
> *as*
> we are,
> that
> we may be
> as he is.

Nowadays we are very conscious of the end as determining narrative, partly because of Frank Kermode's *The Sense of an Ending.* Here is Sartre's Roquentin, in *Nausea:*

> Nothing happens while you live! The scenery changes, people come in and go out, that's all . . . . [Events follow one another in] an interminable monotonous addition. . . . But everything changes when you *tell* about life; it's a change no one notices: the proof is that people talk about true stories. As if there could possibly be true stories; things happen one way and we tell about them in the opposite sense [or direction]. You seem to

start at the beginning . . . and in reality you have started at the
end. . . .The end is there, transforming everything.[2]

In reality, and in Blake, things are a little more complicated.
In Blake, the end is immensely clarifying when it comes—in
Night IX of *The Four Zoas*, for example. But the poetic action
is in finding and unfolding the end. One might say that Blake
begins with the end in his mind in abstract form, as in "that
we may be as he is," or "So, and with the same infinite
variety, all are alike in the Poetic Genius." But it is more to
the point to note that Blake begins with the *whole* in his
mind. He begins in 1788 with an immense condensation—
"Therefore God becomes as we are, that we may be as he
is"—from which the whole of his subsequent myth unfolds.
That statement is neither theology nor philosophy, though
the Tractates, where it appears, look like philosophy. Like the
Tractates as a whole, it is a poetic statement. Its condensation
is too great to suggest that Blake had the whole of his unfolded myth in mind or that he had the unfolded end in
mind, both of which possibilities are nearly unimaginable.

It is all still to be worked out, and the process of working it
out, often blind and requiring correction and reforming and
transformation, is the action of the poetry: the poet's action
in the poetry imaged in his protagonist, Los, whose action
includes Blake's in a much larger action, and who gradually
subsumes other figures—the devil, Milton, Ezekiel, Elijah,
Isaiah, and Christ of *The Marriage of Heaven and Hell*, for
example. As the *Marriage* moves from the devil toward
prophets and toward a revelation of Christ, so Los in Blake's
myth moves from Orc toward prophecy and self-
annihilation.

Los looks a little like other Romantic poet-figures, like
Wordsworth in the *Prelude*, for example, but the *Prelude* looks
simply like autobiography compared with *The Four Zoas* or
Milton or *Jerusalem*. It does not try to contain all of history,
nor does Wordsworth present himself or anyone else as creating the world or saving it. Los also looks a little like Byron

2. Quoted by Gordon S. Wood, in a review of Robert Middlekauf's *The
Glorious Cause: The American Revolution, 1763–1789*, in *The New York Review of
Books*, 12 August 1982, p. 8.

"the poet" in *Don Juan,* where Juan resembles the young, adventurous Byron, passive object of sexual advances, with Byron the older poet—Byron/Los—making great play with the language and order and "plot" of the poem. But for Byron it *is* play; and though *Don Juan* is a serious comedy, Blake is more serious. *Don Juan* looks as if it had been written straight off; however it began, it did not begin as a whole, but more likely as a style and voice. For Blake, poetry proved to be a continually transforming and self-correcting process—almost like science—which approaches closer and closer to the shape of a religion or a prophecy. "God becomes as we are, that we may be as he is" is for Blake a faith as well as the root statement of his myth, a statement which expresses belief and contains poetic potentiality, and which at the same time rounds on and completes itself as form.

Blake's mind is not on himself but on his myth. He looks within, but he is no solipsist or narcissist: the Byron of *Manfred* and *Cain*—the "Lord Byron in the Wilderness"—is closer to that. To look within, for Blake, is to look everywhere, at the whole insofar as it can be heard or envisioned. And the whole sometimes appears and grows in its parts. So Blake turns his attention from whole to part, and back from the newly developed part that has occupied his attention to its place in his now-altered view of the whole. "The eye altering alters all" comes to mind, but so does Blake's polypus. A runner develops and enroots itself; the body regenerates a lost part; the building begins to build a new wing. The whole may of course be radically altered by being seen from a new point of view, by a different figure or character, or from a different time-place.

Blake's "Arguments" and "Preludiums" are often condensed wholes of which the whole poem can be seen as the unfolding, but the poem often begins with a new set of figures and a new point of view. Or a passage may condense the whole six thousand years of mythical history into six lines of landscape, as Blake does in *The Song of Los*:

> For Adam, a mouldering skeleton
> Lay bleach'd on the garden of Eden;
> And Noah as white as snow

On the mountains of Ararat.
. . . .
Orc raging in European darkness
Arose like a pillar of fire above the Alps. (7:20–23, 26–27/
  E68/69)

Blake begins with wholes and elaborates both by changing the point from which we view the whole and by expanding the whole, which he does in part by multiplying figures or characters, and thus points of view. To present an analogy, one might see "Kubla Khan" unfolding into at least as long a poem as *The Marriage of Heaven and Hell.* One might see it, for example, as the argument to the "Rime of the Ancient Mariner," as if "Kubla Khan" presented the Bard, while the "Rime" presented the Bard's Song. Dropping down—as in "down to a sunless sea" and "Merrily did we drop / Below the kirk, below the hill, below the lighthouse top,"—appears in both poems, and both end in a counterbalancing rise. Both poems form a spherical cosmos of height and depth, of sea and sky, of daylight sky and night sky, and both image that cosmos in the glittering eye of the poet or teller of tales. The circular form of the "Rime" is perhaps more obvious, but "Kubla Khan" also comes round to its beginning, so that it would form a neat "Preludium" to the "Rime." "Tintern Abbey," similarly, is a Blakean "Preludium" to—and the 1799 "Prelude" manuscript is the containing seed of—the expanded *Preludes* of 1806 and 1850. I do not argue that Blake's way of working by expanding wholes is unique, but only that his imaginative condensations and leaps have greater and more spectacular force than those of other poets.

The same may be said of Blake's points of view. Part of what makes "The Mental Traveller" a strange poem in Blake's canon at the place where it comes is that the point of view is so rigidly limited and controlled. It is the negative-ironic form of Blake's myth presented through only two figures, but figures whose aspects multiply while we continue to see them from outside, from an "objective" (really a diminishing and withering) point of view: male/female, age/youth, riches/poverty, person/world, and so on. We expect the multiplying aspects, but not their conjunction with the single vision or viewpoint. *The Four Zoas* explodes this single vision.

If what most strikes one about the development of Blake's myth is the active, even gigantic struggle through which it was composed (Leopold Damrosch, Jr., is very good on this), one later sees that the struggle is largely between contending points of view. *The Four Zoas* is a mosaic or cacophony of contending laments, accusations, personal narratives, dreams, and delusions, a struggle of embattled voices trying to learn to speak and finally coming into a clarity of speech and vision. As in "The Mental Traveller," Blake seems almost to be traveling around a circle, but now he is viewing the same matter or action from all points of view. The parts of the whole are points of view, and the differences in point of view provoke conflict. That is one account of the fall.

Los emerges as the focus of energy and the directing vision of that struggle, and it is Los who begins the apocalyptic conclusion by tearing down the sun and moon. In *Europe,* earlier, Los does something similar when he calls all his sons to the strife of blood. Here *Europe* stops short. But Blake in *Europe* had not yet presented Los as the creator-demiurge: he did that later, in *The Book of Urizen.* It looks as if Los is an apocalyptic figure in Blake's imagination before he is a creator or demiurge. Here Blake might seem to begin with the end, but it is the end seen only abstractly. What Blake in fact begins with is the whole, and in that whole, end matches beginning. Change re-establishes the original state (with a difference, to be sure), so that Blake's whole form is a spiral from Eden to Eden. This is certainly not tragic form, and unlike Aristotelian form it emphasizes the form of regaining or redemption more than the structure of change.

"The Mental Traveller" is the clearest example of a poem whose beginning is its end and of a poem which contains the whole form of Blake's myth, though it is the "shadow" cast by it. It is the erroneous form of "turning back"—a turning back to a misconceived primitivist beginning in mother earth, and thus a beginning in error. One imagines an earlier draft in which Blake arrived at the end—"nails him down upon the Rock"—and made that the beginning. It is likelier, however, that "The Crystal Cabinet" (also in the Pickering

Manuscript) is the "Preludium" to "The Mental Traveller." If "The Mental Traveller" begins with a fall into dream presented as the awakening from a fall, the fall itself is presented in "The Crystal Cabinet," where it is a fall through threefold Beulah into Generation-Ulro. There it is a failed sexual act, which ends with a weeping babe and a "Weeping Woman pale reclind" who seems to have given birth to him. In "The Crystal Cabinet," in which sexual intercourse is presented as birth into a fallen world, not only the male seed is the whole man. The penis is, too, and has "hands of flame." One synecdoche generates another, so to speak, and both seed and penis emerge from the vagina as a child being born. Blake's identifications of part and whole are part of the extraordinary holism that sees a world in a grain of sand and eternity in an hour.

But "The Crystal Cabinet" is a poem of sight as well as touch, so that the womb is a fallen, visual "England" as well as "London" space and contains both the Thames and a "pleasant Surrey bower." The speaker is not seeing *through* the eye (as we are urged to do in "Auguries of Imnocence" in the Pickering Manuscript), but has to be imagined as *in* it. The crystal-cabinet womb is the eye. The speaker has been seen, captured, reduced, contained, and kept at a distance by the "eye of love":

> I strove to sieze the inmost Form
> With ardor fierce & hands of flame
> But burst the Crystal Cabinet
> And like a Weeping Babe became. (21–24/E480/488–89)

The babe is born as a tear. The conjunction of tear and babe, frequent in Blake's poetry, is here an identification. He is born also as Eros himself, denied. This Eros, or lack, dominates "The Mental Traveller," with the male so frustrated that his final, frowning form as male babe suggests Eros turned into Mars, both of which are linked with Venus, with Enitharmon as both Aphrodite (in the poem's first phase) and Artemis-Diana (in its second phase) as sides of a coin.

The "Soldiers sigh" and "new-born Infants tear" of "London" have been reduced to a single form of woe, which is now threatening because frustrated Eros has become Mars.

We have seen the making of a soldier, as in "I must rush again to War: for the Virgin has frownd & refusd" (*Jerusalem* 68:63/ E220/222). We have also seen the making of "a Vegetated Christ and a Virgin Eve" (*Jerusalem* 90:34/E247/250). "The Mental Traveller" balances pagan and Christian elements in a single total negative form that clearly implies the positive form of which it is the shadow, as "London" is the shadow of "And did those feet in ancient time," the poem of which *Jerusalem* is the expanded form.

As the Generation-Ulro into which the faery speaker of "The Crystal Cabinet" is born, "The Mental Traveller" also has the form of a womb: it converts the straight-line pursuit of a fleeing form into a globe from which escape is difficult, possible at only one point—downwards—and only in the reduced form of an infant. Seeing the crystal cabinet as eye/ globe/womb and as "Preludium" to "The Mental Traveller" would help to account for the globular world and vision of "The Mental Traveller," where it is as if we were inside the globe of earth, perhaps like the iron/brass, silver, or gold men who emerge from mother earth in the myth of *Republic* X. Blake's mother earth is Enitharmon, both earth and heaven-space: the first phase of "The Mental Traveller" shows an eye of earth; the second shows a cold and remote heaven eye, the moon.

If there is a way back from the Generation-Ulro of "The Mental Traveller," it is through the wrathful, innocent vision of "Auguries of Innocence": "A Robin Red breast in a Cage / Puts all Heaven in a Rage" (5–6/E484/490); "The Soldier armd with Sword & Gun / Palsied strikes the Summers Sun" (77– 78/E486/491). The frowning babe at the end of "The Mental Traveller" may, of course, suggest the wrath of the innocent vision and the power "To see a World in a Grain of Sand and . . . Hold Infinity in the palm of your hand." If so, Blake cuts these implications short. In "Auguries of Innocence,"

> God Appears & God is Light
> To those poor Souls who dwell in Night
> But does a Human Form Display
> To those who Dwell in Realms of day. (129–32/E484/493)

"The Mental Traveller" suggests all of this, but only by shadowing it. It is one of Blake's "night" poems, like "The Tyger"

and "Earth's Answer" and *Europe,* and one of its major subjects is light. If "The Mental Traveller" is a whole, it is also
half of a greater whole that it repeatedly suggests. It is one of
the nodes in the growth of Blake's whole myth. And the
Pickering Manuscript, which contains it and "The Crystal
Cabinet" and "Auguries of Innocence," is itself such a node,
but somewhat more inclusive.

To choose a metaphor that Blake might reject, Blake's
whole is generated by the division of root or seed that grows
into the whole body of the flowering tree. Blake presents two
trees, one the shadow of the other. "The Combats of Good &
Evil is eating of the Tree of Knowledge. The Combats of Truth
& Error is eating of the Tree of Life" ("A Vision of the Last
Judgment," p. 86/E558/563). Through Los, a tree of life, Blake
flowers into a whole body of poetic prophecy and of myth, so
that his poetry may be seen as the poetry of prolific generation: the generation of poetic images and acts and characters,
and their shaping into the forms of prophecy and epic. In the
terms Shelley uses for imagination in his "Defence of Poetry," Los is both "root and blossom" of the creation, both the
poem and the world.

*   *   *

As tree of life, Los stands, though fallen, as an image of the
unfallen body, of the fully human prolific, which appears first
in the family, but ends in "Births of Intellect" ("A Vision of
the Last Judgment," E552/562).

In Los, Blake centers action in the human family. In *The
Book of Urizen* he shows the genesis of sexuality and the
family, but shows it very briefly; in *The Four Zoas* he develops
it. Family history, as in Hesiod and the Old Testament, is
mythical history. In Blake's history of family conflict and proliferation in *The Four Zoas,* Urizen is the first-born, oldest
brother to Luvah and Vala (as David Wagenknecht observes).[3]
His attempt to put a stop to further generation—to stop his
siblings at the source—makes him a kind of Cain. Urizen as
first-born in *The Four Zoas* is really "first fallen," as in *The
Book of Urizen,* or most seriously fallen, as Cain is in Genesis.

3. *Blake's Night,* p. 233.

The great turn in *The Four Zoas* comes when Urizen's attempt to prevent the birth of the brother is finally converted, in Los's relations with his Spectre, into loving fatherhood tending toward brotherhood (in Night VII), and Los's son, Orc, begins to feel and reflect these changes. Urizen and Los are two images of fatherhood/elder brotherhood. Urizen is the father and older brother who wishes his son/brother *not* to be. Los moves from Urizen's jealousy to love.

Blake's first long prophecy is the history of a marriage, its internal conflicts, and the opposition it suffers, through which Los and Enitharmon develop into fully human characters capable of learning and change, with their children unfolding what is implied in the parents, developing as agents of Mental Fight, and changing their parents. *Milton* begins with this human family and gives us a kind of psychoanalysis of it and of Los, so that in its dynamics we see city, nation, and all mankind. Blake's history of "Parents Marriages & Friendships" (*Jerusalem* 16:65/E159/161) is in part a turning from Milton to the Old Testament. In his own *Milton* he gives us not God in heaven with his angels, but a family; and he shows us the fall in the family, instead of in a rebellion and battle in heaven, as it is in *Paradise Lost*. Seen in the family, the fall is a universal and familiar human event intensified. Seen in heaven, it is political theater—a king and his court. (Blake's observation about *Paradise Lost* goes back at least as far as *The Marriage of Heaven and Hell*, where God is identified as a magnified king.)

In *Milton* and *Jerusalem*, finally, Los as progenitor completes his change and becomes Los as brother. Blake makes brotherhood—not filial or feudal obedience—his political human tie when Los becomes a democrat and levels the old hierarchy of king and priest, which Blake finds even in the work of Milton. The greatest and boldest "bringing home" is in seeing every man as divine and "loving the greatest men best." The words, from *The Marriage of Heaven and Hell*, repeated in *Jerusalem* 91, sound aristocratic or meritocratic. Blake offers a democracy, but a democracy which opens careers to talents and an aristocracy of effort and skill, an aristocracy of artists who transpose warfare between nations into international competition-exchanges of art, as in "Now

Art has lost its mental Charms . . . With works of Art their Armies meet" (E471/479).

If the great turn in Blake's conception of Los is in the letter poem to Butts and in Night VII of *The Four Zoas*, the great development in Blake's and Los's consciousness is in *Milton*. Choosing Milton as his poet-prophet, Blake turns to his own nation and approaches his own times, so that when Milton arrives in Blake's garden the poet-prophet reaches the present and incarnates himself in Blake. In *Milton* Blake can enter his own poem beside Los and Milton because he has understood in Los both himself and his task. We can see in *Milton* that Los, at least from *The Four Zoas* on, has been the poet's self-discovery and self-criticism revealed in the poem, acting as the poem's source and center. If in the Tractates and the *Book of Urizen* Poetic Genius is shown fallen into its component parts, in the Bard's Song of *Milton* Los is projected into the poem as the image of the poem's creator in his created world, shown as divided into a "family" that provides the characters of the poem. And *Milton* derives its characters not only from Los's but also from Milton's psyche.

The major figures in the Bard's Song of *Milton* are treated symbolically as psychological forces in the poet-prophet himself—Los's offspring and their Emanations. Los alludes to or "presents" Milton, and the Bard's Song alludes particularly to *Paradise Lost*. So *Milton* reveals the psychic structure of *Paradise Lost*: it shows Milton's psyche as revealed in *Paradise Lost*. And in Los, of course, Blake's poems have increasingly revealed their own psychic structure. In the Tractates, Los appears simply as "Poetic Genius," which consists of reason, desire, and the object of desire. In *The Four Zoas*, that structure appears as an obscure and sometimes chaotic battle among Zoas and between Zoa and Emanation, which comes into clear form and action only at the end, in the magnificent Night IX. In *Milton*, finally, Blake and Los become one and then separate again. Blake has become fully conscious of his task and powers as a poet and is able to enter the poem to correct his errors. One or two errors are in *The Marriage of Heaven and Hell*, where Blake had only angels and devils— what in *Milton* he calls "Elect" and "Reprobate"—and from which Emanations are absent. (The "prophets" in the *Mar-*

riage—Isaiah, Ezekiel, Elijah, Jesus—are "devilish," are "Reprobates.") Now he provides a new class—the "Redeemed"—which makes conversion without violence possible; and *Milton* ends in the marriage that is hard to find anywhere in *The Marriage of Heaven and Hell* outside the title. Distinct separation of Shadow from Emanation, error from truth, is clearer in *Milton* than in any earlier poem of Blake's because in *Milton* the poet for the first time has clearly and dispassionately observed himself and measured himself against the task of the poet-prophet as revealed in Los.

The temptation-agons and identifications between Milton and Satan, Blake and Milton and Los, Milton and Blake and Christ, form the core of *Milton*. They are especially complex in the scene in which Blake, in his garden at Felpham, receives the lark as a mighty angel, a messenger from Eden. The lark's nest is in Golgonooza, at Luvah's empty tomb. The first lark leaves the tomb of the resurrection, in Joseph of Arimathea's garden (Los in Night VIII of *The Four Zoas* has such a tomb), and the twenty-eighth lark meets Ololon descending into Blake's garden—an "annunciation" to Blake by the thirteen-year-old virgin Ololon. The message has come to us through the twenty-seven churches of time, each with its own day and night, and it has arrived on the instant. Blake is showing time as the swiftest of all things and as a space in which we can move around freely. We have begun at the place of death and resurrection and arrived earlier at the time of the Annunciation—or at a later annunciation, the annunciation of a second coming. (Annunciations may occur in any "moment . . . that Satan cannot find.") When Milton arrives and is confronted by his Shadow/Spectre, he corrects the crucifixion-as-atonement by annihilating his Selfhood. Ololon does the same.

If we compare this garden scene with the Los/Spectre/Enitharmon three-figure confrontation in Night VII of *The Four Zoas*, Blake/Milton appears as the Los, and Catherine/Ololon as the Enitharmon, of Night VII; and Blake/Milton's Shadow (his error) appears as Los's Spectre of Night VII. But the confrontation is now clear, unambiguous, and decisive. Milton knows exactly what he is doing. The two males/one female pattern, we remember, goes back to Blake's early prophecies, to *America* and "A Song of Liberty" and *Visions of the Daughters*. Two males quarreling over one female show that the Emanation has ceased to be an exchange of Mental Gifts, or the open bosom which reveals one to others in communication. This breakdown is the start of warfare, as in the rape of Helen and the quarrel between Agamemnon and Achilles at the start of the *Iliad*. Oothoon in *Visions of the Daughters* is an Emanation who tries to offer herself as a gift—in a reversal of the Agamemnon-Achilles quarrel over female prizes—but is prevented by Bromion's rape and his contemptuous gift of her to Theotormon as his harlot. Ololon as Emanation, then, is a new Oothoon, an Emanation who reveals Milton to Blake; Emanations, we remember, stand both male and female at the gates of each humanity. As the Emanation by which one reveals oneself to and greets another, Ololon helps correct Blake's relations with his own "sweet shadow of delight."

Blake in his garden at Felpham enacts the career of Christ, as Los in Night VII enacts in one form the temptations of Adam and of Christ. In the garden Blake receives an annunciation from a virgin angel, "agonizes" (as at Gethsemane) over the question of what he is now to do, "dies," is "buried" and "resurrected" as a new man. Blake as poet alludes rapidly to the whole earthly career of Christ in himself as a figure in his own poem, conceived and reborn as the latest in the line of poet-prophets in England. We might compare Blake's ironic allusion to himself as the resurrected Jesus early in the *Marriage* (and Keats's "death" and "rebirth" in *The Fall of Hyperion*). But Blake (like G. M. Hopkins) apparently sees every conversion or "Last Judgment" as an imitation of Christ. Every just man

> Acts in God's eye what in God's eye he is—
> Christ. For Christ plays in ten thousand places
> . . . .
> To the Father through the features of men's faces. ("As Kingfishers Catch Fire")

Looked at differently, Blake in the garden "conceives" a new Milton—Milton in his second coming reincarnated or re-embodied in Blake, born again in Blake's poem *Milton*. In

Milton, Blake and Catherine receive an annunciation from the angel-virgin Ololon, who is followed by Milton. And, like Mary and her lover (in Blake's view of it), they conceive and give birth: to a reborn Milton. Alternatively, if Milton arrives in the garden as the Holy Spirit, who recreates himself through Blake and Catherine, the Holy Ghost who was "vacuum" in *Paradise Lost* (as Blake alleges in the *Marriage*) has now been filled by Milton himself. If Blake has a disagreement with Milton, he presents it with extraordinary tact. In any case, since what Blake and his wife actually produce is the illuminated poem *Milton*—an Eros "Birth of Intellect from the divine Humanity" ("A Vision of the Last Judgment," E552/562)—we are apparently to see the poem itself as the conception and rebirth or second coming of Milton as if he were Christ: Milton's corrected vision of Christ mediated by Blake. We see again that for Blake the poem is a person.

At the same time, when Milton decisively identifies and annihilates Satan as his Selfhood, he re-enacts and corrects the Christ of his own *Paradise Regained.* Satan as the Selfhood is infinitely closer to one's apparent identity than he is in *Paradise Regained,* and the figure being tempted is now seen by Milton—shown by Blake—to be the poet himself. More accurately, Blake now shows both Satan and Christ to be the poet himself. (Eve also, as the poet's feminine portion, is the poet himself.) We see that the course of Blake's myth is determined as much by his intent to identify Satan as to identify Christ: both are parts of the poet, or recreated in the poet, and both are parts of the same act of identification.

In *Milton* the poet creates anew the Divine Vision: the image of Christ seen in the figure of the poet—Milton/Blake/Los—who has cast out Satan from himself. In *Jerusalem,* it is the poem itself that "rises" as Christ. At the end of *Jerusalem,* when Albion sees the poet-prophet Los as Christ, Los has "become what he beholds" (and so has Albion, most clearly in the double or mirroring crucifixion stance in pl. 76, read nonironically); and the authors of the four Gospels—the four Zoas—rise as Christ. (Blake looks behind the figure of Christ to the Gospel writers. If Christ is a figure created or envisioned through poet-prophets, we can avoid idolatry by seeing the creators as the "greatest men" whom we should "love best," and the creative power as God, as in *The Marriage of Heaven and Hell*.) The poem itself "rises" and comes to life in "Conversation" and "Words of Life." The Ololon of *Milton* is subsumed in Jerusalem, woman and city and poem, and the poem-city is centered in Christ as the human temple. The poem as act is Christ-Jehovah, the highest humanity we can imagine. The poem as image or form—Emanation—is Jerusalem, the exchange of the unique Mental Forms that identify us and thus build community. Christ as Divine Vision has been created by, has created himself through, Blake/Los, much as Milton in Blake's Felpham garden reconceived and recreated himself through Blake and Catherine. "God is a man not because he is so concieved by man but because he is the creator of man" (Annotations to Swedenborg's *Divine Love and Divine Wisdom*/E592/603).[4]

* * *

What is missing from *Milton* is Jerusalem herself and Albion as active fourfold agent. *Milton* is the regaining of identity; *Jerusalem* is the regaining of community: the regaining of identity multiplied fourfold in Albion, who rouses his "Cities and Counties" and his "Twenty-Eight Cities," and ultimately the whole of mankind or earth. (When he announces that "the Night of Death is past and the Eternal Day / Appears upon our Hills" [pl. 97:3–4/E254/256], he might almost be the earth of "Earth's Answer," for Albion answers the plea in the "Introduction" to *Songs of Experience* as the Bard would have wanted, and as earth can now do.) If Jerusalem is that community regained, she is regained in—returns to—London. Blake's turning back now completes itself as a turning toward what is nearest, and also a turning inward like Milton's. In *Jerusalem* 27, Blake delineates the necessary source and end of his myth: that the "Everlasting Gospel" of Jesus that follows the Old Testament in the Bible came first, before the Druids and the patriarchs of the Old Testament, and that its home is London. "'All things Begin & End in Albions Ancient Druid Rocky Shore'" (E170/171).

4. "Every image of God is thus a symbolic expression of the human imagination, in which God dwells" (Leopold Damrosch, Jr., *Symbol and Truth in Blake's Myth*, p. 275).

Jerusalem 27 gives us Blake's Gospel myth in its clearest and sunniest form in Jerusalem and Jesus. Jerusalem here is less Dante's *figlia del* [*suo*] *figlio* than bride of her offspring:

> Her Little-ones ran on the fields
> The Lamb of God among them seen
> And fair Jerusalem his Bride.

Whether or not this Beulah stems from Blake's portrayal of "Los's world" in the center of *Milton,* the poem in *Jerusalem* 27 "answers" the epigraph poem to *Milton*: "And did those feet in ancient time." (*Jerusalem* 77 completes the answer.) But *Jerusalem* 27 juxtaposes Jesus and Satan more closely than "And did those feet" does, where Satan appears only in "dark Satanic Mills." London in *Jerusalem* 27 is both the Beulah of *Songs of Innocence,* where "every English Child is seen, / Children of Jesus & his Bride," and the place of the fall, "Where Satan the first victory won." The lines "He witherd up the Human Form, / By laws of sacrifice for sin: / Till it became a Mortal Worm," together with "Weeping in weak & mortal clay" and "Entering thro' the Gates of Birth / And passing thro' the Gates of Death," include and enlarge "To Tirzah," suggest the womb as tomb of "For the Sexes," and suggest furthermore that the final form of the male babe in "The Mental Traveller" has been "witherd up" so that he can pass through the gates of death.

What is remarkable in all these poems is the juxtaposition of Satan and Jesus and their convergence in Adam or in Los or in Blake. When Blake confesses to having slain the "Lamb of God . . . in my dark self-righteous pride," and this conversion-recognition is immediately reinforced in "My Selfhood! Satan! armd in gold," Milton's self-annihilation has passed to Blake (as it had already done, more subtly, in Blake's Felpham garden in *Milton*). Furthermore, Blake here seems to speak as Albion: it is "Spectre of Albion" that he acknowledges as his Selfhood.

When Albion rouses himself in *Jerusalem* 95, then, it is the conclusion of a long-drawn-out Mental Fight waged by Blake and Los, and we remember that Albion's partial awakening in *Milton* was composed of Blake-Milton-Los. In

> Thou seest the Sun in heavy clouds
> Struggling to rise above the Mountains. in his burning hand
> He takes his Bow, then chooses out his arrows of flaming
>   gold
> Murmuring the Bowstring breathes with ardor! (95:11–14/
>   E252/255),

we are taken back through the weapons of Mental Fight: in plate 52—

> When Satan first the black Bow Bent
> And the Moral Law from the Gospel rent

and

>   the bitter groan of a Martyrs woe
> is an Arrow from the Almighties Bow—

through plate 27, when "the Druids golden Knife, / Rioted . . . / in Offerings of Human Life" to "Albion gave his deadly groan, / And all the Atlantic mountains shook." (The "groans" connect *Jerusalem* 52 and 27, and the multiplication of suffering even to the shaking of the Atlantic mountains is the same linking of moral cause and physical effect that we see in "Auguries of Innocence.") We are taken back also through the epigraph poem to *Milton*—"Bring me my Bow of burning gold: / Bring me my Arrows of desire" (where Blake is the "fighter," as he is in *Jerusalem* 27)—and to the bows and arrows of Mental Fight in the letter poem to Butts of 22 November 1802:

> Los flamd in my path & the Sun was hot
> With the bows of my Mind & the Arrows of Thought
> My bowstring fierce with Ardour breathes
> My arrows glow in their golden sheaves
> My brothers & father march before
> The heavens drop with human gore
>
> Now I a fourfold vision see. (E693/722)

Here, successive multiples of vision yield "thistle," "old Man grey," and Los as the sun ("Twas outward a Sun, inward Los in his might"). Los does not appear as Jesus: his conversion has evidently not yet occurred, and Blake's "Now I a fourfold vision see" remains a mysterious leap. At the end of *Jerusalem*—after Night VII of *The Four Zoas* and after *Milton*—

the multiples of vision go further, and Los is no longer
Apollo, a classical Satan or "God of this world." Blake has
freed himself as poet from the "Covenant of Priam." If his
defiance of Los has helped change both Los and himself (as I
suggested in chapter III), in the final plates of *Jerusalem* this
conversion is intensified into Los's appearance as Jesus and
Albion's fourfold annihilation of the Druid Spectre. In *Jerusalem* 95, then, it is Albion, not Los, who is sunlike. It is Albion
as the sun who is the archer—not Blake—and he is fourfold.
But his bowstring still "breathes with Ardour," as Blake's
does in the Butts poem. Albion as fourfold archer, then,
seems to include both the Los and the Blake of the poem to
Butts. But Blake and Los are of course no longer at odds, and
the family is no longer Blake's "brothers & father" but "a
Male & Female" whose "Children" are arrows, and this family is finally modulated into brotherhood. We have followed a
long hard road from Blake's family and vocation conflict on
the Felpham shore to this humanity.

The end of *Jerusalem* takes place mostly between Albion
and himself. Albion as Jehovah compels his Zoas—all but
Los—to their work, each to his own place: Urizen to his
furrow, Tharmas to his sheepfold, Luvah to his loom. (This is
the last such compulsion; from now on, the Zoas are free and
equal.) Los-Urthona has never left his anvil and is praised for
having "kept the Divine Vision in time of trouble" (95:20/
E252/255). When Albion, having brought his Zoas into order,
sees Jesus and the danger to Los-Jesus from his Selfhood,
sacrifices himself for his friend, rises as a fourfold bowman,
and annihilates his Satan Selfhood, this is, at last, Jehovah's
fourfold self-annihilation, which infinitely multiplies
Milton's self-annihilation in *Milton* and Blake's on plate 27 of
Jerusalem. (Though it also changes the violence of the Night
IX Apocalypse of *The Four Zoas* into the forgiveness of sins, it
has enough "Damn" in it to remain very bracing.)

In this climax of Mental Fight on the verge of eternity, Los,
who from *Europe* on has been Jehovah's thunder, is still
thunderous—"a Bow of Iron terrible thundering"—yet the
fourfold bow is "a Bow of Mercy & Loving kindness" (97:11,
12/E254/256). In rapid succession, weapons become sexual,
become the family, and yield to "humanity" and "human."

"Male & Female" become a bow. "Bow" suggests Apollo and Jehovah, Eros, and male and female forces in tension. The male and female are grasped "between" by the "Hand" of man, the bowstring "breathes with Ardour," and the "Druid Spectre"—Albion's Satan—is "Annihilate." As bows come to life, Eros's "Arrows of Love" become "Children." Male and female having become a bow in the "Hand" of man, sexes are modulated into the Zoas and man—the "Universal Humanity"—and "Words of the Mutual Covenant Divine" on "Chariots . . . with Living Creatures," "Humanize / In the Forgiveness of Sins" (98:41, 45/E255/258). The warfare "Covenant of Priam" has become the "Covenant of Jehovah."

We have passed rapidly through Beulah and Generation and Mental Fight to humanity entering Eden. Blake has included Eros and Apollo, but he has chosen to focus on Jehovah and on Jehovah's mercy—the rainbow covenant after the Flood. And the covenant is now mutual. Albion as the Sixth Eye of History, Jehovah, yields to Albion as the Seventh Eye of History, Jesus. (Los has of course been all the "Eyes" of history, especially Elohim, Jehovah, and Jesus; and from Night VII of *The Four Zoas* on, he has been the Seventh Eye "preparing.") Since Jehovah's "Mutual Covenant Divine" is identified as "the Forgiveness of Sins," it is clear that Jehovah and Jesus have been reconciled in the "Everlasting Gospel" of Jesus. Furthermore, as in more earthly human families, identity as father, brother, and son gets confused. Albion-Jehovah is "the Universal Father"; yet he addresses Jesus as "my Lord," "my Creator," "my Redeemer." He seems to be *figlio del suo figlio*. The jealous God of the Old Testament has disappeared into the forgiving God of the Old Testament and the New, and Albion/Jesus is "the universal Humanity."

As the "Sexual threefold" chariots turn to paradises, four rivers, and four "faces" of humanity "fronting" the cardinal points, "going forward irresistible from Eternity to Eternity," we see that there are two waves of "humanizing." First, Mental Fight becomes "Fourfold," and fourfold vision becomes one complex sense—"sensual enjoyment" energized and improved. Then, weapons yield to "converse": "And they conversed as Man with Man" (Albion and Jesus, pl. 96); and

"they conversed together" (the Zoas, pl. 98). This "conversation" on plate 98 retains the Beulah of plate 27, the Mental
Fight of plate 52 ("When Satan first the black Bow Bent"), and
the exhortation to the Christians of plate 77, all of which are
addresses to the reader as Deist, Jew, or Christian. And it
retains its immediate context—the thunder, fire, bows, arrows, paradises, rivers, faces, and the transcendence of male
and female in the bow of Mental Fight grasped "between" by
the "Hand" of man, ending in "Wars of mutual Benevolence
Wars of Love" (97:12/E254/256), so that sexuality has become
"Wars of Love." In all this, Los, who has prepared it and
shown the way, who has been husband and father and finally
brother and friend, becomes Urthona and ceases to be further named or described. Los's disappearance is the elevation of the fallen humanity we know in ourselves into the
"universal Humanity" or "mutual Covenant Divine."

The line "And the Divine Appearance was the likeness &
similitude of Los" subtly distinguishes Los from Jehovah/
Jesus. In the final plates of *Jerusalem*, all is presented as
Blake's vision, in which identification of Albion with Jehovah
or Los with Jesus is never quite complete or allowed to stand.
More notably, identification of Albion with God never quite
occurs. In

> And Urizen & Luvah & Tharmas & Urthona arose into
> Albions Bosom: Then Albion stood before Jesus in the Clouds
> Of Heaven Fourfold among the Visions of God in Eternity
>   (96:41–43/E253–54/256),

Albion is "among the Visions of God in Eternity." Fourfold
vision seems a kind of ultimate, and Blake shares this vision.
But it is, to repeat, "among the Visions of God in Eternity."
Whether we are being told that Albion is a vision or appearance of God, or one vision among several which God
has, is not clear. At the end of *Jerusalem* we are repeatedly
baffled in our desire to know or to identify God. And *Jerusalem*'s end in "All Human Forms identified," going forth, re-
posing in "the Planetary lives of Years Months Days & Hours
. . . And then Awaking into his Bosom in the Life of Immortality" (99:1–4/E256/258), leaves "his Bosom" unidentified,
though earlier it was Albion's.

*   *   *

If the four Zoas appear to end things, that is perhaps because, as epic-heroic-gigantic forms, they provide the
thunder and lightning of Blake's poetry. But they remain one
of several myths in Blake's composition. By the end of *Jerusalem* these myths are so familiar that they may be described as
voices making up the fourfold harmony of the end.

One is the myth of the bodily life and senses of the Zoas,
with their Spectres and Emanations. A second is the classical
myth of the demiurge and the genealogy of the gods. As
warlike, this is Blake's "Covenant of Priam"; Urizen is as
much Priam and Zeus as Jehovah. A third is the Old Testament myth focused in Elohim-Jehovah, Adam and Eve, the
prophets, Job, the Flood. Blake finally focuses this in "the
Covenant of Jehovah." A fourth—the Gospel myth of
Jesus—has two forms: Gospel as love and Gospel as art, both
of which are redemptive. The triumph of the Gospel myth in
Jerusalem through changing and subsuming the others is a
late and complex development of the conversion of an angel
to a devil in *The Marriage of Heaven and Hell* (a conversion
which results from a radical reading of the Gospel), and of
course it develops Los's conversion in Night VII of *The Four
Zoas.*

The relations among these myths of the Zoas, the classics,
the Old Testament, and the Gospel are of course fluid and
complex. Blake wants to weave them together, and at the
same time to make one of them triumph. The Zoas-Albion
relation that ends in justice and integration is tinged with the
classical genealogy of the gods myth and with the demiurge
of the *Timaeus* and the psychology of the *Republic* and the
Phaedrus.[5] The Spectre of the Zoas myth is identified with
the Satan of the Old Testament (the Satan of Job is the prime
"Accuser") and with the Selfhood. When the Selfhood is
annihilated, and "the Covenant of Jehovah" becomes "the

5. The madnesses of the *Phaedrus* are not distributed evenly among the
fallen Zoas. The prophecy of Apollo and the poetry of the Muses attach to
Los; the wine/enthusiasm of Dionysus and the love-madness of Eros attach
to Luvah; Urizen and Tharmas, being incapable of enthusiasm or inspiration, are left as the extremes of rigid order and chaotic disorder—rock and
sea.

forgiveness of sins," we have passed from the Zoas through the Old Testament to the Gospels. (The Spectre's claim to be God, furthermore, is classical in that he may be the Satan-Selfhood disguised as Zeus as well as Jehovah.) The Emanation branch of the Zoas myth, which ends in the return of Jerusalem, alludes to the classical Eros division of the sexes and also to the Old Testament Jerusalem/harlot—both moving toward the Gospel fruition in the woman taken in adultery and in the descent of Jerusalem as woman/city in the Book of Revelation.[6]

The change of Jehovah into Jesus—or the change of Albion/Jehovah into Albion/Jesus—in the last plates of *Jerusalem* is the final and complete taking up of the Old Testament into the Gospel. When the "Covenant of Jehovah" as the merciful rainbow covenant after the Flood is converted into the mutual forgiveness of sins, we have poetically achieved the promise of "Ye are united O ye Inhabitants of Earth in One Religion. The Religion of Jesus: the most Ancient, the Eternal: & the Everlasting Gospel" (pl. 27). It is, of course, Blake's understanding of "the Eternal: & the Everlasting Gospel," and we have been reading a "poetic tale." (See Blake's deeply ironic "Choosing forms of worship from poetic tales," pl. 11 of *The Marriage of Heaven and Hell*.)

I have said enough about Los as classical demiurge or Hephaestus becoming the Zoa of prophecy, the Seven Eyes of God, and a visionary of Jesus so that it needs no repeating here. But it is worth pointing out that Los is central to all four myths. The change or modulation of one myth into another occurs largely in Los, and when Los's acts and conversion are repeated in the awakened, fourfold Albion, all is complete. Looking at Blake's fourfold composition differently, as a complex set of relationships, yields much the same result. The man-Spectre relation that ends in self-annihilation, the man-Emanation relation that ends in the return of Jerusalem, the Zoas-Albion relation that ends in justice and integration,

6. Athena's emerging from the head of Zeus makes her an Emanation, and her association as Athena Polias with the city associates her with Jerusalem, so that she would be a classical reminiscence of Jerusalem in Blake's view. For Athena Polias, see Vincent Scully, *The Earth, the Temple, and the Gods*, chapter 9, "Poseidon and Athena."

and the change of Jehovah into (or the superseding of Jehovah by) Jesus all end in an annihilation of self or forgivenesss of sins, first by Los and finally by the awakened Albion. Blake's poetry progresses partly by showing the same act in different agents, so that the instrument or voice changes; in this way the act changes, usually by being enlarged or intensified or both.

Blake's nuclear forms persist to the end. "The Ghost of Abel" is such a form, with Jehovah, the devilish or Orc-like "he, who dwells in flaming fire" of the *Marriage,* now preaching the forgiveness of sins: this Jehovah has very nearly become Jesus. Since Adam and Eve are here beset by two voices, Jehovah's and that of the Satan who has made the ghost of Abel his "house," the poem is a Satan-Jesus confrontation like "For the Sexes," "The Everlasting Gospel," and the addresses to the reader in *Jerusalem,* plates 27, 52, and 77. If "The Ghost of Abel" (like the Job series) is a nuclear form of the Gospel as love, redeeming Adam and Eve and Jehovah, then the "Laocoön" is a nuclear form of the Gospel as art. The "Laocoön" is not myth, though it suggests the outlines of one: it is an aphoristic manifesto that gets its force from its identification of art with the life and Gospel of Jesus. The myth of the Gospel of Art, which runs all through Blake's poetry, of course forms around Los. Wherever we turn in Blake's poetry, we are confronted by Los.

*   *   *

The preceding account has shown Los as the generating force in the growth of Blake's systematic myth, the advancing edge of Blake's imagination projected into the poem, the embodiment of the principle of change through imagination as work. It has treated Los as the seed principle, the Poetic Genius, of Blake's first illuminated work—"All Religions Are One"—brought to life and then divided into its component parts of reason, desire, and the object of desire, and embodied in Urizen, Orc, and Enitharmon. This coming to life, division, and interaction in Los is the model of the process by which Blake's later prophecies are built. Through the whole of Blake's poetry, powerfully condensed nuclear phrases and acts and images are elaborated, and sometimes hammered again into passages of diamond intensity. Los's work at hammer and anvil is the image and enactment of this process. The course and shape of Blake's poetry is the line described by the career of Los.

Los prophesies by embodying in himself not only what is to come in the poem, but also in the growing city of Blake's poetry. Thus, I have argued that Los's conversion in Night VII of *The Four Zoas* marks the great turn in Blake's own poetry: as Los the poet-prophet turns back from the pagan corruptions suffered by Hebrew poetry to the true source in the Everlasting Gospel of Jesus, Blake's poetry increasingly converts its pagan elements, which remain in the poetry, into Christian ones. Through his developing imaginative grasp of the character Los, Blake finally learns to write the original, active, architectonic conversation of eternity in which *Jerusalem* ends. Blake, like Los, moves toward the end by turning back to the origin, regains the Golden Age by working through to the end. In the final form of Blake's myth of history, Albion—mankind asleep, fallen into warfare and deadly dreams of good and evil—is reawakened into the brotherhood of Eden by Los, the artist as awakener.

Finally, Los is identified with the community of mankind. We have followed the course by which Los as demiurge and artist, poet and prophet, awakener and redeemer, becomes in Blake's last, long prophecies the creative powers of all men acting through the individual person to create a human world. We have seen that Los ends as the single identity that stands metonymically for the whole community of men: it is in and through Los that Blake works out the prophetic words of "There Is No Natural Religion" of 1788: "God becomes as we are, that we may be as he is."[7] I have argued that these words, more than any others, imply the whole of Blake's poetry.

7. In seeing Los as the "likeness & similitude" of Jesus, the body of the divine human community, I have largely ignored the "part" of Christ that appears in or as "Luvah's robes of blood" and is put off at the crucifixion. I treat all the immense blood and struggle, negation and death, in Blake's poetry as falling back at the end. For a learned and formidable view of Blake which focuses on negation and the problematic in him and in Los and in Los's creation—and which asserts that *the incarnation is the crucifixion* (p. 284)—see Damrosch, *Symbol and Truth.*

The figure of Los, then, is the necessary center of Blake's long prophecies. Without him they would be unimaginably different. In Los as the image in the poem of the poet at work, we see Blake's myth coming into existence as a world being created, with its embodied souls; and it is Los whose example finally awakens the poem *Jerusalem* as a divine community of persons speaking in actions. Finally, Los is the figure who shows us that identity and community are the same supreme state seen differently, by contracted or expanded senses. Identity-as-community is the exercise of one's unique Mental Gifts in the creation and exchange of the Mental Forms of a human world. It is revealed first in Los, and Los remains its strongest image.

Bibliography

Primary Sources

Collected Letters of Samuel Taylor Coleridge. Edited by Earl Leslie Griggs.
6 vols. Oxford: Clarendon, 1956–1971.

The Complete Works of Percy Bysshe Shelley. Edited by Roger Ingpen and
Walter E. Peck. 10 vols. London: E. Benn; New York: C. Scribner's
Sons, 1926–1930.

The Notebook of William Blake: A Photographic and Typographic Facsimile.
Edited by David V. Erdman and Donald K. Moore. Oxford: Clarendon, 1973. Rev. ed., New York: Readex, 1977.

The Poetry and Prose of William Blake. Edited by David V. Erdman with
commentary by Harold Bloom. Garden City, N.Y.: Doubleday,
1965. Newly rev. ed., as *The Complete Poetry and Prose of William
Blake,* Berkeley and Los Angeles: University of California Press;
Garden City, N.Y.: Anchor/Doubleday, 1982.

Secondary Sources

Background Sources

Abrams, M. H. *The Mirror and the Lamp: Romantic Theory and the Critical
Tradition.* New York: Oxford University Press, 1953.

―――. *Natural Supernaturalism: Tradition and Revolution in Romantic
Literature.* New York: Norton, 1971.

Arendt, Hannah. *The Life of the Mind.* 2 vols. New York: Harcourt Brace
Jovanovich, 1978.

Barfield, Owen. *Poetic Diction.* London: Faber and Faber, 1952.

―――. *The Rediscovery of Meaning.* Middletown, Conn.: Wesleyan
University Press, 1977.

Bloom, Harold. *The Visionary Company: A Reading of English Romantic
Poetry.* New York: Doubleday, 1961. Rev. and enl. ed., Ithaca, N.Y.:
Cornell University Press, 1971.

Butler, Joseph. *The Analogy of Religion Natural and Revealed.* London: J.
M. Dent, 1906. Reprinted 1927.

Cassirer, Ernst. *Rousseau, Kant, Goethe: Two Essays.* Translated by
James Gutmann, Paul Oskar Kristeller, and John Herman Randall,
Jr. Princeton, N.J.: Princeton University Press, 1945.

Freud, Sigmund. *The Interpretation of Dreams.* Translated by James
Strachey. New York: Norton, 1959.

Friedman, Maurice. *To Deny Our Nothingness.* London: Gollancz, 1967.

Frye, Northrop. *The Anatomy of Criticism.* Princeton, N.J.: Princeton University Press, 1957.

———. *The Educated Imagination.* Bloomington, Ind.: Indiana University Press, 1969.

———. *The Stubborn Structure.* Ithaca, N.Y.: Cornell University Press, 1970.

Jung, Carl. *Answer to Job.* Translated by R. F. C. Hull. Cleveland and New York: World, 1960.

Langbaum, Robert. *The Mysteries of Identity.* New York: Oxford University Press, 1977.

Leibniz, Gottfried Wilhelm von. *Monadology and Other Essays.* Translated by Paul Schrecker and Anne Martin Schrecker. Indianapolis and New York: Bobbs-Merrill, 1965.

Morley, Edith J., ed. *Henry Crabb Robinson on Books and Their Writers.* London: J. M. Dent, 1938.

O'Brien, Denis. *Empedocles' Cosmic Cycle.* London: Cambridge University Press, 1969.

Panofsky, Erwin. *Studies in Iconology.* New York: Harper & Row, 1962.

Ponsot, Marie, and Deen, Rosemary. *Beat Not the Poor Desk.* Montclair, N.J.: Boynton/Cook, 1982.

Rad, Gerhard von. *The Message of the Prophets.* New York: Harper & Row, 1965.

Russell, Bertrand. *A Critical Exposition of the Philosophy of Leibniz.* London: G. Allen & Unwin, 1937.

Scully, Vincent. *The Earth, the Temple, and the Gods.* New Haven and London: Yale University Press, 1962. Rev. ed., 1979.

Wilson, Milton. *Shelley's Later Poetry: A Study of His Prophetic Imagination.* New York: Columbia University Press, 1959.

Blake Criticism: Books

Adams, Hazard. *William Blake: A Reading of the Shorter Poems.* Seattle: University of Washington Press, 1963.

Ault, Donald. *Visionary Physics: Blake's Response to Newton.* Chicago and London: University of Chicago Press, 1974.

Beer, John. *Blake's Humanism.* Manchester and New York: Manchester University Press, 1968.

Bindman, David. *Blake as an Artist.* Oxford: Phaidon; New York: E. P. Dutton, 1977.

Bloom, Harold. *Blake's Apocalypse.* Garden City, N.Y.: Doubleday, 1963. Rev. ed., Ithaca, N.Y.: Cornell University Press, 1970.

Damon, S. Foster. *William Blake: His Philosophy and Symbols.* Gloucester, Mass.: P. Smith, 1958.

Damrosch, Leopold, Jr. *Symbol and Truth in Blake's Myth.* Princeton, N.J.: Princeton University Press, 1980.

Erdman, David V. *Blake: Prophet Against Empire.* Princeton, N.J.: Princeton University Press, 1954. Rev. ed., 1969. 3d ed., 1977.

Fox, Susan. *Poetic Form in Blake's "Milton."* Princeton, N.J.: Princeton
University Press, 1976.

Frosch, Thomas R. *The Awakening of Albion: The Renovation of the Body
in the Poetry of William Blake.* Ithaca and London: Cornell Uni-
veristy Press, 1974.

Frye, Northrop. *Fearful Symmetry: A Study of William Blake.* Princeton,
N.J.: Princeton University Press, 1947, 1969.

Gallant, Christine. *Blake and the Assimilation of Chaos.* Princeton, N.J.:
Princeton University Press, 1978.

Hirsch, Eric D., Jr. *Innocence and Experience: An Introduction to Blake.*
New Haven: Yale University Press, 1964.

Mellor, Anne Kostelanetz. *Blake's Human Form Divine.* Berkeley, Los
Angeles, and London: University of California Press, 1974.

Mitchell, W. J. T. *Blake's Composite Art: A Study of the Illuminated Poetry.*
Princeton, N.J.: Princeton University Press, 1978.

Murry, John Middleton. *William Blake.* London: Jonathan Cape, 1933;
New York: McGraw-Hill, 1964.

Nurmi, Martin K. *Blake's "Marriage of Heaven and Hell": A Critical Study.*
Kent, Ohio: Kent State University Press, 1957.

———. *William Blake.* London: Hutchinson, 1975.

Paley, Morton D. *Energy and the Imagination: A Study of the Development
of Blake's Thought.* Oxford: Clarendon, 1970.

Percival, Milton O. *William Blake's Circle of Destiny.* New York: Columbia
University Press, 1938; Octagon, 1964.

Raine, Kathleen. *Blake and Tradition.* 2 vols. Princeton, N.J.: Princeton
University Press, 1968.

Schorer, Mark. *William Blake: The Politics of Vision.* New York: Henry
Holt, 1946; abridged ed., Anchor, 1959.

Wagenknecht, David. *Blake's Night: William Blake and the Idea of Pastoral.*
Cambridge, Mass.: Belknap, 1973.

Wilkie, Brian, and Johnson, Mary Lynn. *Blake's Four Zoas: The Design of
a Dream.* Cambridge, Mass.: Harvard University Press, 1978.

Wittreich, Joseph Anthony, Jr. *Angel of Apocalypse: Blake's Idea of Milton.*
Madison, Wis.: University of Wisconsin Press, 1975.

Blake Criticism: Collections of Essays

Curran, Stuart, and Wittreich, Joseph Anthony, Jr., eds. *Blake's Sublime
Allegory: Essays on The Four Zoas, Milton, and Jerusalem.* Madison,
Wis.: University of Wisconsin Press, 1973.

Erdman, David V., and Grant, John E., eds. *Blake's Visionary Forms
Dramatic.* Princeton, N.J.: Princeton University Press, 1970.

Paley, Morton D., and Phillips, Michael, eds. *William Blake: Essays in
Honour of Sir Geoffrey Keynes.* Oxford: Clarendon, 1973.

Pinto, Vivian de Sola, ed. *The Divine Vision: Studies in the Poetry and Art
of William Blake.* London: Gollancz, 1957.

Rosenfeld, Alvin H., ed. *William Blake: Essays for S. Foster Damon.* Providence, R.I.: Brown University Press, 1969.

Blake Criticism: Essays

Curran, Stuart. "The Structures of *Jerusalem.*" In *Blake's Sublime Allegory*, edited by Stuart Curran and Joseph Anthony Wittreich, Jr., 239–45.

Doskow, Minna. "William Blake's *America*: The Story of a Revolution Betrayed." *Blake Studies*, vol. 8, no. 2, pp. 167–86.

Enscoe, Gerald. "The Content of Vision: Blake's 'Mental Traveller.'" *Papers on Language and Literature* 4 (1968): 400–413.

Erdman, David V. "*America*: New Expanses." In *Blake's Visionary Forms Dramatic*, edited by David V. Erdman and John E. Grant, 95–114.

Frye, Northrop. "Notes for a Commentary on *Milton.*" In *The Divine Vision*, edited by Vivian de Sola Pinto, 97–138.

Johnson, Mary Lynn. "'Separating what has been Mixed,': A Suggestion for a Perspective on *Milton.*" *Blake Studies*, vol. 6, no. 1, pp. 11–18.

Kiralis, Karl. "The Theme and Structure of William Blake's *Jerusalem.*" In *The Divine Vision*, edited by Vivian de Sola Pinto, 139–62.

Mitchell, W. J. T. "Blake's Radical Comedy: Dramatic Structure ˀs Meaning in *Milton.*" In *Blake's Sublime Allegory*, edited by Stuart Curran and Joseph Anthony Wittreich, Jr., 281–307.

———. "Poetic and Pictorial Imagination in Blake's *The Book of Urizen.*" *Eighteenth Century Studies* 3 (1969): 83–107.

Nurmi, Martin K. "Joy, Love, and Innocence in Blake's 'The Mental Traveller.'" *Studies in Romanticism* 3 (1964): 109–17.

Paley, Morton. "The Female Babe and 'The Mental Traveller.'" *Studies in Romanticism* 1 (1962): 97–104.

Rieger, James. "'The Hem of Their Garments': The Bard's Song in *Milton.*" In *Blake's Sublime Allegory*, edited by Stuart Curran and Joseph Anthony Wittreich, Jr., 259–80.

Rose, Edward J. "Blake's Metaphorical States." *Blake Studies*, vol. 4, no. 1, pp. 9–31.

———. "Los, Pilgrim of Eternity." In *Blake's Sublime Allegory*, edited by Stuart Curran and Joseph Anthony Wittreich, Jr., 83–99.

———. "The Structure of Blake's *Jerusalem.*" *Bucknell Review* 11 (1963): 35–54.

Sandler, Florence. "The Iconoclastic Enterprise: Blake's Critique of Milton's Religion." *Blake Studies*, vol. 5, no. 1, pp. 13–57.

Schleifer, Ronald. "Simile, Metaphor, and Vision: Blake's Narration of Prophecy in *America.*" *Studies in English Literature, 1500–1900* 19 (1979): 569–88.

Simmons, Robert E. "*Urizen:* The Symmetry of Fear." In *Blake's Visionary Forms Dramatic*, edited by David V. Erdman and John E. Grant, 136–71.

Sutherland, John. "Blake and Urizen." In *Blake's Visionary Forms Dramatic,* edited by David V. Erdman and John E. Grant, 244–62.

Tannenbaum, Leslie. "Blake's Art of Crypsis: *The Book of Urizen* and Genesis." *Blake Studies,* vol. 5, no. 1, pp. 141–64.

Tolley, Michael J. "*Europe:* 'To Those Ychain'd in Sleep.'" In *Blake's Visionary Forms Dramatic,* edited by David V. Erdman and John E. Grant, 115–45.

Index

Abraham, 146, 191

Abrams, M. H., 5–6, 12n, 13, 14n, 90n

Accusation of Sin, 55, 145, 148, 212–18, 221

Achilles' shield, 109–10, 114

Act: creative, 3, 20; unique, 4; dramatic, 25; desperate, 233; as speech, 236; in poetry, 239

Adam, 14, 62–63, 72, 117, 121, 127, 128, 140, 144, 146, 148, 155, 197–99, 201, 213, 222–25, 233, 259

Adams, Hazard, 92n, 115n

Adonis, 85, 93–97

Agape, 122, 198

Ahania, 128–29, 137, 161, 162

Albion: speaking, 25, 226–28; implied in *French Revolution*, 28, 29; as containing figure, 45, 59, 78, 154; fallen, 124–31, 190–93, 196–99; conversion, 151; entering Eden, 159–61, 219, 251, 252, 260; Blake and Milton as, 182–83; and Los, 202–4, 233; as Jehovah, 236, 254–56, 259

Alcestis (and Admetus), 158

"All Religions Are One," 21–25, 207, 209, 232, 259

America, 49–51, 57n, 59, 60, 61, 62, 83, 248

Angel, 35–39, 40–42, 45, 46

Annunciation, 248

Apocalypse, 14, 27, 30, 61, 65, 85, 117, 159, 164, 181, 230, 232, 242, 245. *See also* Revelation

Apollo, 80–81, 254, 255

Arendt, Hannah, 122n

Aristophanes (in *Symposium*), 13, 113

Aristotle, 231, 236

Ark and secret place and tabernacle, 196, 198–99, 201

Art: true and false, 99–100; as energy freed, 144; and Christianity, 154; and Los, 235–36; replacing war, 246–47

Artemis, 119n, 243

Athena, 106, 108, 110, 113, 258n

Atom, 4, 19, 23, 72, 233, 235

Atomism, 72, 233–34

Atonement, 147–48, 170

Augustine: *City of God*, 14, 103–5, 117, 121; *Confessions*, 14, 15

Ault, Donald D., 20n, 92n, 226n

Awakener, 164, 232, 236

Ball, Robert Hamilton, 192n

Barfield, Owen, 3n, 15n

Beer, John, 25n, 34n, 86n

Beulah, 15, 59, 80, 89n, 114, 116, 117, 120, 124, 131, 133–34, 141, 152–53, 157–60, 186–87, 188, 189, 243, 252, 256

Bible: biblical plot, 13–14; poetry of, 33, 108, 110, 162; as source of art, 153; symbolism, 198n

Binding: of desire, 53–55, 65, 69, 71–72, 87; of body and senses, 70, 85–86, 195; of Orc, 71–72, 106n, 111–12, 134–36; erotic, 88, 93

Bindman, David, 106n

Blake: and Los, 70, 78–83, 154–57, 210, 232, 237, 239, 247, 248–50, 253–54, 260; and Milton, 164–65, 166, 180, 182–84, 248–50, 252; and Satan, 183; "identified," 189, 209; as Urizen, 210–11; in *Jerusalem*, 220, 256; and Catherine, 248, 250, 251; and Christ, 249; and Albion, 254

Bloom, Harold, 37n, 190n

Boccaccio, 107n

Body: of poetry, 1, 19; of energy, 20; fallen and mortal, 21, 102, 152, 157; and Poetic Genius, 23, 24; as nation, 29–30, 34, 41–42; unfallen, Edenic, 44, 128; as spiritual, 152, 157, 227; created by Los, 186, 205, 235; as garden and building, 186; as language, 236

Boehme, Jacob, 90n

Book of Ahania, The, 54, 60, 70–71, 130

Book of Los, The, 7, 53, 60, 70, 71–74, 80, 88, 159, 236